Inflation, Unemployment, and Poverty

Inflation, Unemployment, and Poverty

John L. Palmer

Lexington Books
D.C. Heath and Company
Lexington, Massachusetts
Toronto   London

Library of Congress Cataloging in Publication Data

Palmer, John Logan.
   Inflation, unemployment, and poverty.

   Based on the author's dissertation, Stanford University, 1971.
   Bibliography: p.
   1. Inflation (Finance). 2. Unemployed. 3. Income—United States.
4. Poor—United States. I. Title.
HD5707.P32   332.4'1'0973   73-11679
ISBN 0-669-90464-3

Published simultaneously in Canada.

Printed in the United States of America.

International Standard Book Number: 0-669-90464-3

Library of Congress Catalog Card Number: 73-11679

Contents

List of Figures

List of Tables

xii

Acknowledgments

This study is based almost entirely upon my Ph.D. dissertation, "Inflation, Unemployment, and Poverty," completed in late 1971 for the Department of Economics of Stanford University, which, in turn, grew out of an earlier study I coauthored with Robinson G. Hollister, entitled "The Impact of Inflation Upon the Poor" (first released as a discussion paper by the Institute for Research on Poverty of the University of Wisconsin in 1967, then published in 1972 in *Redistribution to the Rich and Poor: The Grants Economics of Income Redistribution*, Boulding and Pfaff (eds.), Wadsworth, Belmont, Calif.). I am grateful to Rob Hollister for the initial idea of the study, considerable subsequent encouragement in continuing it, and permission to utilize herein portions of the empirical analysis (contained in Chapters 7, 8, and 9) appearing in our earlier aforementioned paper.

I wish to acknowledge the indispensable roles played by two of my dissertation advisors in the development of this study. John Pencavel was invaluable as a reader and critic of all chapters except 10 as revised in this work. Melvin W. Reder was responsible for generally guiding me throughout my efforts and, in doing so, contributed considerably to my intellectual growth.

I am also indebted to Philippe DeVille, Charles Anderson, and Denton Marks for able research assistance, and to the Office of Economic Opportunity, the Institute for Research on Poverty, the Institute for Public Policy Analysis (Stanford University), and the Stanford University Department of Economics for financial support at various stages of my work.

Inflation, Unemployment, and Poverty

1 Introduction

The domestic economic policy of the United States since World War II can probably be most succinctly characterized as an attempt to maximize the level of employment through appropriate monetary and fiscal measures subject to the constraint that there be little, or no, sustained inflation.[1] However, the maintenance of a desirably high level of employment (in the absence of strong federal controls) seems destined to be frustrated, given the present structure of our economy, because of the proclivity toward inflation at even moderate levels of unemployment. In the sixties, it had become commonplace to presume that there is a fairly "tight" functional relationship between the rates of inflation and aggregate unemployment and to talk of steering the economy on a course which achieves some appropriate balance between the two. The experience of the American economy in the very early seventies has caused many economists to reevaluate their notions about the degree of "tightness" of this relationship; however a strong belief in our ability to steer such a balanced course is still prevalent.

The achievement of such a goal presents two broad difficulties to policymakers and their economic advisors. One concerns the determination of the alternatives which may be feasible for the economy at any given point in time, and over time. This difficulty has two major components. First, there is the controversy, which recently has been so heated, about the exact nature of the relationship (tradeoff?) between inflation and unemployment. Both the shape and stability of the conventional Phillips curve are at issue here. And, secondly, even assuming that we have knowledge of structurally feasible time paths of rates of inflation and aggregate unemployment, there is a question as to how reliable are the various aggregate economic policy instruments for enabling us to attain any given desired, and structurally feasible, goal. Policymakers do not have direct control over the prevailing rates of inflation and unemployment even within the structural constraints; in the short run they must rely upon monetary and fiscal tools which are often imprecise in their effects. In fact, these two components are not as separable as our categorization above suggests. We shall argue in Chapter 10 that the nature and degree of the policy instruments employed have considerable influence on the determination of what time paths of inflation and unemployment are feasible.

The economics profession in general recognizes that these are issues about which much more must be known in order for optimal policy decisions to be made. The proliferation of research on these topics is an indication of this

1

awareness. Nevertheless, policies still must be implemented (on a best-guess basis), and these policies presumably are based upon an evaluation of the welfare implications of the rates of unemployment and inflation which are believed to be feasible, or are prevailing. Herein lies the second of the two difficulties. The profession often seems to be operating under the assumption that there is a good understanding of these welfare implications.[2] The presumption of all too many economists, when confronted with what they consider to be an improper balance between inflation and unemployment as implicitly, or explicitly, reflected in the actions of the monetary and fiscal authorities, is to assume that the weights given to the various costs and benefits are different from their own[3] perhaps because certain kinds of "peripheral" political issues overrode the more obvious economic ones.

Just how good is the economics profession's understanding of the implications of different rates of inflation and unemployment for distribution and the efficiency of allocation over time? It is our contention that it is not nearly so accurate as it could and should be. One of the recurrent arguments that addresses the undesirable aspects of inflation emphasizes that it is particularly harmful to the poor. There seems to be a great deal of "conventional wisdom" and very little supportive analysis on this subject. Arthur F. Burns expresses a view that is not at all uncommon among both economists and laymen when he asserts that, "unhappily, much of the public as well as private effort to reduce poverty is being nullified by inflation. There can be little doubt that poor people, or people of modest means generally, are the chief sufferers from inflation."[4] We know of no evidence that would validate such a categorical statement. More importantly, focusing attention only upon inflation is a very partial and (we believe) undesirable approach. What if the inflation is accompanied by, and necessary for the achievement of, low unemployment rates (as the Phillips curve suggests)? Should not the effect of these unemployment rates also be considered and policy decisions made on the basis of the total impact of aggregate economic conditions experienced by various income groups? Clearly, better information about these issues than we presently have is required since the attempt to optimize the mix between inflation and unemployment is going to continue to be a primary concern of public policy.

Our intention when embarking upon this study was to evaluate empirically the impact of various rates of inflation and unemployment on the economic well being of the poor[5] so that more knowledgeable policy decisions could be made on this basis. However, as we progressed it became clear that it would be interesting to analyze more extensively the theoretical considerations that should logically precede such an empirical analysis—particularly regarding the relationship between inflation and unemployment—and to examine the linkage between macroeconomic policy instruments and the economic welfare of the poor. Consequently, the bulk of our efforts in this study can probably best be described as the development of a theoretical framework for the analysis of the effects of macroeconomic policy (as reflected in various rates of unemployment and inflation) on the distribution of income and wealth and the efficiency of allocation of economic resources. In dealing with distributional considerations, we focus explicitly on low-income groups whenever possible. Finally, we are able to report on some casual empirical analysis that bears directly on the costs and benefits to the poor of various rates of inflation and aggregate unemployment.[6] As a result, we believe that this study helps lay the foundation for future analyses that should lead to more enlightened macroeconomic policies, as well as makes some immediate contribution to such policies.

Chapter 2 deals with the concept and measurement of inflation. Inflation and some of its primary exogenous causes are discussed in the context of aggregate supply and demand curves of an economy. A section on the construction, interpretation, and limitations of price indices as measures of inflation is also included. In Chapter 3 we present a critical treatment of the more traditional views of inflationary processes in the context of a particular typology which emphasizes their incompleteness. The failure of any one of these views to present us with an adequate conceptual framework for our purposes is discussed. Chapter 4 turns to the more recent literature on informational (or search) unemployment, Phillips curves, and the "natural rate of unemployment" concept. We discuss in some detail the nature of this latter concept, particularly with reference to the role of expectations. A somewhat different view of inflationary processes than those contained in Chapter 3 emerges from this literature, and we attempt a partial integration of the various approaches.

The material in Chapters 2, 3, and 4 provides us with sufficient background to construct a broad conceptual framework for our analysis. This is done at the beginning of Chapter 5, which emphasizes the need for: (1) a general equilibrium model in which inflation and unemployment are treated as jointly determined, endogenous variables and are related to macroeconomic policy instruments; and (2) a theoretical examination of the implications of various rates of inflation (anticipated and unanticipated) and aggregate unemployment for distribution and the efficiency of allocation. Chapters 5 and 6, which treat inflation and unemployment in a partial equilibrium context, contain frameworks for these latter analyses.

Chapters 7, 8, and 9 contain what empirical analysis we were able to perform with regard to the impact of various rates of inflation and aggregate unemployment across income groups (with emphasis on the poor). The theoretical considerations contained in Chapters 5 and 6 guide this analysis. Chapter 7 deals with expenditure effects. Here we examine the recent past and possible future experience of the poverty population and some of its demographic subgroups, with respect to cost-of-living increases, and compare this experience to that of other income groups. In Chapter 8 we present a profile of income sources for different income groups and discuss the redistributional implications of inflation for nonwage and salary sources. We briefly analyze some potential wealth effects in Chapter 9 by ascertaining the extent to which inflation might have caused a redistribution against the poor through its influence on asset prices.

In Chapter 10 we construct a simple model in the spirit of (1) above and estimate it with quarterly data for the United States, 1956I-1969IV. This model provides us with interesting empirical results as well as a vehicle for illustration of some important conceptual points. We discuss the implications of both. Finally, Chapter 11 explores briefly the implications of our analyses for both future research and policy.

2 The Concept and Measurement of Inflation

Anyone who has ever ploughed through a significant portion of the literature on inflation cannot help but be struck by the amount of time and effort that various authors have spent trying to define the concept of inflation with some precision before dealing with it in substance. To do this in any but a preliminary sense seems to us to be a fruitless task. A precise and meaningful definition of inflation can be presented only in the context of a more detailed discussion of inflation—in particular, in the context of its causes and measurement. We shall enter into just such a discussion shortly, but prior to this we need to mention a few things in relation to a preliminary definition of inflation—i.e., *inflation* is a sustained increase in the general level of prices.

First, we must confront our usage in this definition of "the general level of prices." It is rises in this which interest us rather than of specific prices. To be sure, the general level of prices, however defined, must necessarily be a statistical construct derived from certain selected specific prices. However, inflation is often meant to imply that many prices are moving together over time because they are being subjected to some common pressures. In this sense the general level of prices is the inverse of the value of money, a fact that emphasizes the peculiar role that money must play in any treatment of inflationary processes. After we have dealt at some length with the causes of increases in the general level of prices in the first two sections of this chapter, we shall return to the subject of its measurement in the third section.

Secondly, what do we mean by "sustained increases"? How fast and over what period of time does the general level of prices have to rise before we consider there to be an inflation? Any distinction that we might endeavor to make here would be arbitrary. As a general guideline we might offer that the increase should be sufficient so that it is unlikely to be simply the result of an upward bias in the relevant price index, and it should continue to occur over a long enough time period that it is unlikely to be only the result of a one-time upward adjustment of prices to a specific change in structural circumstances[1] rather than reflecting more general continuing conditions in the economy. Conventional usage of the term would seem to indicate that it is appropriate to label what we are experiencing an inflation whenever an increase in the general level of prices has occurred in excess of 1.5 to 2 percent for two or more consecutive years. However, as we shall see in this chapter's last section, such an increase need not satisfy the casual guidelines set out just above.

Finally, what of the situation that exists when the general level of prices

5

would increase substantially were it not for government control and regulation of part or all of the economy? For the most part, we shall exclude the treatment of this phenomenon from our discussion. Such a "repressed inflation," as it is often referred to, is usually the result of an attempt by the government to prevent rationing by means of price increases and to substitute instead a distribution system based partially upon legal controls.[2] We are primarily interested in the situation in which the economy operates "normally," where prices are permitted to ration the excess demand for goods and services and factors of production.[3] However, we should distinguish from a repressed inflation what for our purposes we shall label a "suppressed inflation." There is no clear line between a suppressed inflation and an open one. Our use of the term "suppressed" is intended to indicate that, even if legal controls are not placed upon the economy to prevent price increases, the behavior of certain sectors of the economy, certain institutional arrangements, and government policies may serve to head off or greatly slow down an inflation that would occur much more rapidly in their absence. When these factors are relatively important, it might be useful to think of the inflation as more suppressed than open. We will discuss some of these factors in more detail as the study progresses.

The Derivation of Aggregate Demand
and Supply Curves

It will prove useful at several points in this chapter and throughout this study if we first construct in some detail aggregate supply and demand curves for the economy. Since these curves explicitly relate the level of real income (Y) to the general price level (P), one initial value of them will be to enable us to isolate those exogenous variables whose change can cause an increase in P.

Figures 2-1 and 2-2 depict the derivation of an aggregate demand curve (DD in graph a) for an economy.[4] The central ingredient to this derivation is in graph b which contains the Hicksian IS and LM curves, whose intersection determines the equilibrium level of real income and the interest rate. A change in the general price level does not enter explicitly by causing movements along these curves (as do changes in the rate of interest and the level of real income) but is reflected implicitly by a shift in the IS and/or LM curve if it causes a shift in one of component curves underlying either the IS or LM curve.

Graphs c, d, and e show the relationships that underlie the IS curve. Graph c displays the marginal efficiency of investment (MEI) curve which depicts the assumed inverse relationship between the amount of potential investment over the appropriate time period and the expected rate of return on this investment. This can be interpreted as a demand for investment function when it is assumed that all investment projects whose rates of return are in excess of the market rate

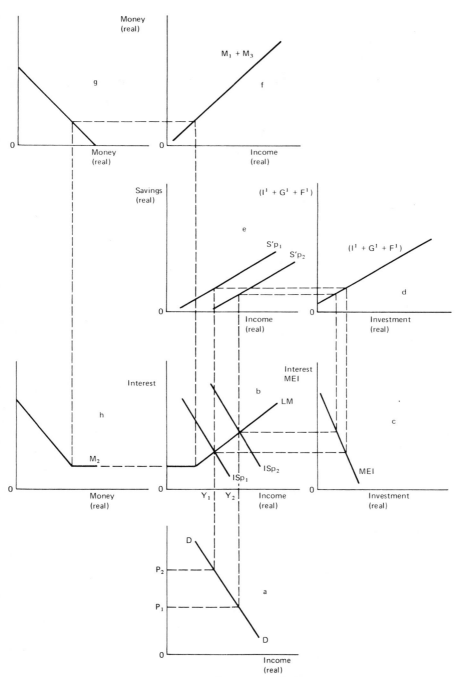

Figure 2-1. Derivation of Aggregate Demand Curve (1)

8

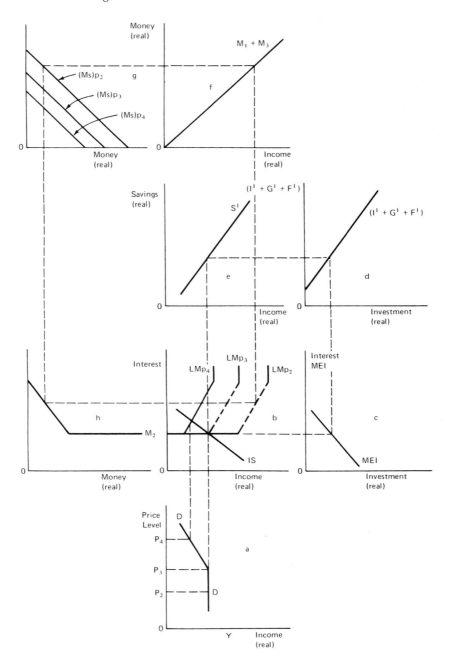

Figure 2-2. Derivation of Aggregate Demand Curve (2)

of interest are desirable (and those whose are less are not). Graph d displays the total "injections" into the system by adding to the investment component, I', the government expenditures component, G', and the foreign trade balance, F'. All components are in real terms. In equilibrium the "injections" must be equal to the "leakages," S', which includes both private savings and taxes.

Graphs f, g, and h show the relationships that underlie the LM curve. Graph f displays the component of the demand for money that is presumably related to the level of real income, the sum of the Keynesian "transactions" and "precautionary" components. Graph h displays the component of the demand for money that is related to the interest rate, the Keynesian "speculative" component. Graph d intermediates between the two, indicating that under the assumption of a constant real supply of money $[(Ms)p]$, the two components must sum to the whole. The LM curve is thus the set of values of Y and the rate of interest that are compatible with equilibrium in the money market.

There is considerable controversy as to the exact shape of the aggregate demand curve in (P, Y) space. The shape depends upon what we assume will be the effect of a change in the price level (ceteris paribus) on the curves in the graphs underlying the IS and the LM curves. The aggregate demand curve in Figure 2-1 is derived by assuming that the effect of a decrease in P is to shift downward the savings function, and thus shift upward to the right the IS curve. This yields a downward sloping aggregate demand curve. In Figure 2-2 the effect of a decrease in P is shown to be an increase in the real value of the money supply, which in turn causes an outward shift of the LM function. This, too, yields a downward sloping DD to the point where the IS curve intersects the LM curve in the liquidity trap, at which the DD curve becomes perfectly vertical— unless we also assume that the IS curve is shifting outward as in Figure 2-1. But we need not be concerned with the various subtleties regarding the exact shape of DD. For our purposes it will be sufficient to assume that it is downward sloping, without specifying the degree of the slope. This assumption does no injustice to any of the prevalent views on the shape of the DD function.[5]

Figures 2-3 and 2-4 depict the derivation of an aggregate supply function for the economy. Graphs b and c are the same in each figure. Graph c shows the assumed relationship between the level of employment (N) and the level of output (Y) which is read from the total product (TP) curve. Here we assume that there is a declining, but positive, marginal product contributed by each additional worker to the ranks of the employed. Graph b displays the labor supply function (Ns), which is assumed to be an increasing function of the real wage, and the labor demand function (Nd), which is assumed to be a decreasing function of the real wage.

The differences in the two figures reflect the various assumptions that underlie graph a. In Figure 2-3 it is assumed that money wages are completely flexible. They will be bid upward by employers if, at the prevailing real wage, there is an excess of labor demand over labor supply; however, money wages will

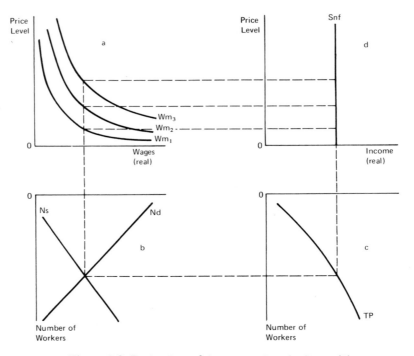

Figure 2-3. Derivation of Aggregate Supply Curve (1)

be bid down by workers if there is an excess of labor supply over labor demand at the prevailing real wage. The result is an economy that is in equilibrium only at that level of real wages that equates labor supply with labor demand; thus the aggregate supply function (*Snf*) is perfectly vertical at the corresponding level of real income. In Figure 2-4, graph a, it is assumed that money wages are flexible upward, but rigid on the down side. This yields an aggregate supply function (*Sni*) that is upward sloping over the range of output that corresponds to real wages for which the labor supply is in excess of the labor demand (thus the money wage is not bid upward, but is fixed at Wm_2 in Figure 2-4), but which is perfectly vertical at the level of output corresponding to level of employment occurring where *Ns* and *Nd* intersect since no higher level of employment than this can be obtained. (In the event of excess demand for labor, money wages and prices would increase together, maintaining the same real wage.)

We will be interested in both aggregate supply curves—the standard neoclassical one in Figure 2-3 and the modified one with money wages inflexible downward in Figure 2-4. It is also possible to make a more standard Keynesian

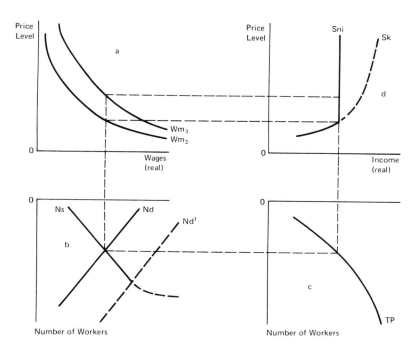

Figure 2-4. Derivation of Aggregate Supply Curve (2)

assumption concerning the labor market which yields an aggregate supply curve of the same general shape as that in Figure 2-4, but one which does not become vertical until the full employment level of Y is obtained. The necessary prerequisites for the derivation of this aggregate supply curve are that money wages be inflexible on the down side, and that workers be subject to "money illusion," such that if prices rise, they continue to offer the same supply of labor even though money wages have not increased proportionately. Thus the demand for labor, still expressed as a decreasing function of the real wage, is the only constraint on the level of employment until the full employment level of Y is approached. If the labor demand function intersects the labor supply function close to where it turns out[6] (as does Nd' in Figure 2-4), then the neoclassical aggregate supply curve with inflexible wages on the downside is more or less the same as the Keynesian one in shape and location; but, if Nd intersects Ns short of where it turns out, then Sni will become vertical at a lower level of Y than would the Keynesian aggregate supply curve (such as Sni compared to Sk in Figure 2-4).[7]

Exogenous Causes of Increases in the General Level of Prices

Now that we have constructed some models of the economy, as embodied in our various aggregate supply and demand curves, we are able to catalog in a very simple fashion the principal causes of increases in the general level of prices in terms of our exogenous variables. This does not constitute an explanation of inflationary processes since we are not focusing on sustained increases in P or dP/dt (the rate of change of P). To accomplish this, these models would have to be supplemented with other assumptions that render them less static. However, as we shall see in our discussion of traditional views of inflationary processes in Chapter 3, shifts in these exogenous variables[8] often are cited as causes of inflation for, presumably, one of two possible reasons: (1) the shift in the exogenous variable continues over a considerable time period and leads to sustained increases in P over that period, and/or (2) a shift in the exogenous variable is instrumental in initiating a dynamic process which results in sustained increases in P. We will address these possibilities in the next chapter.

Let us focus first on the aggregate demand curve. Since each of our aggregate supply curves has a positive slope over its entire range, any shift of the aggregate demand curve upward to the right will result in a price increase. We can see from Figures 2-1 and 2-2 that this can come about as the result of a shift outward, independent of P, of either the IS or LM curve—so we need to turn to the graphs underlying their derivation in order to isolate the relevant exogenous variables. With regard to the LM curve, clearly one possibility is an exogenous increase in the nominal supply of money. Such increases have come about as the result of deliberate action on the part of monetary authorities and have often been cited as the cause of historical inflations. A properly specified autonomous shift in either of the curves in graphs f or h will also shift outward the LM curve and thus could lead to an upward shift in the aggregate demand curve. There are a number of factors that could contribute to such shifts, but it is unlikely that many of them have had much significant historical importance for price level increases over a short period of time.[9] However, one such factor that is perhaps the strongest candidate for a cause in an outward shift of the LM curve (other than an increase in the nominal supply of money) is a shift in people's expectations concerning inflation. A change in expectations of inflation, ceteris paribus, could shift the speculative and transactions demand for money curve and, in this manner, lead to an increase in the general level of prices.

There are also a number of factors that could result in an outward shift of the IS curve, some of which have been historically important. An obvious candidate here is an exogenous increase in G' without a balancing increase in taxes. The causes of the present inflation are often traced back to such an occurrence. A downward shift in the savings function (again, independent of P) could have a similar effect. It is believed that the pent-up demand for durable goods after

World War II led to such a shift. Another cause of a downward shift in the savings function could be a change in inflationary expectations. The belief that the general level of prices is going to be significantly higher tomorrow than today can lead to an increased consumption in the present relative to the future. Expectations can also play an important role in the determination of the level of investment. The prevailing "climate of opinion," which can undergo exogenous changes, plays a role in the determination of the location of the MEI curve.[10]

Now let us turn our attention to the aggregate supply curves. As in the case of the aggregate demand curve, there are numerous exogenous variables which, if they change in value, can cause a shift in the aggregate supply curves. A shift to the left of an aggregate supply curve, ceteris paribus, will cause an increase in P since the aggregate demand curve is downward sloping, except in the instance where only the upward sloping portion (as opposed to the vertical portion) of an aggregate supply curve is affected and the aggregate demand curve is intersecting the aggregate supply curve on its vertical portion.

The first instance that would produce a leftward shift of the entire aggregate supply curve of each type that we have discussed is an exogenous change in labor productivity. This would be reflected in a shift of both the demand for labor and the total product curve. Such an occurrence could be precipitated by such factors as technical regress, natural disaster, or a large shift in the composition of demand. A shift in labor demand alone could also occur because of a change in the expectations of employers about their ability to sell a given amount of goods at prevailing prices—assuming that prices are somewhat inflexible.

Higher costs of production could lead to increases in P whether they be labor or nonlabor costs. An increase in the money wage will shift upward the sloping portion of the two aggregate supply curves (Sni and Sk) that have such a portion, while an increase in nonwage costs of production would be reflected in a downward shift of the labor demand function and a leftward shift of all portions of Sni and Snf, but just the upward sloping portion of the Keynesian aggregate supply function. If an increase in money wages represents an attempt on the part of labor to obtain and maintain an increased real wage (*ceteris paribus*), then this would cause a shift in the labor supply curve that would shift to the left the neoclassical aggregate supply curves. Such a shift in labor supply could also be brought about by a change in the size or composition of the labor force.

The prices of some commodities may be set by arbitrary administrative procedures rather than determined in the market by the interaction of supply and demand forces. Such "administered prices" can result in increases in P which can be conceptualized in our models by a movement of the economy up along the aggregate demand function even though the location of aggregate supply curve remains unchanged. This is the exercise of monopoly power on the part of producers which has often been cited as a cause of inflation.

There is one final cause of an increase in P that cannot be conveniently conceptualized in the context of these models. This is the index number bias which may be implicit in the nature of the construction of whatever index it is we are using to measure *P*. We shall see in the next section, however, that the degree of the bias also can depend upon the nature of composition of aggregate supply and demand in the economy.

This completes our catalog of causes of increases in *P* in terms of those exogenous variables which can be identified as the primary contributors to said increases. As we mentioned earlier, it may also be appropriate to utilize this catalog to label inflations. A common approach to such an endeavor has been to distinguish among different inflations as "cost-push" or "demand-pull," according to whether sustained increases in *P* are initially caused by (or perhaps primarily characterized by) shifts in aggregate supply (including administered prices here) or in aggregate demand, respectively. While these are useful labels for some purposes, we shall see when we deal with theories of dynamic inflationary processes that inflation can be a much more complex phenomenon than has been indicated so far, and the distinction between a cost-push and a demand-pull inflation is not always an easy or fruitful one to make.

The Measurement of the
General Price Level

The mention of index number bias in the preceding section as a possible cause of an increase in the general price level should serve as a reminder that a discussion of the measurement of *P* is in order. It would be of dubious marginal benefit for us to examine in detail the three major indices which are relied upon as measures of *P* and, therefore, of inflation; however, we do need to deal with some broad characteristics of these indices since they have implications for inflationary processes that are relevant to our purposes in this study. The three indices to which we are referring are the Consumer Price Index (CPI), the Wholesale Price Index (WPI), and the Implicit Price Index (IPI).

First, let us note that there are two primary, and presumably quite different, reasons for which we might desire to have a measure of *P*. One is as a measure of the degree of general inflationary pressure that exists in the economy, while the other is as an indicator of the cost increases (or decreases) that face firms and consumers as they perform their normal functions in the economy. A common problem in the construction of an index for either of these purposes is the decision with regard to which items should enter into the base, with what quantity weights, and what measurement of their prices. An index designed to measure the degree of increase in the general level of prices should reflect as broad a base of quantities and prices as possible. Although the IPI has the largest universe of the three price indices, it nevertheless does not include such items as land, securities, and labor (except where the output of a sector is measured by its labor input). Another problem with these indices is that they can incur a significant increase because of developments affecting supply in a single sector. For example, a significant part of the price advance in 1965 reflected the decrease in the supply of livestock with the accompanying rise in prices of livestock, hides and skins, and meats.[11] To be sure, this can be considered inflation as we have defined it, but often what one has in mind by inflation is more of a broad upward pressure on prices.

If a price index is going to be utilized as a measure of the price increases facing a firm or consumer (i.e., a measure of the cost of living), then the quantities and weights in its universe should reflect the set of conditions appropriate to the relevant economic unit. We shall see shortly that the CPI serves this purpose to some extent for a certain subclass of consumers, but there is no corresponding index for industry. The WPI could be constructed to achieve this purpose; however, one of the major criticisms leveled against it is that, as it is presently defined, it has no adequate frame of reference. It is a composite of costs and prices from all stages of the manufacturing process, and its transaction coverage is not descriptive of any definable set of producers or purchasers in the economy. The primary value of the WPI (given the way it is presently constructed) is that, because it reflects price movements at early stages of the production-distribution process, it may provide warning of the future trend of finished goods prices.

The CPI is the most widely used measure of the general level of prices and rate of inflation. The justification for the extensive use of this index is that it is a measure of a market basket composed of only those goods and services for final consumers, the provision of which is the primary purpose of our economy. As a general measure of inflation, then, it is lacking because it excludes not only those items we mentioned earlier (land, securities, labor), but also (among other things) the price of government output. As a measure of the cost of living for consumers it is more useful; however, there are also significant problems associated with it in this respect. First, it is inappropriate to label it a "cost-of-living" index since it does not measure price increases of many items that influence directly the standard of living of a consumer unit (such as, again, the price of real estate, labor, and securities). Perhaps it would be more aptly labeled a "cost-of-consuming" index. Secondly, we must take into account the well-known theoretical problems in using a price index as a welfare indicator even over these narrowly defined grounds.[12] Thirdly, we must realize that the CPI is not based upon a market basket of goods bought by all consumers, but only by urban wage earners and clerical workers within a given middle-income range. Thus this index might differ significantly from ones constructed for other special consumer groups. If we are interested in the differential impact of inflationary processes on the well-being of various subgroups of the population, we need to examine the appropriate indices.[13] Finally, there is the problem of index bias discussed below.

The IPI has the widest coverage since it attempts to measure the general level of prices of all goods and services produced in the economy during a specified period. It differs fundamentally from the CPI and the WPI in that it represents the ratio between current dollar GNP and constant dollar GNP multiplied by 100. Thus it is an aggregate price index which is affected by changing expenditure patterns each year.[14] Price series for components of the CPI and the WPI are among those used to deflate the various components of current dollar GNP in order to arrive at the IPI.

The IPI has severe problems that restrict its usefulness as a measure of inflation. Since it contains shifting quantity weights in its base, changes in its value might be reflecting changes in the composition of GNP as well as changes in the prices of goods and services entering into GNP. This may, or may not, be desirable depending upon the purposes for which the index is being used. Other difficulties are centered about the treatment of government output. Many of the goods produced by the government sector have no close counterpart in the private sector so that it is difficult to know what price to impute to them. Also there is no attempt to adjust for changes in output per man hour that might have taken place among government employees. This is particularly critical since the price of government services is measured by the payments to its employees. Finally, no attempt is made to adjust for labor productivity increases that have taken place in the construction industry. All of these factors can, and probably have, resulted in a significant upward bias of the IPI.

The CPI has also been criticized for having an upward bias built into it. Some of the primary arguments in support of this contention are:[15]

1. The CPI does not fully reflect the quality improvements which are constantly taking place. This is particularly true of the service sector which is becoming an increasingly more important component of the CPI.
2. New items are not added to, nor old ones subtracted from, the CPI's universe with sufficient speed.
3. There are delays in reflecting the effect of new methods of distribution at lower prices.
4. There are technical problems associated with the sampling and the representativeness of the price data reported to the BLS which could be causing an upward bias.

It is impossible to determine the degree to which the above factors have caused an upward bias in the CPI on the basis of the available evidence. Expert opinions differ widely on this issue. However, there is no doubt that the potential upward bias of the CPI could easily be upwards of 2 percent in any given year. One would have to examine the specifics of the time period involved in order to discover how important a contribution each of the above reasons might have made. Once we take into account the probability of these upward biases, the appropriateness of the CPI (as it is presently constructed) as a welfare indicator, and of all of the indices as measures of changes in P, is greatly vitiated. There may be a considerable gap between "measured" and "real" changes in the cost of living and between "measured" and "real" changes in P.

Since the universe of the three indices are not the same, we would not expect them to move too closely together except, perhaps, during a very broad inflation. Thus a close examination of the indices and their components might help determine when a measured (and real) inflation is more the result of circumstances that are unique to a particular sector of the economy rather than a widespread phenomenon. However, differences in the rate of change of these indices can also be caused by alterations in the structure of the economy and by the particular nature of the inflation (and/or the accompanying antiinflationary policy that the government is pursuing) even if it is a broad one.[16] This is an important fact, especially when considered in conjunction with the index bias, because of the uses to which these indices are put in our economy.

The WPI, or its components, is employed in many long-term contracts to provide automatic upward or downward adjustment of prices.[17] The effect of the CPI is even more widespread:

The CPI plays an important role in collective bargaining, particularly during periods of rising prices. In addition, contracts contain clauses which provide for automatic adjustments—cost-of-living escalator clauses—every 3 or 6 months. The CPI is used to convert money wages into real wages, and thus to determine the extent to which workers are sharing in the rising levels of living. . . . A number of the components of the CPI are used to build up the implicit price index. Finally, the rent component is sometimes used as part of an escalator clause in long term leases.[18]

To this list we might also add the importance of the CPI in determining legislated welfare increases, particularly OASDI. These are just some of the most direct ways in which the use of these indices to measure yesterday's price increases has an effect on today's and tomorrow's price increases. In a more general sense, the use of these indices to measure inflation creates certain expectational patterns and, in this way, significantly influences the nature (particularly the rate) of the inflation we get. The crucial role of expectations in inflationary processes will become more evident as we proceed in this study—thus emphasizing the need for us to be cautious about the construction, interpretation, and utilization of price indices.

3 Traditional Views of Inflation

Economists and others have classified inflations in many different ways. The distinction between an open and a repressed inflation is one that we have already made. We have also seen that an open inflation can be thought of as demand-pull or cost-push depending upon whether it is primarily characterized by exogenous shifts in the aggregate demand curve or the aggregate supply curve. For our purposes we need to look beyond exogenous causes of increases in P and obtain a more comprehensive understanding of inflationary processes. To do this, we first turn to an exposition of some traditional views of inflation.

A fact so obvious that it is often overlooked is that a person's approach to a particular problem and the solutions he finds depend upon the framework within which he tends to think—a framework that to a great extent is dictated by his view of the world. This seems to be especially so when the issue is inflation and the person an economist. Economists' views of inflation often tend to be by-products—albeit, too casual ones—of their conception of the economy. This is not to say that a theory of inflation should not be derived from a larger view of an economy. Indeed, a fully developed theory of inflation can only be conceptualized in the context of a complete model of an economic system. Our point is that the models of an economic system which have yielded most traditional views of inflation are not such. They often have been incompletely stated and were developed for purposes other than the analysis of inflationary processes.

The bulk of this chapter will be devoted to a discussion of the theories of inflation most prevalent in the literature in the context of a particular typology which we believe is useful in understanding and emphasizing the incompleteness of these views. In this discussion we will point out some of the advantages and limitations of each approach, occasionally making a modification or extension of our own. This is not intended to be a complete survey of inflation theory, but only a brief attempt to elucidate aspects of certain prevalent models which may be useful for the purposes of this study. After examining each of these models, we will remark on their general characteristics and indicate the direction in which we must move in order to construct a model of inflationary processes that is appropriate to our task.

An Approach to Traditional Models of Inflation

Consider the following expression, which contains numerous terms of aggregate economic variables—each of which is equivalent by definition to the gross national product (GNP) due to conventions adopted in the national income accounts:

$$\overset{(a)}{\text{GNP}} \equiv \overset{(b)}{PY} \equiv \overset{(c)}{MV} \equiv \overset{}{C + I + G + F} \equiv \overset{(d)}{kwN} \equiv \overset{(e)}{W + R + B + Z} \tag{3.1}$$

Each of the variables is described below. The flow variables must all be defined over the same appropriate time period (say, one year), while the stock variables must be averaged over that same time period.

GNP = the money value of Gross National Product.
P = (an index of) the general price level.
Y = real output.
M = the nominal value of the money supply.
V = the velocity of turnover of money in the purchase of newly produced goods and services.
C = the money value of personal consumption.
I = the money value of gross private domestic investment.
G = the money value of government expenditures on goods and services.
F = the money value of net foreign investment.
k = a scalar that is equal to PY/wN.
w = the average money wage/worker.
N = the number of workers (workers = employed people).
W = the money value of workers' compensation (wN).
R = the money value of corporate profits.
B = the money value of property income.
Z = a miscellaneous term which equates (e) to (a). It includes indirect business taxes, the current surplus of government enterprises, business transfer payments, and a statistical discrepancy.

We have used the triple line equality sign ($\equiv$) to indicate that, as we have formulated it, (3.1) expresses the exact equivalence of the terms (a) through (e); i.e., (3.1) is a series of identities.

Now consider term (a) pairwise with each of the terms (b), (c), and (d). When certain assumptions are made with regard to the determinants of the variables appearing in (b), (c), and (d), these pairwise associations are injected with behavorial content and become simple models of the economy expressing the equilibrium relationship among the relevant variables (or constants, as the case may be). We shall make explicit these assumptions since it is in the context of these three simple models of the economy that most traditional views of inflation can be developed and that we shall proceed in our discussion of these views. Our purpose in displaying (3.1) is to emphasize that, *a priori*, none of these views has a corner on the market;[1] changes in PY must be accompanied by changes in (b), (c) and, (d).[2] Also, each theory of inflation—as embodied in the different simple models—has to have implications for income distribution—as embodied in (e). We shall return to these points later.

The Quantity Theory View of
Inflationary Processes

The quantity theory view of inflationary processes takes as its starting point the familiar "equation of exchange" of our terms (a) and (b): (3.2) $MV \equiv PY$. Under certain assumptions this is transformed into an equilibrium relationship that yields an explanation of inflation in its "purest" form as an entirely monetary phenomenon. To understand this, assume that Y is normally at (or, if in disequilibrium, tending toward) its full "natural" employment level. The neoclassical mechanisms embodied in our aggregate supply curve of Figure 2-3 insure this. Assume also that the velocity of money, V, is constant. Then M and P must vary in proportion to one another: the degree of expansion (or contraction) of the nominal money supply dictates the degree of inflation (or deflation) that will take place. The stability of prices can be insured over time if the money supply is expanded at that rate which offsets increases in productivity as embodied in rightward shifts of the neoclassical aggregate supply curve.[3]

This crude approach has been modified and refined until it has become a sophisticated theory of the demand for money whose leading spokesman today is Milton Friedman.[4] He suggests that the amount of money that people wish to hold is chiefly determined by two factors: total wealth and the opportunity cost of holding money. His empirical studies indicate also that as real permanent income increases there is a tendency for people to increase their demand for money somewhat more than proportionately. That is to say, the desired value of the ratio M/PY rises, or desired V falls, slightly as real permanent income increases. The opportunity cost of holding money is determined by the prevailing rates of return that are available on other types of assets as well as people's expectations about the future movements in the prices of these assets. Friedman believes that neither of these determinants appears to have considerable influence on the demand for cash in normal times, although major changes in them will produce significant effects on V.

Changes in M affect P in the following manner: Suppose that the economy is in equilibrium, then an autonomous increase in the nominal supply of money occurs with no concurrent alteration in the demand for money. Because of this excess supply of money, many people will be in asset disequilibrium and, in their attempt to restore equilibrium, will drive up the level of prices and (or) real output until the desired ratio of PY/M prevails once more. Short-run supply adjustments may be such that Y surpasses full employment level of the neoclassical model in Figure 2-3, but in the long run, competition within the labor market and flexible prices and wages insure that the economy will operate at the full employment level of Y.[5] Thus, any changes in M will be fully reflected in changes in P (taking productivity into account) unless V also is altered.

The conclusions of this modern, more sophisticated quantity theory of money are very similar to those of the older school, but there are numerous qualifications that we should emphasize.[6] Velocity is not considered to be constant through time, but is subject to a secular downward drift due to the increase in aggregate real income.[7] Also, it is recognized that there can be significant short run shifts in V, but they require sizeable changes in either the real rate of interest or expectations of a fairly rapid inflation, or both. The short-run correlation between M and P is further weakened by possible changes in Y, although in the absence of wage rigidities and a liquidity trap, equilibrium at less than full employment is not possible (as it is in a Keynesian model), and underfull and overfull employment can be only transitory.[8] Finally, one has to recognize that increased productivity in the long run will continue to put downward pressure on P so that if a stable level of P is desired, the nominal supply of money will have to be increased at the same annual rate as increases in productivity.

This modern version of a quantity theory does become, with the addition of these qualifications and the recognition of the full range of influences on the primary variables (especially V), a more general approach than the earlier one. But still, this approach to inflation places great emphasis on the stability of V and Y, and thus on the degree to which M influences P even in the short run. It is valuable for the insights that it offers regarding the crucial, causal role that the nominal money supply might play in some inflations, as an active agent whose increases in size can, under certain conditions, lead to increases in P.[9] The danger is that, if one views inflation only in the context of this model, then one thinks of it only as a monetary phenomenon and tends to ignore other variables that can have, and often have had, direct influence on determining the nature of inflationary processes. We shall discuss many of these factors in the context of our other two models, but let us mention just two here. First, the nature of the assumptions about the labor market are sufficiently restrictive that they do not permit us to analyze very meaningfully disequilibrium relationships between M and P and Y, which may be of important concern (see note 5 of this chapter in the endnotes). Secondly, the quantity theory gives us no insights into what might be occurring when M is increasing with regard to the distribution of income among the various terms in expression (e) of (3.1) and how a shift in this distribution, which is likely to occur during an inflation, might in turn affect P, V, and Y.

Markup Models of Inflation

We now turn to another model which provides a very different context in which to view inflation than does the quantity theory. We shall follow the same format here as before, first presenting a crude formulation of the model, attributable to Sidney Weintraub,[10] then a more sophisticated one. The focus here is on the identity (3.3): $PY \equiv kwN$. Solving for P yields $P \equiv kwN/Y \equiv kw/A \equiv kU$, where A is the real output/worker and U, unit labor cost. This ceases to be a mere identity and becomes the wage-cost markup equation when certain behavioral assumptions are ascribed to the variables.

Consider the form $P = kw/A$. Weintraub argues that in the short run A varies very little and in the long run for most economies tends to rise at a slow, steady, predictable rate, while k (the average markup of prices over unit labor costs) is as close to a constant as we could hope to find in the behavioral sciences. Thus movements in P are directly related to movements in w. The key to inflation is the rate of increase of money wages. In the short run P is closely related to w; in the long run, we have to take into account changes in A. In order to maintain a stable P we need only require that w rise at the same rate as A.

The type of inflationary process that emerges from this view is an example of what is usually labeled wage-push, a special case of cost-push, in the economics literature. Weintraub does not distinguish it in exactly this manner; for him all inflations are both cost-push and demand-pull since as money wages are permitted to mount, they put cost-push pressure on prices from the aggregate supply side and demand-pull pressure from the aggregate demand side. We recognize that once such an inflationary process is underway these two aspects of pressure on prices cannot be separated out (except conceptually). However, it seems to us that the designation of this particular type of inflationary process as cost-push is appropriate because of the emphasis on money wage increases as its cause.

Weintraub defends the value of his model on the basis of the relative constancy of k (analogous to Friedman's belief in the stability of V). He has collected data from many different countries which presumably substantiate his claim that, both secularly and cyclically, k has fluctuated less than V. If this is true, then perhaps Friedman would want to concede that w is a better predictor of P than is M; but, of course, we can in no way infer from Weintraub's model that, even granting the constancy of k, changes in w are the causes of changes in P. Changes in P may occur for some entirely unrelated reason and then themselves cause movements of w.

But let us take a closer look at k. Note that $1/k \equiv wN/PY \equiv W/PY$, labor's share of income. Thus this model is more than just a theory of inflation; it also has direct implications for the distribution of income which the quantity theory did not. Weintraub's model can be viewed as an example of a markup theory of distribution—by which we mean those theories which make the distribution of the receipts of a firm, industry, group of industries, or an entire economy depend solely upon the relative prices of factor services and products, but regard these prices as being independent of relative quantities. That is, the ratio of price to average cost is "explained" as the outcome of oligopolistic agreements (explicit or implicit), conventional profit margins, and the like, and not by the presence and amount of excess capacity (of capital goods). Similarly, the wage rate is supposed to reflect union and employer bargaining power rather than the amount and sign of the excess demand for labor.[11]

If we can assume that in general unit labor costs are constant, then labor's share of income and the general level of prices are determined by k, which, in turn, is determined by the degree of market power of various constituents. The relative constancy of k, then, is "explained" by the fact that this is the result of how market power in the aggregate has evolved over time.

This is a beginning in an understanding of price determination in mark-up models, but we would like to be able to relate market power more systematically to price-level determination, as well as analyze the implications of relaxing the assumption of constant unit labor costs. To do this we need to develop a more general formulation of a markup model. Assuming imperfect competition and profit maximization, a generalized price markup equation for a representative firm can be given by:[12]

$$p = \frac{1}{a} \cdot \frac{e}{e+1} (MC) = \frac{1}{a} \cdot \frac{e}{e+1} \cdot \frac{w}{MPP_N} \tag{3.4}$$

where e is the point elasticity of the firm's imaginary demand curve for its output, p is the price of the firm's output, w is the average wage of homogeneous labor defined over an appropriate time period, MPP_N is the marginal physical product of that labor over the same time period, and $1/a$ is a factor which takes capital costs into account in the markup. We can now discuss a number of types of inflationary processes that can be profitably viewed in this context.

In the first case, consider that a shift in the imaginary demand curve of the firm may result in the decrease of the elasticity of the curve along its relevant portion. This would cause an increase in the degree of monopoly power of the firm as represented by $e/(e+1)$ which, in turn, could lead to an increase in the price of its output if the expectations of the firm are that it can sell its output at the higher price. Note that we can obtain the same result without any shift taking place in the imaginary demand curve if the firm was previously pursuing a conscious policy of profit nonmaximizing and then decided to exploit its untapped market power. In these situations the price can rise even though measured marginal costs have remained the same, although such a revision in pricing policy is likely to occur in conjunction with an upward shift in the firm's imaginary demand curve. If the general level of prices is affected by this type of process, perhaps because a large number of firms find themselves in the same position or because it occurs for a particular firm that is considered a price leader and others follow,[13] then the result can be what is often labeled a "profits inflation"—a subclass of cost-push inflations.

In the second case we assume that the marginal cost curve shifts upward for the firm, thus causing an increase in the price of its output. In our model this could occur most obviously because of an increase in the money wage, although the same thing could happen to other variable costs.[14] Again, this price increase could affect the general level of prices if similar circumstances prevailed over a sizeable portion of the economy, or if a wage increase in a particular firm or group of firms that is critical leads to a "spiral" or "round" effect with many other wages and prices following.[15] This is the wage-push of Weintraub's model. Note that for a fuller understanding of the inflationary process we should be seeking answers to questions concerning the cause of the initial wage increase. Was it due to an increase in union power, employers' expectations of being able to sell their product at higher prices, or some other cause?

The final type of inflation that can be best viewed in the context of a markup model is that which has been labeled "sectoral" or "demand-shift."[16] This theory focuses on the prices of capital goods and wage rates in the more strongly organized sectors of the economy. The hypothesis is that such prices rise in response to increased demand (due to, for instance, increased monopoly power or movements up an increasing marginal cost curve) or costs (shifts in the marginal cost curve), but do not fall when demand or costs decrease; i.e., they are downward rigid. The same is true for money wages, which increase in response to increases in the cost of living or business profits, but do not fall when these decline. The result of this one-way movement in money wages and prices is that shifts in demand have inflationary effects (even though aggregate demand may remain constant) by raising the two in those sectors to which the demand has shifted, and leaving them as high in those sectors from which demand has shifted. We can visualize this process in terms of our graphs as a shifting upward of the upward-sloping portion of either the Keynesian or relevant neoclassical aggregate supply curve.

It is important for us to note the essential (theoretical) emptiness of markup theories. Exactly what determines the degree of markup? Most firms do not know with any precision the exact nature of the demand curve for their product. There is also considerable dispute as to whether most firms utilize marginal costs (estimated), or average costs (estimated), or some function of the two as a basis for their markup. Furthermore, there is no reason to believe that for the economy as a whole the *ex ante* markup will be equal to the *ex post* markup. In a general equilibrium context, the degree of realized markup is clearly an endogenous variable, perhaps best thought of as a markup function whose determinants are usually poorly specified (if at all) in most markup models.

Nevertheless, we might gain some insight into certain inflationary processes by utilizing this model when it is more appropriate to emphasize shifts in supply rather than demand. We must keep in mind, however, that the implications of changes of presumably exogenous variables in this model for price level determination are by no means as simple as they appear in this context, particularly when inflation is viewed as a dynamic process. Our discussion in the last section of this chapter should help to further clarify these issues.

The Neo-Keynesian View of
Inflationary Processes

The basic ingredients of the neo-Keynesian model are contained in the graphs underlying the derivation of our aggregate demand curves in Figures 2-1 and 2-2 and in the derivation of a Keynesian aggregate supply function which we described in that same section. For this reason our description here of the neo-Keynesian view of inflationary processes will be sketchy in many areas that have already been covered. We will emphasize primarily the differences of this approach from others, discuss aspects of the model that relate particularly to inflation and were not explicitly considered in Chapter 2, and indicate some possible extensions of this view we believe to be fruitful.

The neo-Keynesian approach to inflationary processes focuses on the identity:

$$PY \equiv C + I + G + F^{17} \tag{3.5}$$

In this view V is not stable, particularly in the short run, so that the emphasis is on studying the behavior of aggregate demand components of desired expenditure flows rather than monetary stocks. It is believed that these components can be expressed as reasonably stable functions of a small number of other variables, some of which are treated as exogenous, others endogenous. Thus (3.5) becomes an equilibrium condition where Y is the equilibrium level of real output and the realized aggregate demand components are the desired ones.

This approach does not preclude M from having any effect on P and Y, but any such impact of M is presumed to operate indirectly through its influence on the rate of interest, the degree of credit availability, and other such determinants of desired C, I, G, and F. If the various factors that determine the desired levels of C, I, G, and F are such that there is an increase in aggregate demand, then V will have to increase if M does not; and, since V is believed to be quite capable of fluctuations in the short run under ordinary conditions, the stable relationship between M and money income is broken. If there is an increase in the supply of money, people may be content to absorb this in additional money holdings or use some or all of it to purchase securities which may reduce the rate of interest.

In an extreme case (the liquidity trap) the increase in M would have no effect on aggregate demand; in other instances it could be stimulating to the extent it altered those variables that are determinants of desired C, I, G, and F.

Within the broad framework of the neo-Keynesian approach, there are many possible ways of disaggregating expenditures. The particular choice in (3.5) represents a method that seems to make sense from an accounting point of view and also because it is believed that the determinants of demand are likely to be more similar within each of these categories than across categories. Further disaggregation within these sectors of the economy is often suggested on similar grounds. A typical example follow:[18]

I.   Personal consumption expenditures (C)
        A. Durables
        B. Nondurable goods and services
II. Gross private domestic investment (I)
        A. Fixed business investment
        B. Residential construction
        C. Inventory investment
III. Net foreign investment (F)
IV. Government expenditures on goods and services (G)

Let us focus on consumer durables to demonstrate some possible determinants of one subcomponent of aggregate demand. We shall not give the exact form of the demand function, but only an indication of the direction of influence of the variables that *a priori* theorizing would predict to be relevant. In general it is believed that the demand for durables varies: (1) positively with the level of permanent income; (2) negatively with the level of existing stock of durables; (3) negatively with the relative price of durables; (4) positively with the degree of availability of credit; and (5) positively with the expected future rate of inflation.

Note the role of expectations in (5). In general, expectations about future economic conditions, particularly the degree of inflation, will effect the various components of desired aggregate demand—although often not in well specified ways. Note also that an indirect influence of the money supply can be through (4). The desired level of expenditures in other subsectors of the economy can be similarly expressed as a function of some small number of relevant variables. G is usually treated as being exogenously given in money terms.

Perhaps the most difficult question that must be faced in the neo-Keynesian model of inflation is that of whether aggregate demand is more appropriately specified in real or money terms. When there is little or no inflation occurring, or when the aggregate demand curve (in Y, P space) intersects the aggregate supply curve on its upward sloping portion, this distinction may not be so crucial since an increase in money aggregate demand will increase real income and output.

However, when the economy is at, or near, full employment, it definitely is an important distinction.[19] Undoubtedly, it is unrealistic to assume that desired expenditures are either all in real terms or all in money terms. The traditional Keynesian approach is to assume that desired aggregate expenditures are in real terms. In this case, if an increase in aggregate demand occurs when the economy is at full employment, then the new equilibrium value of P is not readily apparent.[20] In the extreme, the inflation could continue indefinitely.

The method with which this problem was dealt was to study the behavior of the aggregate demand curve at higher and higher levels of P to see if desired real expenditures were not decreased by such things as real balance effects, money illusion, progressive taxation, lags, and so forth, which would influence consumer, business, and government behavior. One example of this would be the possibility that the inflationary process would cause a shift in the distribution of income by increasing the share of a group with a low marginal propensity to consume at the expense of a group with a high marginal propensity to consume. This would be consistent with the theory of income distribution illuminated by Kaldor and others for the full employment situation—a theory that is in the Keynesian tradition since it stresses the equilibrium condition of *ex ante* savings equal to *ex ante* investment and different, but constant, marginal propensities to consume for different income groups in the economy.[21] If such effects as this do not serve to reduce desired real expenditures until they are once again in line with the full employment level of real output, then monetary and/or fiscal policy would have to be used in attempts to halt the inflation.

In order to gain insight into the exact nature of some types of inflationary processes that can profitably be viewed in the context of a neo-Keynesian model and to discern the necessary antiinflationary policy, we believe that it may be useful to disaggregate desired expenditures into those defined in real and those in monetary terms as well as in the conventional $C + I + G$ manner.[22] To be specific, consider first the desired level of government expenditures.

In most models of inflation, G is considered to be exogenously given in money terms over some period of time (such as the fiscal year). While G is defined in money terms in current prices some of the appropriations are fixed in real terms.[23] When inflation has taken place in past years, the amount budgeted to the Office of Economic Opportunity has not been increased, but the amount going to the Defense Department has, since many of its contracts were issued on a cost-plus basis and there were considerable overruns of cost estimates. Similarly, some of HEW's budget had to be revised upward over original intentions because HEW pledged to deliver real amounts of services such as health care. If the level of the governmental budget and the size of the deficit are planned with consideration to their overall impact on the economy, then, unless an inflation is correctly anticipated and its effect on the money value of actual governmental expenditures and taxes correctly predicted and taken into account in these plans, the federal policymakers' objectives will be thwarted.[24] If recent experience can be taken as a guide, during an inflationary period the actual deficit is more likely to be greater, not less than, the planned deficit; the result is more expansionary than was intended.

In an analogous manner to these two different components of G, it seems clear that in the private sector there are various subsectors of the economy that are more likely to make their planned purchases in real terms and to be able to carry them out even in the face of appreciable inflation and restrictive monetary policy. We refer here to areas where there is a significant market power—the monopolistic, oligopolistic, and regulated industries such as the public utilities and some transportation and communications companies. The extremely high rates of interest (often in excess of 10 percent) that were necessary to sell bonds in late 1969 and early 1970 did not prevent some public utilities from floating such issues to finance previously planned expansion. Higher than anticipated costs and interest payments were financed by raising the prices for their output, with the benevolent permission of the appropriate regulatory agency, of course.[25]

This method of compartmentalizing aggregate demand within the context of a neo-Keynesian model seems to us to illuminate what may be an important ingredient in the understanding of the dynamics of some inflationary processes, particularly the one that this country experienced in 1968 and into 1969. It helps partially to account for the continued strength of aggregate demand in the face of extremely restrictive monetary and (presumably) nonexpansionary fiscal policy. A recognition of this possibility may be crucial to the choice of an appropriate, effective antiinflationary policy.

An Overview of Traditional
Inflationary Processes

Let us now utilize the views of inflation that we have just sketched to obtain an overview of the types of inflationary processes that are predominant in economic literature prior to 1965.[26] Refer to Figures 3-1, 3-2, and 3-3, which again employ our aggregate supply and demand curves. Figure 3-1 depicts the purest form of demand-pull inflation which occurs when the economy operates on the vertical portion of the aggregate supply curve.[27] An initial shift of the aggregate demand curve, say from D_1 to D_2, leads to an increase in prices from P_1 to P_2. But how can a dynamic inflationary process be generated whereby the aggregate demand curve will continue to shift upwards over time to D_3 and above? The quantity theory approach offers two quick answers already discussed. The first is by continued rises in the nominal supply of money that are in excess of productivity gains. The other possibility is through the effect of expectations of inflation on the velocity of circulation of money (V). V can increase with M constant if future price increases are expected, thus leading to

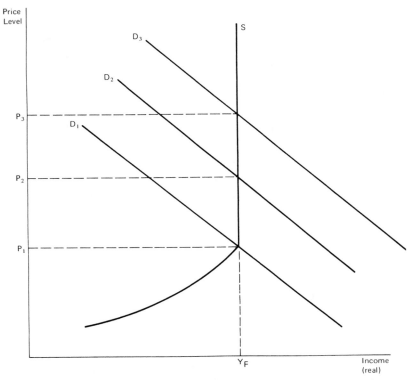

Figure 3-1. Depiction of Traditional Theories of Inflation (1)

increases in $P.$[28] In the neo-Keynesian view there are numerous forces at work which can affect the size of the inflationary gap at the full employment-output level of Y, once the price level has initially risen. One can construct almost any dynamic inflationary process (both stable and unstable) by choosing appropriately from a selection of such items as the real balance effect, redistribution of income, and attempts to maintain real aggregate expenditures at a level greater than capacity output. It is usually recognized that expectations of continued inflation are likely to cause further increases in aggregate demand, but, as we have seen, expectations can enter the model in many different places with many different assumptions about their effect.

Figure 3-2 reflects the kind of inflationary process that policymakers would prefer to encounter (if there is to be inflation at all). Here the aggregate demand curve is intersecting the aggregate supply curve on its upward sloping portion (as does D_1). The aggregate supply curve can be of this shape for reasons of either neoclassical or Keynesian assumptions. In this case, if increases in aggregate demand take place for any of the reasons indicated in Chapter 2, there are

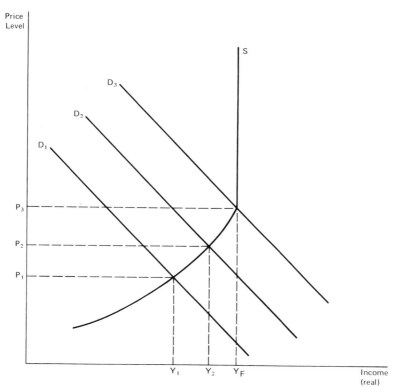

Figure 3-2. Depiction of Traditional Theories of Inflation (2)

permanent increases in output and employment "bought" by one-time increases in P up to the point of D_3. There is no dynamic process to mention here. We would expect no feedback affecting the aggregate supply curve because in the Keynesian case money illusion exists—so even though P increases, money wages do not—and in the neoclassical case there is excess labor supply due to the rigid downward money wage, so money wages are not bid up.

Figure 3-3 can be utilized to depict three different types of inflationary processes. The first is the pure cost-push inflation of our markup model. In this view, due to market power of various types, the aggregate supply curve continues to shift upward over time (say from S_1 to S_2 to S_3) quite independently of aggregate demand. This presents the monetary authorities with the dilemma of a choice between "validating" the wage and price increases by expansive policies, or permitting real output and employment to decline. Y_f is maintainable only continually increasing price levels, and the policymakers are relegated to the passive role of ratifying the seller's decisions.[29] In this case the price output path of the economy may look something like *a-b-c-d-e*. The same

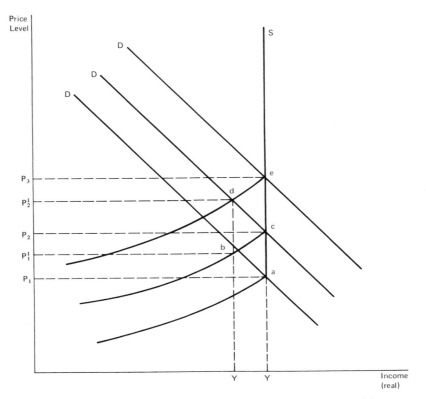

Figure 3-3. Depiction of Traditional Theories of Inflation (3)

type of result could come about as the result of a demand shift inflation. We mentioned earlier that it could be depicted as an upward shift in the aggregate supply curve.

It also is possible to depict a more mixed inflation in the context of Figure 3-3—a process that emphasizes the possibility of interrelated shifts in the aggregate supply and demand schedules inducing less than full-employment inflation with larger shifts in S being more likely as increases in D bring the economy closer to Y_f.[30] In particular, the economy may experience what Turvey calls an "income inflation."[31] The basic idea involved here is that at, or near, full employment, different groups attempt to maintain or raise their real incomes by raising their money incomes. Such a process can be started by any number of means, but once it begins it may be difficult to halt. If output cannot be expanded to satisfy all objectives then some groups' are going to be frustrated.

The process continues as long as frustrated groups . . . try to change monetary arrangements to suit their economic objectives. The process stops when everyone adapts to the new monetary arrangements. This may occur when those who have no power to change their money incomes (say rentiers) are sufficiently expropriated through rising prices to satisfy the demands of the other groups; through money illusion, or, in general, when the course of the inflation has caused a sufficient reduction in employment and real expenditures that the power to make excess income claims ceases.[32]

The Limitations of These Models

The various macro models that we discussed in the previous section each present a different view of inflationary processes. Attention is focused in turn on three main elements of any inflationary process: (1) the balance between desired and actual stocks of money; (2) between desired demand for, and potential supply of, goods and services; and (3) increases in the various cost components of output. Each model contains its own assumptions about which variables are endogenous and exogenous and in a stable relationship with PY.[33] Proponents of each view believe that changes in PY are best understood by focusing on changes in those aggregate variables which appear in the appropriate term (c), (d), or (e) of (3.1).[34] Movements in other variables may have an effect on PY, but their influence is assumed to operate through the endogenous variables of the terms of (c), (d), and (e) rather than directly on PY. By specifying the structure of the model, one has determined the nature of the impact that the various variables can have on one another. The particular structure chosen may or may not be a reasonably valid reflection of some facet of reality, but at best it will represent only a limited view of inflationary processes.

Recall that changes in PY must be accompanied by changes in some or all of the variables in all of our equivalences in (3.1) for GNP. Depending upon the exact nature of a particular inflationary process and one's concern about this process, one model may be a more appropriate mode of analysis than another, but it is unlikely that the same model will be the most useful one for analyzing all inflationary processes. As we noted in Chapter 2, price increases can take place for many different reasons; thus different inflationary processes can best be understood by altering one's perspective of the economy to suit the particular characteristics of the inflation about which one is concerned. These simple models may be useful in highlighting for a particular inflation some variables and relationships that are crucial to a comprehension of its nature.

Clearly, a more general model of inflationary processes would be desirable for most purposes. This is especially true for the needs of this study since we have to achieve a fuller comprehension of the relationship between prices and wages on the one hand, and output and employment on the other, than is possible in the context of these traditional, partial views. In particular, we require a theory of price and wage behavior that will enable us to better understand shifts of, and movements along, the economy's aggregate supply curve in relationship to aggregate demand. The explanations of money wage behavior that we have examined so far are obviously inadequate in this regard if we are to understand the dynamics of inflationary processes. In the next chapter, we will explore some more recent literature which will provide some grist for this mill. Once this is done, it will be possible for us to construct a very simple general equilibrium model in which the rate of inflation and level of unemployment are jointly determined. The problems of causality, which are so confounded in such a model where mutual interdependence of many variables becomes obvious, can be circumvented to an extent by focusing our attention on the relationship between those instrumental policy variables over which the policymakers have control and the endogenous variables (inflation and unemployment) about which we are most concerned.

4 The Relationship Between Inflation and Unemployment: Its Nature and Implications

There are many possible definitions of full employment. For each such case, efforts to attain and maintain full employment as defined probably will have implications for the level or rate of change of prices which would be compatible with this goal. Complete analysis of this relationship would require a theory of labor-market activity and knowledge of the nature of the policy measures that would be applied in the attempt to reach full employment. There were such theories implicit in our neo-Keynesian and neoclassical aggregate supply curves of Chapter 2, but they were not sufficiently well formulated to enable us to deal adequately with our problem. Our aim in this chapter is to focus directly on labor-market activity, particularly a recently developed approach to "voluntary" unemployment, in an attempt to develop an understanding, which is necessary for the purposes of this study,[1] of the nature and implications of the relationship between inflation and unemployment.

Unemployment and Inflation in a Neo-Keynesian Model

Full employment in a neo-Keynesian model incorporates a capacity, billet view of jobs and workers. A characteristic definition of full employment in such a model would be that of Lord William Beveridge. For him, *full employment* existed whenever the number of job openings, or vacancies, was as great as, or greater than, the number of men willing to work.[2] Regardless of how one wishes to interpret "willing" in this context, this definition implies that the level of employment is nearly as high as the stimulation of aggregate demand can obtain. As such, it is consistent with the full employment-output level of real income of our neo-Keynesian model of Chapter 2 and is almost surely inflationary—a fact which Beveridge recognized. This concept of full employment appears to be the same as Lerner's high-full employment and for Ohlin definitely represents a situation of what he terms overfull employment.[3]

The typical view of wage and employment dynamics that flows from this approach is one that yields a stable Phillips curve for an economy.[4] There are a number of *a postiori* explanations which generally focus upon market power as a primary element in determining this inverse relationship between money wage changes and the unemployment rate, but the commonly accepted starting point for a theory of labor-market activity which could underlie such a phenomenon is to be found in Lipsey's article[5] that was published shortly after Phillips'. His basic assumption was that the rate of change of the average money wage rate ($\dot{w}$) in the economy is proportional to the degree of excess demand for labor, which, in turn, could be approximated by the unemployment rate (U). Thus,

$$\dot{w} = f(U) \tag{4.1}$$

Primarily because of the importance for stabilization policy of the relationship between $\dot{w}$ and U, research on this subject proliferated in the early and middle 1960s. The basic model of Phillips was extended through the addition of variables to the right-hand side of (4.1) relating to changes in the cost of living, profit rates, and others as "explainers" of the rate of change of money wages along with various forms of the unemployment rate.[6] These models generally were empirical in their orientation; the choice of the additional independent variables was often determined by the degree to which they improved the goodness of fit rather than because any rigorous *a priori* theorizing indicated their relevance. The state of the theory of labor-market activity that underlay these models' derivations advanced little beyond that of Lipsey's, and the models relied on partial, rather than general, equilibrium analysis. It is not surprising, therefore, that estimates of the position and shape of the Phillips curve for the United States in the 1960s were often at considerable variance with one another.

Informational Unemployment and the Natural Rate Hypothesis

Recently, there have been some theoretical advances in our understanding of the dynamic processes of the labor market which have other implications for the inflation-unemployment relation. We refer here to the so-called informational theories of unemployment.[7] While most of the models developed in this area are only theoretical and have not yet resulted in any convincing empirical testing, they do serve to clarify some of the critical issues surrounding the Phillips curve relation.[8] For this reason an examination of this literature will be useful to us in the construction of a conceptual framework for our analysis. In the discussion that follows, we will assume that the reader is familiar with the relevant works; thus we will focus only on certain aspects of the models rather than attempting a complete summary.

The common thread running through all of these models is an adherence to the neoclassical postulates of lifetime utility and/or net worth maximization, while at the same time relaxing the usual Walrasian assumption of complete information concerning the present and future states of the economy. Once we recognize that there is a great deal of incomplete information concerning both present and future wage rates and prices on the part of both firms and workers, then, even under the condition that the labor market is continuously clearing,[9] a certain amount of "frictional" unemployment is the normal thing in a complex economy such as ours. A period of unemployment can be viewed as an investment on the part of an individual worker since it allows him time to accumulate knowledge about job opportunities and wage rates that should aid him in his utility maximization process. But, not being employed has its costs as well as its benefits, the primary cost being the foregoing of present employment and income that would be possible for the individual if he were willing to take the first job that became available, whatever the wage rate. Presumably, there is some equilibrium rate of unemployment that reflects a balance between the above-mentioned costs and benefits as they are assessed by workers. This is the so-called natural rate of unemployment,[10] which is independent of any monetary variable, in particular the anticipated rate of increase of money wages.[11] Its level is determined by structural characteristics of the labor market such as certain institutional arrangements, the nature of mobility, the demographic distribution of labor-force participants, and so forth. Only if there is a discrepancy between the actual and anticipated rates of increase of money wages can employment deviate from this natural level, because such a discrepancy would cause workers to assess wrongly the relative costs and benefits of employment, thus causing disequilibrium in the labor market (i.e., a move off of Ns in Figure 2-3).

Phelps distinguishes among three types of unemployment as determined by the motivations of workers. They are "search," "precautionary" (or "wait"), and "speculative."[12] Search unemployment has its roots in the lack of perfect information on the part of an individual worker concerning job vacancies and wage rates that are appropriate to his supply characteristics. Time spent by the worker collecting this information and soliciting specific offers of employment may be a profitable investment on his part. Precautionary unemployment depends upon incomplete information on the part of suppliers of services for their frequency of demand over the future at given prices.[13] Speculative employment comes about as a result of workers offering greater than usual labor supply at a given real wage rate because an unanticipated inflation has prompted them to hope that the higher present money wages can be spent partially on future consumption goods whose prices are expected to return to the old lower level.[14]

The picture that emerges from this literature is that of an economy which can be characterized by an inverse relationship between the rate of unemployment and the discrepancy between the actual and anticipated rates of increase of money wage rates. A long-run stable Phillips curve exists only to the extent that workers do not revise their anticipation (and behavior) regarding the trend rate of money wage changes to conform more to reality. If they do so, then the maintenance of some given less-than-natural rate of unemployment requires an ever-accelerating rate of inflation in order to preserve a constant discrepancy between the actual and anticipated rates. In addition, once people are antici-pating some positive rate of inflation, then a return to the natural rate of unemployment accompanied by price stability may be possible only by engineer-ing a temporary, greater-than-natural rate of unemployment in order to break the inflationary expectations.[15] Given these alternatives, some proponents of this view advocate that the maintenance of the economy on a balanced growth path at the natural rate of unemployment and price stability is the most desirable situation.

The above relationship was derived solely by concentration on the supply side of the labor market. It has also been shown to be compatible with a view from the demand side by Phelps and others, for roughly the following type of reasoning. If a firm finds it profitable to expand its output, it will want to increase its money wage offer relative to money wage offers elsewhere in order to reduce the difficulty it would otherwise have in filling its vacancies.[16] But, if money wages are rising in general as during an inflation (due to other firms' attempts to reduce vacancies), then the firm cannot increase its relative wage offer unless it explicitly takes into account this general rise in money wages. As long as a large number of employers are seeking to raise their relative wages, the average money wage must continue to rise. Employers as a group will be in equilibrium only when the expected rate of money wage increases equals the actual average rate since they will then have the success that they desire in filling their vacancies. However, all solutions in which the actual and expected rates of money wage increases are equal lie at the natural rate of unemployment. Thus this natural rate of unemployment

is the equilibrium rate in the sense that it is characterized by equality between the average rate of increase of money wage rates and the expected average rate of increase of money wage rates. This equality results when (and only when) firms on the average are having roughly the success (or failure) they were expecting to have in recruiting and retaining employees, and workers are having roughly the same success (or difficulty) on the average that they were expecting finding jobs of the type and pay that they were hoping for.[17]

Now let us drop the assumption that the labor market is continuously clearing. Money wage rates are notoriously rigid on the downside, and when, for instance, after a particularly long recession, employers might be tempted to lower them, there always exist some obstacles (particularly the minimum wage laws and general social approbation). No doubt, conditions such as those that prevailed in the 1930s would lead to some money wages falling, but this is not as likely to be the case during the downswing of the kinds of business cycles that we have been experiencing in this country since World War II. This opens the door wide for job rationing on a nonwage basis to a much greater extent than might exist with downward flexible money wages.[18] Under these conditions, it is possible for there to be considerable "involuntary" unemployment as opposed to the "voluntary" informational unemployment that we have emphasized above.[19] In such a situation, when there is an increase in aggregate demand, it is likely that many employers can attract the additional labor that they require without having to increase their money wage offers.[20] Money wages of already employed workers will have to be increased to keep pace with the rise in prices that accompanies the increase in aggregate demand if firms wish to retain their larger labor force, but it is not clear that in the short run continued money wage increases in excess of mean expectations are necessary. Eventually, as firms and workers (particularly those who were previously unemployed) adjust to the new situation and become convinced that the boom is going to continue, it will become necessary for there to be a discrepancy between the actual and anticipated rates of inflation if this higher level of employment is to be maintained.[21]

Some Clarifications of the Natural Rate of Unemployment Hypothesis

Under the conditions described in the previous section, there is no stable short-run Phillips curve, but a family of momentary ones with the long-run curve tending to a vertical line at the unique natural rate of unemployment. This is an extreme case—and one which does not seem to be in accord with the historical experience of many Western economies. The issue of expectations and the degree to which they are modified is clearly the critical factor in distinguishing this view from that which yields a stable long-run Phillips curve with considerable downward slope. For this reason, we need to examine their role in more detail.

Let us assume that there are no productivity increases, with all wages and prices generally moving together in the longer run. In this case, we can talk of "the" rate of inflation, which we shall designate by $\dot{p}$. The Phillips curve formulation is given by

$$\dot{p} = f(X) \tag{4.2}$$

where X is a vector of relevant real characteristics of the economy—in the simplest case, only the unemployment rate, U. The natural rate hypothesis states that the correct formulation is really

$$\dot{p} = f(X) + \dot{\overline{p}} \tag{4.3}$$

where $\dot{\overline{p}}$ is the expected rate of inflation.[22] $\dot{\overline{p}}$ must enter with a coefficient of unity, otherwise the value of X would vary with that of p even when $\dot{p} = \dot{\overline{p}}$.

Something needs to be said here about how expectations are formed. The usual assumption in this regard is that of "adaptive expectations" of the form

$$\dot{p}_{t+1} - \dot{p}_t = b\,(\dot{p}_t - \dot{\bar{p}}_t) \tag{4.4}$$

with $0 \leq b \leq 1$.[23] If the actual rate of inflation is maintained at some constant level, then the expected rate will tend toward this level with the rate of adaptation being determined by the value of b. If, however, $b = 0$, then there is a stable short-run Phillips curve which is also the unique long-run one. It is also possible to imagine many, not unrealistic, assumptions such that b might be a function of $\dot{p}$, t, and/or certain exogenous variables—with the result that there would be a stable, downward sloping Phillips curve over some ranges of $\dot{p}$, either temporarily or permanently.[24] But, if one adheres strictly to the adaptive expectations mechanism, then a given less-than-natural rate of unemployment can be maintained only at the expense of an ever-accelerating rate of inflation.

We have examined the implications of incorrect expectations, but what of the situation in which, for various reasons, complete adjustment to expectations is not made? To illustrate this possibility and its consequences, we can modify (4.3) to yield

$$\dot{p} = f(X) + g(Z)\dot{\bar{p}} \tag{4.5}$$

where $0 \leq g \leq 1$ and Z is a vector of variables which we will discuss shortly. If people do not adjust at all to their expectations, then $g = 0$ and (4.5) reduces to (4.2); if they adjust completely, then it reduces to the strict adaptive expectations hypothesis of (4.3) and (4.4); and if they adjust only partially, then $0 \leq g \leq 1$ and we can combine (4.5) and (4.4) to yield

$$\dot{\bar{p}}_{t+1} = [1 - b(1 - g)]\dot{\bar{p}}_t + bf(X) \tag{4.6}$$

which describes the time path of the relationship between $\dot{\bar{p}}$ (and indirectly $\dot{p}$) and X. In this case, for a given X, both $\dot{p}$ and $\dot{\bar{p}}$ tend to $f(X)/(1 - g)$.[25] There is a tradeoff between the rates of inflation and unemployment so long as $g < 1$, even if the actual rate of inflation is expected.

There has been a considerable amount of work done recently on this subject (in many cases in response to the natural rate literature) which indicates that many economists take issue with some of the inferences drawn by the natural rate proponents.[26] These authors point out that there is definitely a considerable short-run tradeoff between inflation and unemployment,[27] and that, while the longer run Phillips curve is likely to be steeper than the short-run one due to a revision of expectations, it is by no means clear that it approaches verticality within any operationally meaningful time period, if at all. The arguments in support of this view are many and varied, but they essentially boil down to a belief that the nature of the adjustment of the participants in the labor market to inflation and inflationary expectations is such that there can be a reasonably permanent tradeoff between inflation and unemployment without the rate of inflation having to accelerate continually in order to maintain some given low rate of unemployment.[28] In order to obtain a short-run tradeoff, these arguments can rely upon a b with a very low value, or high costs to, or the inability of, adjustment to an expected inflation (i.e., $a g(Z) \ll 1$).[29] However, for there to be a stable less-than-vertical long-run Phillips curve, it is necessary that one postulate dynamic money illusion and/or failure of anticipation of inflation on the part of labor-market participants.[30] Otherwise people would fully anticipate and adjust to a long-term constant rate of inflation (unless they are deliberate nonmaximizers).

The belief on the part of the authors (note 26) that there is a stable long-run Phillips curve is based not only upon a priori grounds, but also in many instances upon empirical estimations of (so-called) longer run Phillips curves that explicitly incorporate a revision of expectations into the model forumlation. However, two things should be noted about these models in general. First, expected prices and wages are usually determined by some weighted sum of actual past money wages and prices in lieu of any observable series of better theory or expectations formation. This means that there is considerable experimentation with different formulations with no particular theoretical justification as to which is appropriate. Secondly, and more importantly, the models utilized for this estimation are still only partial ones. We have stressed before the need for a more general equilibrium approach to this problem; specifically, a model that treats inflation and unemployment as jointly determined, endogenous variables and which also includes the relevant exogenous policy instruments. This does not mean that those who believe there is a stable, downward-sloping, long-run Phillips curve are wrong, but it does mean that their empirically based arguments in support of this view are little more conclusive of its reality than are the a priori theoretical arguments of the natural rate proponents to the contrary.[31]

The Natural Rate of Unemployment, A Neoclassical Aggregate Supply Curve and Inflationary Processes

Since the natural rate of unemployment hypothesis is derived from essentially neoclassical postulates of labor-market behavior, we should be able to relate it to our neoclassical aggregate supply curve of Chapter 2 in an attempt to understand more fully its implications for inflationary processes. Refer to Figure 4-1 to see how such an endeavor might proceed. LS is the perfectly vertical aggregate supply curve (Snf) of Figure 2-3. The natural rate of unemployment hypothesis indicates that this aggregate supply curve occurs at the equilibrium level of real

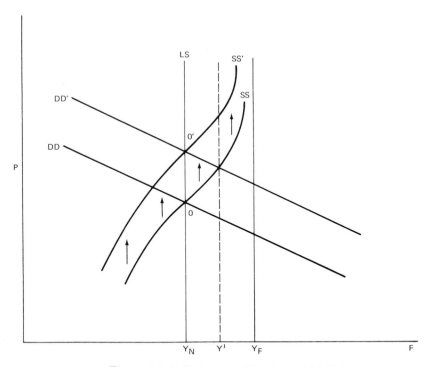

Figure 4-1. Inflation in a Neoclassical Model

output (corresponding to the natural rate of unemployment) and is the relevant supply curve for the economy whenever $\dot{p} = \dot{\bar{p}}$.[32] At any time there is also a disequilibrium short-run (assuming adaptive expectations) aggregate supply curve, SS, which is relevant whenever $\dot{p} \neq \dot{\bar{p}}$. SS can be thought of as being anchored to LS at point X with X moving up along LR over time at the rate $\dot{\bar{p}}$. SS is assumed to approach verticality at the level of real output, Y_f, which corresponds to a full employment-output capacity concept of a Keynesian model.[33]

Now, assume that initially the economy is in a state of equilibrium with aggregate demand equal to DD, $\dot{p} = \dot{\bar{p}} = 0$, and $Y = Y_n$. Then an autonomous shift in aggregate demand takes place such that the new aggregate demand curve becomes DD'. In this case the economy moves up along SS to the new level of employment and output, Y', and P increases. With adaptive expectations after workers learn of the increases in P, SS will begin to shift upward at some rate $\dot{\bar{p}}$. If Y' is to be maintained, then DD' has to continue to shift upward at an appropriate rate which will become faster and faster as $\dot{\bar{p}}$ increases since $(\dot{p} - \dot{\bar{p}})$ must be maintained constant. If DD' does not continue to shift upward, then Y

will gradually decrease to Y_n, and the natural rate of unemployment will again prevail—but this time with some positive expected rate of inflation equal to the actual rate. Hopefully, this one example of a method of translating the implications of the natural rate hypothesis into visual terms is sufficient for the reader to generalize.

When it is viewed in this context, we can see that what some authors have termed a cost-push (wage-push) inflation may be partially the result of adaptive expectations operating after an initial demand-induced increase in the general price level has taken place. Other authors, however, do seem to have in mind a definition of cost-push that can be conceptualized in terms of a leftward shift of the LS aggregate supply curve and an increase in the natural rate of unemployment, for whatever reason. From a policy point of view, it could be very important to distinguish between the two possibilities, since in the former case the proper application of monetary and fiscal policy could have some success in returning the economy to an earlier configuration of unemployment and inflation (particularly the same natural rate with $\dot{p} = \dot{\bar{p}} = 0$), while in the latter case such efforts would be misguided. Only a structural change in the economy would permit this result. Similarly, what was earlier called an incomes inflation seems to contain some of both these elements, since it can be the result of groups trying to increase their money incomes during an inflation in order to maintain their real incomes at some given level or may reflect a desire to increase one's real income independent of any expectations of inflation.

The material presented in the earlier parts of this chapter have led us to a different and more appropriate (for our purposes) view of the inflation-unemployment relationship than was explicit in the traditional approaches contained in Chapters 2 and 3. Notice, however, that this has been with reference only to aggregate supply; we have not yet said anything about factors influencing aggregate demand in this chapter. Indeed, the same factors that we now see are crucial to an understanding of movements in the aggregate supply curve in an inflationary period—namely, the actual and anticipated rates of inflation—are very likely also to cause shifts in the aggregate demand curve, which is drawn in P, Y space under the assumptions of constant money income and no inflationary expectations. The possible influences of these variables were mentioned when we constructed aggregate demand curves, discussed briefly in the context of the quantity theory of money, and then in more detail with reference to a neo-Keynesian approach to inflationary processes. One cannot assume that it will be an easy matter for policymakers to control the position of the aggregate demand curve through monetary and fiscal policies in order to achieve a desired, feasible inflation-unemployment configuration since the actual and anticipated rates of inflation also will be influencing private demand for goods and services.

The discussion in this section should emphasize further the degree of interdependence of aggregate supply and demand considerations in an inflationary process, thus recalling again the need for a more general equilibrium approach to the problem of inflation-unemployment relationship. There is one further point in this regard that should be made, and which recalls the discussion at the end of the last chapter. We have so far been treating expectations as adaptive only, implicitly assuming that their formulation was independent of anything except past price movements, and also assuming that past price movements were not dependent on the particular nature of aggregate demand, in particular the method by which it was stimulated, but only by its level. It may well be that the implications of expansionary fiscal and monetary policy are quite different with regard to their effect not only on actual but also expected prices.[34] Thus we will want to explicitly enter variables representing fiscal and monetary policy into any general equilibrium model for this reason as well as the fact that, since they are the available policy tools, it is ultimately their effect on inflation and unemployment in which we are interested for policy purposes.

5 Theoretical Aspects of the Effects of Inflation on Distribution and the Efficiency of Allocation

The Conceptual Framework

We have defined the primary analytical task of this study to be the development of a conceptual framework for the evaluation of the impact on the poor of macroeconomic policies as they are reflected in various rates of inflation and aggregate unemployment. Our examination of inflationary processes in Chapters 2, 3, and 4 has provided us with sufficient background to broadly sketch this conceptual framework. We shall do so here as a preliminary to the more detailed treatment to follow.

First, a general equilibrium model is required, one that contains the ingredients our previous discussion has indicated are essential. In particular, this model should incorporate explicitly the relationships among monetary and fiscal policy on the one hand and the rates of inflation and unemployment on the other. Here we know that $\dot{p}$, $\ddot{p}$ and U should all be treated as jointly determined, endogenous variables. A fairly simple example of such a model is developed and tested in Chapter 10. Secondly, knowledge is required of the implications for the welfare of the poor of the various indicated feasible time paths of rates of inflation and unemployment. To obtain this, the dimensions of inflation and unemployment that are crucial to an understanding of their effects on the efficiency of allocation and the distribution of economic resources over time have to be identified.

We have already seen that an important distinction that must be made with regard to inflation, if we are to understand its relationship with unemployment, is the degree to which it is anticipated. Other theoretical considerations indicate that the degree of anticipation of inflation, as well as the actual rate of inflation, is also a crucial dimension in determining the potential effects of inflation on distribution and efficiency of allocation. These theoretical considerations are examined in this chapter;[1] and in Chapters 7, 8, and 9 the results of some empirical analysis on the effects of inflation on distribution are reported.

The crucial dimension of unemployment to be considered is its rate.[2] It will prove useful for us to have some benchmark for comparison when we consider the effects of different rates of unemployment on distribution and the efficiency of allocation. One candidate that suggests itself is the lowest rate of unemployment which at any given time is compatible with price stability under static expectations. We will designate this as the PSR for "price stable rate" of unemployment. Under certain conditions, which were outlined in Chapter 4, the

PSR is the unique natural rate of unemployment. Chapter 6 examines some theoretical arguments and empirical evidence which bear on the effects of a greater- and less-than-PSR on distribution and the efficiency of allocation over time.

The main purpose of this chapter is to examine some theoretical aspects of the possible effects of inflation on distribution and the efficiency of allocation over time.[3] It is our objective to make this analysis as partial as possible, in particular to hold constant macroeconomic employment conditions in the economy.

This chapter would be a lengthy one if we were to attempt to deal with all theoretical considerations relating to the distributional and efficiency implications of inflation. However, primarily for two reasons this is not the case. First, we shall explore many different aspects of the redistributional biases of inflation in our empirical work in Chapters 7, 8, and 9. Consequently, the second section sketches briefly the relevant considerations which are necessary to guide our empirical analysis with regard to this issue. Secondly, the third section on allocative efficiency is much shorter than it might be because we do not believe that very full development of such material is essential to our purposes. We must take into account the effects of inflation on efficiency for the completeness of our study, but (as we shall argue), from a general equilibrium viewpoint, the major impact of inflationary processes on the poor is usually transmitted through changes in labor-market conditions. A fear of the efficiency (and redistributional) costs of inflation becoming excessively high if inflation is not kept at a minimum, however, often does lead to aggregate economic policies that have strong labor-market consequences for the poor. For this reason we must pay some attention to the basis of these fears.

The Redistributional Effects of Inflation

Most of the theoretical issues involved here are generally well known and need not be discussed at any length. In one of the few previous empirical studies done on this topic,[4] Ando and Bach state what they believe to be the four basic analytical propositions concerning the redistributional effects of inflation. We list them here since they provide a useful point of departure for our discussion in this section.

1. Inflation redistributes real purchasing power (over current output and over assets) from those whose income rises less rapidly relative to the prices they pay as a result of the inflation to those whose incomes rise more rapidly relative to the prices they pay.
2. Inflation redistributes real purchasing power from those whose assets rise more slowly in price as a result of inflation to those whose assets rise more rapidly than prices.

3. Inflation redistributes real purchasing power from creditors to debtors, when debts are stated in fixed dollar terms.
4. To the extent that accurate expectations of continuing inflation affect economic behavior, the redistributional effects indicated above will tend to be negated, except where readjustment of terms of economic contracts is prevented or retarded (by government rules, existence of long term contracts, unequal knowledge, unequal bargaining power, etc.).[5]

Item 4 reminds us again of the crucial role that anticipations can play where the effects of inflation are concerned. If today's inflation was expected as far back as before the longest outstanding contract, then its redistributional implications would be minimal. If it is entirely unexpected, then there is the maximum potential for redistributional consequences (for a given rate of inflation); and, if it is partially anticipated, then the potential consequences are in some intermediate range.[6] Let us examine propositions 1 through 3 above with these considerations in mind. We generally will do so with an unanticipated inflation assumed, recognizing that to the extent it is anticipated, the redistributional consequences are reduced.

Item 1 has many different aspects to it, some of which relate to empirical analysis that we undertake in Chapters 7, 8, and 9. These are:

(a) An inflation-induced lag of wages behind prices has often been cited as a source of redistributional bias against low-income groups since they tend to be relatively more dependent upon human capital for income.[7] Recently, however, there has been much work done that casts considerable doubt on the significance of such an effect.[8] We believe that this evidence indicates that the redistributional consequences of this effect are minimal and will not pursue this question further in this study.
(b) Interest and rent income, on the other hand, are a possible source of a redistributional bias against the nonpoor since they tend often to lag prices and are a more important source of income for the nonpoor than the poor.[9] In Chapter 8 we present a profile of income sources for various income and demographic groups of the population. This will enable us to discern just how important the various types of income are to these groups.
(c) We have already discussed the possibility of changes in labor-market activity, particularly the unemployment rate, being implicit in inflationary processes. Such changes may have a redistributional bias for earned income. This is the subject of Chapter 7.
(d) The role of transfer payments in the income of the poor and nonpoor is important. First, there are nonlegislated transfer payments, primarily private pensions and annuities, that are fixed in dollar value so that unanticipated inflation definitely erodes their value. We have to discover how important this effect is on the poor by again examining our profile of income sources.

Secondly, there are the various types of government transfer payments which are subject to legislative action. In Chapter 8 we examine the historical experience and likely future course of the real value of these transfers ar.d discuss the redistributional biases therein.

(e) Finally, there is the question of the appropriate cost-of-living index for various subgroups of the population, particularly the poor versus the nonpoor. Our brief discussion of price indices in Chapter 2 indicated that there are likely to be redistributional effects of inflation due to differential rises in the cost of living for different population subgroups. In Chapter 7 we perform some empirical analysis that sheds some light on this issue and discuss further its implications.

In order to examine the magnitude of the redistributional effects of inflation that are described in items 2 and 3 of Ando and Bach's list, knowledge is required of the quantity and nature of the assets and debts held by different income groups. In Chapter 9 we utilize such data to make a rough estimate of this effect on the poor and nonpoor and also report on the results of another more sophisticated study on the same topic.

Inflation and the Efficiency of Allocation

There are two topics that we shall examine briefly under this heading. The first deals with the dual role of money in our economy as a medium of exchange and a store of value and how this might lead to efficiency costs from illiquidity. The second topic is the related problem that exists with regard to the United States' balance of payments once we consider the economy as open. We will limit our discussion to the mild and/or moderately rapid inflations that have characterized the U.S. experience since World War II. The efficiency costs of a hyperinflation would be enormous, but such a phenomenon does not appear to be a likely consequence of a less rapid inflation.[10]

The Costs of Illiquidity

When an inflation is occurring there is an increased cost to holding money. If the inflation is entirely unanticipated it can have the redistributional implications examined in the last section, but it will have no effect on people's desired liquidity. If, however, the inflation is anticipated, it will affect desired liquidity in a way that may impose efficiency costs. Alchian and Kessell address this possibility:

An increase in the cost of holding money induces a community to divert some resources to the production of money substitutes. Consequently, a good that is nearly costless to society is in part supplanted by goods that have greater costs. These costs constitute the efficiency losses, or the welfare effects of anticipated inflation. Both the duration of an inflation and the rate of change of prices affect the costs of holding money. Hence, both play a role in determining the volume of resources that goes into economizing on cash balances.[11]

The theoretical treatment of the welfare losses of anticipated inflation is dealt with in the literature under the rubric of inflationary finance.[12] The most recent thrust of this literature is to discuss the problem in terms of the optimal level of liquidity. This is the level of liquidity at which the marginal social benefits (of liquidity) and the marginal social costs are equated, and it is consistent with some steady rate of anticipated inflation (or deflation). Depending upon the model used for the analysis of this issue,[13] estimates regarding this optimal rate of anticipated inflation range from the negative of the real rate of interest up to a moderate positive rate. Thus, while there is no doubt that a sufficiently high anticipated rate of inflation does impose efficiency costs through a misallocation of financial resources for this reason, there is considerable controversy as to the level of inflation at which these costs become a significant burden.

In most instances it will probably be the case that an inflation is neither entirely unanticipated nor fully anticipated. People may be expecting some inflation but not the exact amount that occurs. Also, even if their expectations regarding the rate of increase of the general level of prices are correct, there may be a considerable doubt as to which specific prices (particularly of financial assets) will inflate and at what rates. Finally, some effort is involved simply in determining what has happened to various prices as the inflation continues. All these factors indicate that during an inflationary period certain kinds of activity, particularly speculation, may become relatively more rewarding than previous-ly[14] and, in the extreme, more rewarding than work of the usual productive sort. This also results in efficiency costs, but ones that are extremely hard to estimate. It is clear that such costs are likely to become a considerable drag on the economy as hyperinflation is approached in an economy, but their probable magnitude at moderate rates of inflation is a subject about which our knowledge is imprecise. However, it would appear that they are not very burdensome.[15]

International Aspects

We have been treating our economy so far as though it were a closed one, and we shall continue to do so in the remainder of this study. This assumption will not do an injustice to the primary purposes of our analysis. However, we must recognize that the implications of inflation for the international situation are of considerable concern to policymakers and pay some attention to this fact.

Briefly, the problem as usually articulated is this: Inflation in this country raises the prices of our goods and services relative to those of other countries.

This is likely to increase the deficit of the balance of payments over what it would have been had domestic prices not risen. Confidence in American financial policy on the part of foreigners decreases, fear of devaluation of the dollar increases, and more gold leaves the country, thus aggravating the difficulty. Since we are essentially the bankers for the world, this leads to fear of international illiquidity and the concommitent efficiency losses.

While it is true that the international financial situation is worsened as a result of our domestic inflation, it also seems probable that inflation is not the basic cause or, perhaps, even a major contributor to this difficulty. The general level of prices for the United States rose less than that of any other major Western economic power (except Western Germany) in the twenty years following World War II, while our balance-of-payments position continually deteriorated. The fundamental problem seems to be disequilibrium in international markets which has been perpetuated by fixed exchange rates, coupled together with our rigid adherence to the gold standard. Many prominent economists believe that only adjustments in these areas will solve the problem in the long run. In their view, measures aimed at keeping up interest rates and holding down the rate of inflation are only temporary panaceas which treat the symptoms and not the disease. Recent events in international monetary circles indicate that the United States is beginning to adopt more appropriate policies in these regards. Nevertheless, while hoping for a more rational approach to these matters in the future, we must live in the present; and this is a present where the fear of aggravating the balance-of-payments situation for this country places restraints on the monetary and fiscal authorities that make it difficult, if not impossible, to pursue (within the limits of our knowledge and ability) optional policies concerning our domestic economy.

6

The Implications of the Aggregate Unemployment Rate for Distribution and the Efficiency of Allocation

The purpose of this chapter is to examine the effects of various aggregate rates of unemployment on distribution and allocative efficiency in our economy over time. We assume that the aggregative unemployment rate is negatively correlated with the level of economic activity,[1] so much of the discussion is couched in terms of this latter phrase rather than in terms of the unemployment rate, per se. As was the case in the last chapter, the analysis here is intended to be partial. In particular, we are abstracting from the effects of any anticipated or unanticipated inflation that may be accompanying a given rate of unemployment.[2] These were the subjects of Chapter 5.

A given rate of unemployment is said to be efficient if, for some after tax and transfer shares, there exists no other rate of unemployment which can yield greater discounted-over-life, net economic benefits for all members of the economy. Thus the efficient rate(s) is (are) Pareto optimal. We will consider the question of efficiency in relation to the price stable (PSR) or natural rate of unemployment in this chapter's second section.

Under the question of distribution, we wish to consider the implications of the aggregative rate of unemployment or level of economic activity for the relative share of pre tax-and-transfer over life economic benefits of the poor vis-à-vis the nonpoor. This issue cannot be entirely divorced from that of allocative efficiency. In the last section of this chapter, we shall argue that the efficiency losses or gains in movements of the aggregative unemployment rate about the PSR or natural rate of unemployment are not neutral with respect to their distributive effects. Before dealing directly with either of these subjects, however, we must specify some relevant aspects of labor-market structure and their relationship to individuals' employment advancement.

Social Mobility and Labor-Market Structure

In this section we shall present a broad view of some aspects of the relationship between social mobility and labor-market structure. This will provide us with a framework within which we can examine the implications of the level of economic activity on distribution and the efficiency of allocation. The primary view to be advocated in this section has been most cogently developed by Melvin W. Reder and can best be summarized as follows:

Given his individual characteristics, an individual's upward mobility is advanced or impeded by the state of his economic environment. To fix ideas, posit some "natural" or "normal" level of economic activity which roughly approximates the idea of aggregate full employment equilibrium. At this level of activity there will be some normal expected rate of improvement in the rate of earnings and of status for any worker of given age, sex, race, years of schooling, etc. If the level of economic activity falls below this, the observed normal rate of improvement will also fall below the expected normal rate; the reverse will occur if the level of activity rises above the normal. Analogously, the relation of the actual to the normal rate of activity in any given sector of the economy will retard or accelerate the rate of improvement of any given individual.[3]

An important concept underlying this view is that of a job ladder. It is presumed that there is a network of hierarchically organized jobs covering most employment opportunities of the economy.[4] These sets of jobs may be confined to a single firm, but a job ladder can be thought of as cutting across firms that provide similar employment opportunities. It is the accession to, and the movement up, these ladders that constitute the individual improvement which is so affected by the general level of economic activity.[5]

Why does advancement so often take place in the context of ladder climbing? Let us assume, as is generally the case, that excess demand for labor, which is reflected in job vacancies, appears for jobs located at all stages of the lifetime earning cycle. Where well-defined job ladders are in existence, it will usually prove more profitable for employers to recruit a candidate for the $j + $ 1st rung of the ladder from the jth rung rather than from a random selection of workers having a particular set of socioeconomic characteristics.[6] Two of the more important reasons for this relate to the costs of specific training and hiring:

1. One of the general characteristics of ladder jobs beyond the first rung is that they require specific training. A great deal of the training that is necessary to the satisfactory performance of the job at the jth rung is also required for jobs at the $j + $ 1st rung.
2. The same bias toward promotion from within can arise even in the absence of common trainings for jobs at different rungs on the same ladder. This is due to the familiarity that an employer will already have with the characteristics of a current employee, or the relative ease with which he can acquire such information if a potential employee was previously engaged in the same or related line of work elsewhere.

Now let us examine nonladder jobs for a moment. Such employment can be thought of as satisfying two criteria: (1) there is no specific training associated with them; and (2) there is no incentive for the employer of a nonladder employee either to consider him for promotion or to retain him during a period of low activity in order to avoid the costs of rehiring when activity picks up again. At any given time there will only be a certain number of bottom-rung jobs available on any ladder. Workers who are unable to gain access to a particular ladder will have to try others, but in general there will be fewer ladder vacancies than there are applicants and the excess will have to seek nonladder employment or leave the labor force.

The most important characteristic of nonladder jobs is that they are frequented with unskilled workers who experience high unemployment percentages.[7] These high unemployment percentages are a direct, though not necessary, result of the high turnover that is associated with such employment.[8] This high turnover seems to be translated into high unemployment rates due either to a failure of workers to anticipate job separation or to a combination of their unwillingness and inability to reduce the time spent in job search. The result of this is that, for a given demand for unskilled workers, there is an increase in the number of workers unemployed when an increase in the supply of workers for unskilled jobs results from a slower rate of accession to job ladders.[9]

It is useful to think of a pool of unskilled workers alternating between unemployment and temporary, nonladder jobs. This pool is augmented by new entrants into the labor market (who make up a disproportionate number of the unskilled) and depleted by those who gain footholds on job ladders.[10] An increase in the number in the former category relative to the latter will increase unemployment if the ratio of unskilled jobs to unemployed persons remains constant. The opposite of this is also true.

The ratio of unskilled jobs to unemployed persons has three primary determinants. One we have already discussed—the relation of actual to normal economic growth. The second is the relation of the normal growth rate of ladder-associated jobs to the actual growth rate of the labor force.[11] The third is the social minimum wage rate. Reder has the following to say about this concept.

Economic theory would suggest that there is some natural rate of unemployment that would exist when the actual and natural levels of economic activity were equal. This natural rate and the other equilibrium conditions of the system together determine the ratio of the number unemployed to the number with unskilled jobs. If the number of unemployed thus determined involves too many disappointed job seekers, the wage rates on unskilled workers should fall, and vice-versa. However, there is considerable evidence to show that these rates are relatively insensitive to the level of unemployment, and much more sensitive to a variety of institutional forces that work to maintain the reservation price of time despite unemployment. The effect of these forces is to set what is called the Social Minimum Wage Rate which is an exogenous variable of the system, setting a lower bound to unskilled wage rates and partially determining the unemployment percentage.[12]

While it is true that many of the unskilled workers who enter the urban labor force via the pool remain there all of their lives, a significant number do eventually find their way onto a ladder of some sort. The particular ladder upon which they manage to get will depend among other things upon: (1) their demographic characteristics; (2) the current level of economic activity; and (3) such things as luck, ingenuity, and so forth. As a worker's age advances, the probability and profitability of his .switching from one ladder to another diminishes, so that it is while he is young that there is more direct competition of employers for his services. In this view, a sharp increase in the general level of economic activity not only accelerates the rate of ladder ascent for the typical worker, but also increases the probability that a worker of given background can get onto any particular ladder.

The Level of Economic Activity and
Allocative Efficiency

The primary focus of this section is on the implications of the level of economic activity on allocative efficency in the labor market. However, for completeness we shall also have to consider briefly the product market. For this reason, it will be useful to employ the concept of a "natural rate of capacity utilization" which is assumed to prevail on an equilibrium balanced growth path in a manner analogous to that of the natural rate of unemployment—indeed labor is just one of the various resources that is employed (or unemployed) at its "natural" rate on this balanced growth path. This natural rate of capacity utilization will serve as our benchmark; we will consider whether deviations from it are likely to constitute efficiency gains or losses for the economy.

At first glance the question of what is the most efficient rate of unemployment may appear to be easily answered: is it not at just that level of employment at which output ceases to increase with the addition of more workers to the ranks of the employed? This is a naive answer because it focuses only upon current output and ignores the effect of the present level of employment (and concommitant characteristics of the environment such as the vacancy rate) on the time profile of future output. It also fails to take into account whether or not the goods and services that are desired by society are being produced in the proper balance and delivered at the appropriate time. In particular, if a lower unemployment rate is achieved through the deviation of the actual from the expected pattern of price and wage changes on the part of some or all economic participants, then it is not necessarily true that this rate is more efficient than a higher one would be even though the former results in greater current output.

Recall that our discussion in Chapter 4 on informational theories of unemployment indicated that many decisions regarding labor-force participation and employment have an (inventory) investment aspect. This may be true from both a private and social vantage point. From the perspective of private investment, search unemployment can be viewed as a sacrifice of present wage earnings for the expectation of a future improvement over what would otherwise be possible. Precautionary unemployment is an act of investment through waiting in order to be available for more profitable future employment. And the speculative view of labor supply treats unemployment as an intended intertemporal trade of present employment for leisure in response to an expected deterioration in the leisure cost of future consumption. Search and precautionary unemployment can also be viewed as a social investment since they will hopefully result in the placing of a worker in a job where his productivity is higher than it would have been had he not undergone the period of unemployment. If we assume that differences in the marginal social productivity of workers are reflected in differences in their wages, then employment behavior on the part of the workers that increases their discounted future earnings will also result in greater social benefit (in the Pareto sense).

All this is to say that, in a world of incomplete information and uncertainty, some unemployment may be allocatively superior to none. But we can be more precise than this. Recall that our analysis in Chapter 4 indicated that for the economy to be operating above or below its natural rate implies that at least some economic participants are not optimizing; the most likely reasons being either money illusion and/or a divergence between actual and anticipated prices. For this reason, in the absence of certain kinds of market imperfections or externalities, the natural rate of capacity utilization is the most efficient rate. That a less than natural rate of capacity utilization is not as allocatively efficient as the natural rate under such conditions should be fairly easy to accept. However, since it might not be quite so obvious that an increased level of economic activity (beyond that level compatible with the natural rate of capacity utilization) leads to movements away from Pareto optimality, it may be helpful to mention some of the efficiency costs that can develop in such a situation.

We have already elaborated on the fact in Chapter 4, and mentioned briefly at the beginning of this chapter, that a less than natural rate of unemployment may be accompanied by nonoptimal allocations of labor supply on the part of many workers if they suffer from money illusion or are anticipating less accurately the present or future pattern of wages and prices. There may also be costs that are born by employers for similar reasons which have been described by Edmund Nourse:

Even under conditions of the mildly inflationary boom that we have witnessed, scraping the bottom of the manpower barrel has entailed expenses of recruitment, training, absenteeism, spoiled work, and lowered morale that have raised unit costs, direct and indirect, until they have probably exceeded in some instances the unit value of added product.[13]

Finally, many authors have discussed the nature of the efficiency costs that develop in the product market (particularly the capital goods sector) when a less than natural rate of capacity utilization prevails.[14] The primary manifestations of these costs are such things as lowered quality of products and either bad delivery of, queueing for, or simple unavailability of, inputs (nonlabor) and final products.[15] The most important effect of these is to greatly increase marginal unit costs[16] at higher levels of economic activity.

Once we drop the assumption that there are no significant market imperfections or externalities, the waters become very muddied. It is no longer possible to assert that the natural rate of capacity utilization is Pareto optimal.[17] Any examination of the question of what rate (or rates) is most efficient would require detailed analysis in the context of a model that specified the particular nature of the imperfections and externalities and would also be befuddled by second-best problems. The model that we sketched in the first section of this chapter does include some assumptions and implications concerning imperfections and externalities that may exist in the labor market. To the extent that the inferences that can be drawn from this model are consistent with reality it suggests to us that, within the labor market, equal deviations from the price stable rate of unemployment are less detrimental on efficiency grounds on the downside than they are on the upside.[18]

Distribution and the Level of Economic Activity

If unemployment were distributed equally throughout the labor force at all levels of economic activity (and of the aggregate unemployment rate), this country would undoubtedly find itself much more willing than under the present circumstances to endure the aggregate rate of unemployment in excess of 4 percent which may be necessary (given the present structure of the economy) to maintain price stability. There would not be nearly so much reason to be concerned about "the problem of unemployment." This would probably indicate that the dichotomy between ladder and nonladder jobs was not so severe. In general, workers could anticipate their being unemployed for a certain length of time periodically and incorporate it into their longer run work/leisure plans. Much more of the unemployment could be considered "voluntary" and would probably contribute to the lifetime utility maximization of workers in the spirit of the neoclassical, frictional unemployment models.

But unfortunately, as we have noted in the beginning of this chapter (and as our model there implied), such is not the case. Measured unemployment is distributed differentially across the labor force in a nonrandom manner. In particular, it is concentrated among the young, the aged, the unskilled, the uneducated, and certain ethnic minorities—in general, among low-income groups.[19] In fact, not only are the unemployment percentages higher for these groups than for the rest of the population at levels of economic activity within the range common to our economy's experience, but they also fluctuate more in their absolute value as the aggregate unemployment rate varies. These facts, which have received much attention in the past seven or eight years, have led many economists to propose that there is a significant redistributive bias in favor of many low-income groups as the level of economic activity increases.[20] Despite the general prevalence of this belief among economists, there has been remarkably little rigorous analysis of the subject; and most of what has been done is quite recent. The relevant studies are those of Beach, Budd, Metcalf, Mirer, Thurow, and T.P. Schultz.[21] While the approaches taken by the different researchers varied considerably, all focused on the impact of macroeconomic fluctuations on the equality of income distribution, some at a more disaggregated level than others. Not surprisingly, their findings are not entirely consistent, but, in general, do support the notion that the income redistributional consequences of higher levels of economic activity favor the lower income population.[22] Perhaps the most sophisticated study, with the strongest results, is that of Metcalf. He reports that the lower tail of the income distribution makes absolute and relative gains at lower levels of the aggregate unemployment rate and that the magnitude of these gains is larger for the various demographic subgroups of the poor in proportion to the degree of their tendency to participate in the labor force. Thurow found that rising employment has mixed effects for whites but is a powerful force leading to higher and more equal black incomes (therefore reducing the inequality of the overall income distribution). Beach's results indicate that a higher aggregate employment rate results in a greater degree of income concentration among males aged twenty to sixty-four, but has mixed effects among very young and aged males. Overall he finds there to be "a definite pattern of cyclical fluctuation in income-concentration with the strongest impact (occurring at the bottom of the distribution) being on the order of ten percent or so (in proportionate terms)."[23]

In addition to these studies on the redistributional consequences of differing aggregate unemployment rates, there are a number of papers which have explored the relationship between variations in the aggregate unemployment rate and the relative speed with which the poverty population in this country (defined with constant real-dollar thresholds) has been reduced. In a sense, these results reflect the net effect on the poor of both changes in the efficiency of allocation and redistribution as the unemployment rate varies. Although there is some controversy, the evidence in these studies suggests that there is a considerable increase in the rate of departure from poverty during both movements to lower unemployment rates and periods of sustained low unemployment (as opposed to a sustained higher rate). This seems to be true even at very low unemployment rates (3 percent); and (consistent with Metcalf's results) the subgroups of the poverty population most sensitive to this effect are those with the highest labor-force participation rates.[24]

These results are certainly not surprising and do lend support to the validity of a significant, favorable[25] redistributive bias of lower aggregate unemployment rates; however, we should not leap to this conclusion too rapidly lest we mistake a short-run gain for a longer run loss, as when assuming that the greater output forthcoming at less-than-natural rates of capacity utilization necessarily signalled a movement towards Pareto optimality.[26] This does not seem to be a problem, though, if we accept the model of this chapter's first section as an appropriate context in which to analyze this phenomenon. We saw there that it is precisely those low-income workers who are in the unskilled pool that stand the most to gain from increases in the level of economic activity because they are disproportionately engaged in search activity.[27] At higher levels of economic activity they will experience: (1) less anticipated unemployment with its detrimental consequences; (2) greater ease in locating nonladder employment; and, most importantly, (3) greater ease in locating ladder employment with all its implications for their future improvement in human capital and income.[28]

This redistributive bias is further strengthened by two other phenomena relating to the labor market. First, the model in the first section of this chapter also predicts that in the movement from one level of economic activity to a higher one, there will be a narrowing of wage differentials.[29] And secondly, since movement up the job ladder is enhanced by higher levels of economic activity, this will tend to favor those nearer the bottom, whose ranks are more likely to be composed of members of lower income groups than those at the top.[30] In view of all this it appears that on welfare grounds one would want to argue for the maintenance of a higher level of economic activity than would be warranted by efficiency of allocation considerations alone.[31]

7

Inflation and the Relative Cost of Living

The major indication that inflationary processes are underway in the American economy is generally taken to be a substantial annual rise in the Consumer Price Index (CPI). This index is designed to reflect the expenditure pattern of a "typical" family (i.e., an urban wage or salary earner's family).[1] It seems curious, therefore, that discussions of the effects of inflation on various parts of the population have rarely included a careful examination of the expenditure patterns of particular groups[2] and the way in which differences in their expenditure patterns might generate differential inflationary impacts on their costs of living.[3] Theoretical analysis of price indices[4] indicates that, even when tastes are homogeneous across all income groups, one should still expect that a differential "true" index would be applicable to different income classes since the value of such an index depends upon the level of real income. In fact, if we consider a Paasche or Laspeyre's price index series calculated during times of inflating prices, the level of the index tends toward a maximum the greater the correlation between the price changes and relative value weights of the various commodity items. In particular, then, one should expect inflations to have a different relative impact on the poor, and on various subgroups of the poor, than on the "typical" family or other nonpoor groups. Also, the exact nature of these differing relative impacts should depend upon the particular characteristics (i.e., the pattern of relative price changes) of any inflation. Consequently, in the first section of this chapter we construct cost-of-living indices (price indices) which reflect the expenditure patterns of the poor for the recent United States economy and we compare them with cost-of-living indices for other consumer groups. Then in the next section we discuss the limitations of these indices and their comparison and thus the implications that can be drawn from this analysis.

The Construction and Comparison of Cost-of-Living Indices

Some calculations based upon data from the Survey of Consumer Expenditures (SCE), 1960-61, are presented in Tables 7-1 and 7-2. Table 7-1 demonstrates the degree to which families defined as poor according to their incomes have levels of expenditure exceeding the poverty line relevant to their family size and residential location. Table 7-2 shows the percentage distribution among cells defined at a more aggregate level than in Table 7-1. We include data for those

Table 7-1
Unit[a] Income and Expenditures in Relation to Poverty Standards

Income Poverty Line	Total Expenditures/Poverty Line Percentage of Raw Total					
	0-100	100-120	120-140	140-160	160-300	
0-1.0	78.6	9.5	4.5	3.1	4.3	100
1.0-1.1	35.6	31.5	16.0	8.6	8.3	100
1.1-1.2	28.8	32.5	15.9	9.6	13.2	100
1.2-2.0	8.5	8.8	22.8	19.3	40.6	100

[a]Consumer units: families and unrelated individuals
Source: U.S. Department of Labor, Bureau of Labor Statistics, *Survey of Consumer Expenditures*, 1960-61.

Table 7-2
Distribution of Consumer Units by Income and Expenditures

Income Poverty Line	Total Expenditures/Poverty Line Percentage of Total		
	0-100	100-300	Subtotal
0-1.0	26.3	7.1	33.4
1.0-2.0	8.6	58.0	66.6
Subtotal	34.9	65.1	100.0

Source: U.S. Department of Labor, Bureau of Labor Statistics, *Survey of Consumer Expenditures*, 1960-61.

families just above the poverty line as well, in order to give some indication of the extent to which drawing a sharp distinction right at the poverty threshold may distort the picture.

Table 7-1 is of some interest beyond the concerns of this study, since it would seem to suggest that as much as 22 percent of the group defined as poor on an income basis have expenditures exceeding their official poverty level. Many of these might be considered only "temporarily poor" in that their expenditure levels suggest that they may be used to (or anticipating) a higher standard of living than that of the truly poor.[5] Using a combination of expenditure and income levels as applied to the relevant poverty standard, we have tried to separate out a group which would have expenditure patterns most closely representative of those of the "longer term poor."[6] This group is labeled "Poor" in our later tables. The group labeled "Poor and Near Poor" includes those with incomes up to 1.2 times the poverty line and expenditures up to 1.6 times the poverty line.[7]

For these two groups, and some others, we utilized the expenditure data of the SCE to calculate average expenditure weights for each of the broad categories of the CPI. These weights were then used in conjunction with the CPI price series to derive price indices for the years 1947-67 for various subgroups of the population. The results of this effort are reported in Table 7-3.

First note that in Table 7-3 several different indices are reported. The Aged Poor Index is for a subset of the poor including those families with heads sixty-five and over similarly-aged unrelated individuals whose incomes and expenditures fall below the poverty line for their unit size. The Poor and Near Poor Index is based on the expenditure patterns of the population defined in the previous paragraph. The Wealthy Price Index is based on the expenditure patterns of units with incomes of $10,000 and above.

Comparisons of the Poor and Near Poor and Poor Price Index (PPI) with both the CPI and the Wealthy Price Index make it possible for us to obtain some idea of the relative differences in expenditure effects for groups at different income levels that price level changes have had in the recent past. The CPI is based upon the expenditure patterns of urban wage and salary earners with incomes below $10,000 (this income limit was revised upward after 1961). Thus the CPI group includes many poor units. If we wish some idea of how expenditure effects of price level changes are affecting the relative welfare of the poor, it is useful to remember that the gap between the CPI and the PPI will tend to understate any relative changes between the PPI population and the CPI population excluding the poor, since some poor units are averaged into the CPI base.[8] It is for this reason that we constructed the Wealthy Price Index, to further accentuate any differences which might be indicated by a difference between the CPI and the PPI.

The picture that emerges from this table is one which has the PPI very close to the CPI in general. The Aged-Poor Index is more consistently above the CPI and this difference began to widen after 1965. However, we make a rough adjustment to take into account the possible effects of Medicare[9] on the aged poor. This adjustment reduced the Aged-Poor Index back to the level of the CPI. In line with this change in the Aged-Poor Index, we adjusted the PPI to account for the influence of the aged subset of this group on the overall weights. This brought the PPI down by a lesser extent, but still to the level of the CPI. The results of these adjustments are reported in Table 7-3 in the column headed "1967a."

The process of making these adjustments brings to light a further consideration. It turns out that the aged are a considerable portion of the poor as we have defined them by income and expenditure. This suggests that if a Non-Aged Poor Index had been constructed, it would have fallen below the CPI in most years since the aged-poor segment is pulling the PPI up. Also, the Medicare adjustment does not take into account the possible effects of Medicare or Medicaid on the non-aged poor, and in this sense undoubtedly represents a conservative estimate of the effects of this important social legislation.

Table 7-3

Aggregate Price Indices for Various Consumer Groups (1957-59 = 100)

	Year												Expenditure Weights			
	1947	1948	1950	1952	1956	1958	1960	1964	1965	1966	1967	1967[a]	Poor	Aged Poor	Poor and Near Poor	Wealthy
Consumer Price Index	77.8	83.8	83.8	92.5	94.7	100.7	103.1	108.1	109.9	113.1	116.3					
Poor Price Index	77.4	83.1	83.9	92.4	94.8	100.8	102.9	108.2	110.0	113.7	116.6	116.3				
Aged Poor Price Index	76.6	82.3	83.4	91.9	94.8	100.8	103.1	180.4	110.3	114.1	117.1	116.3				
Near Poor Price Index	77.1	80.6	83.8	92.2	94.7	100.6	103.1	108.4	110.2	113.8	116.8					
Wealthy Price Index[b]	76.5	82.2	83.9	92.0	94.5	100.6	103.4	108.9	110.6	113.8	117.0					
Food	81.3	88.2	85.8	97.1	94.7	101.9	101.4	106.4	108.8	114.2	115.2		.349	.344	.317	.219
Alcoholic Beverages	75.4	78.9	82.6	96.6	97.1	99.6	102.1	104.7	105.8	107.7	109.9		.007	.004	.010	.018
Tobacco	73.0	76.3	80.0	86.6	94.1	99.7	107.1	114.8	120.2	126.1	130.0		.023	.016	.021	.013
Housing	74.5	79.8	83.2	89.9	95.5	100.2	103.1	107.2	108.5	111.1	114.3		.356	.422	.339	.278
Clothing	89.2	95.0	90.1	97.2	97.8	99.8	102.2	105.7	106.8	109.6	114.0		.078	.036	.087	.118
Transportation	64.3	71.6	79.0	89.6	91.3	99.7	103.8	109.3	111.1	112.7	115.0		.051	.033	.074	.160
Medical	65.7	69.8	73.4	81.1	91.8	100.1	108.1	119.4	122.3	127.7	136.7		.058	.086	.066	.062
Personal Care	76.2	79.1	78.9	87.3	93.7	100.4	104.1	109.2	109.0	112.2	115.5		.033	.025	.032	.027
Recreation[c]	82.5	86.7	89.3	92.4	93.4	100.8	104.9	114.1	115.2	117.1	120.1		.023	.013	.027	.048
Reading[c]	82.5	86.7	89.3	92.4	93.4	100.8	104.9	114.1	115.2	117.1	120.1		.008	.011	.008	.009
Education[c]	82.5	86.7	89.3	92.4	93.4	100.8	104.9	114.1	115.2	117.1	120.1		.003	.0003	.005	.020
Miscellaneous	75.4	78.9	82.6	90.6	95.8	101.8	103.8	108.8	111.8	114.9	118.2		.011	.010	.014	.029

[a]Adjusted for Medicare

[b]Incomes of $10,00+ in 1960

[c]Reading and Recreation Index Used.

Note: The source of the price statistics in U.S. Dept of Labor, Bureau of Labor Statistics, *The Handbook of Labor Statistics, 1968*, Bulletin No. 1600 (Washington, D.C.: G.P.O., 1969). One difficulty was presented by the fact that price series were listed for Recreation and Reading combined. We simply applied the Recreation had Reading price series to the three weights from the SCE for which we had separate data. A glance at the expenditure weights in this table will suffice to demonstrate that with the possible exception of the Wealthy Price Index, this procedure could make little difference relative to any other arbitrary one.

We were able to refine this analysis even further by taking advantage of the more detailed breakdowns of expenditure patterns that the SCE provides. Wherever these disaggregated weights were compatible with detailed price series information in the 1968 *Handbook of Labor Statistics*, we utilized the information to construct a better price index for the poor.[10] We were also able to construct some price indices for other subgroups of the poor that the earlier calculations suggested might be interesting. These final disaggregated price indices are reported in Table 7-4. The difference between the disaggregated PPI (Table 7-4, column 3) and the earlier approximation of the PPI are striking. Even before the Medicare adjustment is made,[11] the result of the disaggregation is to reduce the PPI two points below that value in Table 7-3. It would appear that much of the reason for this drop is because of the high index for food prepared away from home in contrast to food prepared at home (129 versus 112 in 1967), and the exceedingly high index for hospitalized illness costs. Since the poor spend a much smaller percentage of their incomes on both of these former and latter items than do the nonpoor, the impact of price rises in these detailed indices is smaller for them.

In the last two rows of Table 7-4 we have made an adjustment for Medicare

Table 7-4
Disaggregated Price Indexes for Various Consumer Units (1957-59 = 100)

Year	CPI	All Poor	Aged Poor	Rural Nonaged Poor	Rural Aged Poor	Urban Nonaged Poor	Urban White Poor	Urban Nonwhite Poor
1953	93.2	93.8	93.2	94.3	93.7	93.7	93.4	93.8
1954	93.6	94.3	93.9	94.3	93.9	94.2	94.0	94.3
1955	93.3	94.1	94.0	93.7	93.6	93.9	93.8	94.1
1956	94.7	95.4	95.2	94.9	94.9	95.1	95.1	95.4
1957	98.0	98.2	98.0	97.9	97.9	97.9	98.0	98.1
1958	100.7	100.9	100.7	100.7	100.8	100.6	100.7	100.7
1959	101.5	101.4	101.2	101.3	101.3	101.1	101.3	101.2
1960	103.1	102.9	102.7	102.6	102.7	102.6	102.9	102.7
1961	104.2	103.9	103.8	103.5	103.7	103.6	103.8	103.7
1962	105.4	104.9	104.7	104.5	104.5	104.7	104.8	104.6
1963	106.7	106.4	106.0	105.9	105.8	106.1	106.2	106.0
1964	108.1	107.5	107.1	107.0	107.0	107.2	107.4	107.1
1965	109.9	109.1	108.8	108.7	108.6	108.9	109.1	108.7
1966	113.1	112.5	112.0	112.1	112.0	112.2	112.4	112.0
1967	116.3	114.7	114.2	114.6	114.3	114.7	114.9	114.3
1966[a]		111.8			111.2			
1967[a]		113.5			112.4			

[a]Adjusted for Medicare

on the aged-poor indices. The substantial benefits of this social legislation in protecting the aged-poor from expenditure effects due to the rise in medical costs is reflected in the fact that the Medicare adjustment lowered their estimated price index by 0.7 points in 1967.

The Significance and Implications
of These Indices

There are numerous questions which should be dealt with at this point: for example, what is the exact nature of our indices; how are we to interpret them in the light of theoretical analysis of price indices; and how significant are these results? Even for our most refined results we were forced to use a fixed set of quantity weights (based upon 1960-61 expenditure patterns) for all years for which we calculated the various price indices. This means that our indices up to and including 1960 are Paasche price indices, while from 1961 onward they are Laspeyre's price indices. The CPI, however, is adjusted by the BLS for the 1950-60 period to reflect shifting expenditure weights which occurred because the "typical family" enjoyed a rise in real income in this time span. Thus it is a linked chain index. After 1960 there were no new expenditure studies done, but an attempt was made to continue to take into account the effect of rising real income on expenditure patterns by raising the upper income cutoff for units included in the CPI base. The CPI, therefore, is an upper or lower bound on a true index,[12] which is an estimate[13] of the change of the cost of living to a "typical family" with the recognition that the real income of this family is rising over time. On the other hand, prices indices are upper or lower bounds of true indices which estimate the changes in the costs of living to different representative consumer units under the assumption that their real income is constant over the period. This is indeed the comparison that we would like to make because we are interested in the experience of that portion of the population that is remaining poor as contrasted to that of the typical or higher income consuming unit whose real income rose during most past inflationary periods.

Since we are working with fixed expenditure weights of 1960-61, our poor price indices are probably more reliable estimates of the true indices the closer we are in time to 1960-61. Also, we would expect that those indices which are more narrowly defined with regard to the group of consumers over which they are aggregated will be a better representation of any given individual consumer unit member's experience than are those that are not so narrowly defined. (For example, the Urban Non-White Poor Index versus the PPI, or any of the poor indices versus the CPI).

There are many difficulties with our poor price indices. They are subject to all the criticisms made in Chapter 2 with regard to the CPI. In their construction we have used the same prices series that is used for the CPI. This was necessary since we have no conclusive data on the prices the poor actually pay—particularly, no time-series data.[14]

It is important to note the following, especially in view of the current controversy over whether or not "the poor pay more." We are investigating the effects on economic welfare of increases in the price level. It may be that the level of prices paid by the poor for comparable goods is higher than that for the nonpoor. However, this is not relevant to our task; we need not be concerned unless the *rate of increase* of the price of the market basket purchased by the poor is greater than that of the market basket purchased by the nonpoor during inflationary periods. While there is sound *a priori* reasoning which would indicate that "the poor pay more," there does not seem to be any such basis for the position that the prices they face rise faster as a result of inflation. And even if within each broad expenditure category (such as food) the items that are relatively more important to the poor do show a greater average price rise than those purchased by the nonpoor, this does not necessarily mean that a poor price index will inflate more than a nonpoor price index; only the construction of the full index will yield a valid comparison of the cost-of-living indices for the two groups.[15]

Given the theoretical problems of the construction of price indices and the nature of the indices that we had to construct due to the paucity of relevant data (as well as possible errors in the data we did use), it seems to us that little, if any, significance can be attached to the differences that showed up between our poor indices and the nonpoor indices. The strongest statement that could be justified in this regard is that the results suggest that cost-of-living effects of inflation in the 1960s have been less adverse for the poor than for the nonpoor. On the other hand, we may reject rather emphatically the hypothesis that (given the present state of the theory of index numbers and the availability of relevant data) indications are that the poor and the aged have experienced increases in their cost of living relative to the larger population due to the inflation in the United States in recent years.

In general, there is no *a priori* reason to believe that the effects of inflation on the relative costs of living of different subgroups of the population will be consistently biased either in favor of, or to the detriment of, low-income consumer units. Such effects depend upon the pattern of relative price movements and the expenditure weights characteristic of the subgroups. While the latter demonstrates certain income-related stability over time,[16] the former has varied considerably during different inflationary periods. It may be that in the earlier part of the twentieth century, inflations tended to be more detrimental to the poor because food price increases usually outstripped the increase in the general level of prices, just as present inflations may tend to be less detrimental to the poor primarily because medical costs have soared. But such situations presumably are caused by specific supply and demand conditions that may not persist for any long period of time and (in any event) are not inherent in inflationary processes. A knowledge of these specific conditions may permit us to predict an uneven incidence across income groups of cost-of-living effects of particular inflations, but we cannot generalize from such results.

Inflation and the Redistribution of Income: Some Empirical Evidence

Our primary purpose in the two sections of this chapter is to carry out some of the empirical analysis suggested in Chapter 5 with regard to the determination of the redistributional consequences of inflation. Our approach here is quite casual; nevertheless, there are several valuable insights to be gained from even so cursory an examination of some of the relevant data. In the first section, we present a profile of various income sources and their relative importance to different subgroups of the population. The experience of the poor during inflationary periods with regard to nonearned income other than social security and public welfare is discussed in this context since we are not giving it separate consideration. In the second section, we undertake an examination of these latter two in more detail because of their importance to the economic welfare of the poor—especially the aged.

A Profile of Income Sources

Tables 8-1, 8-2, and 8-3 on the following pages contain certain data pertaining to income for the year 1966 for various families and unrelated individuals (heretofore lumped together under "units") by age, sex (of head, if relevant), and income class. Poverty class 2 reflects the official standards of the federal government and is approximately consistent with the definition of poverty we used in Chapter 7.[1] Poverty class 3, whose members we will designate as near-poor, includes units receiving somewhat higher income than those in class 2, but who are still relatively poor.[2] Poverty class 4 contains those whose incomes were above the upper threshold for class 3. For each age-sex-income group there are three columns of numbers. The first column contains the percentage of all units reporting nonzero income from the source indicated to the left. The second column contains the mean value of this source of income for those units reporting nonzero income of this type; and the third column contains the mean value of this source of income as a percentage of total CPS (Current Population Survey) income for all units including those who reported no income of this type. The entries in the "Source" column are mostly self-explanatory. "Pensions" is the sum of government, veterans', and private pensions. "Benefits" includes workmen's compensation and unemployment insurance. "Welfare" is all other public assistance. "Oth. Inc." (other income) includes private welfare, payments from life insurance annuities, and miscellaneous.

Table 8-1
A Profile of Income Sources for Male-Headed Units

				Sex = Male	Poverty Class = 2				
Source	Non-Z	Nonaged Mean(N-Z)	/CPS	Non-Z	Aged Mean(N-Z)	/CPS	Non-Z	Total Mean(N-Z)	/CPS
CPS Inc.	–	2278.4	–	–	1453.5	–	–	2024.3	–
Earn Tot	88.040	2149.7	83.069	28.500	658.3	12.908	69.700	1961.9	67.551
Non-Earn	46.202	866.4	17.570	98.200	1290.6	87.194	62.219	1072.6	32.969
Rent	3.252	461.4	0.659	7.900	324.3	1.763	4.684	390.2	0.903
Int + Div	15.386	150.6	1.017	26.900	246.8	4.568	18.933	192.7	1.802
So. Sec.	10.568	1004.4	4.659	84.200	1033.8	59.887	33.249	1027.3	16.874
Pensions	4.766	888.8	1.859	11.600	886.1	7.072	6.871	887.4	3.012
Benefits	8.352	470.6	1.725	1.000	520.3	0.358	6.087	473.1	1.423
Welfare	11.862	1287.0	6.701	23.000	816.7	12.923	15.293	1069.1	8.077
Oth. Inc.	3.619	576.4	0.915	4.100	340.9	0.962	3.767	497.4	0.926

				Poverty Class = 3					
Source	Non-Z	Nonaged Mean(N-Z)	/CPS	Non-Z	Aged Mean(N-Z)	/CPS	Non-Z	Total Mean(N-Z)	/CPS
CPS Inc.	–	4083.0	–	–	2326.1	–	–	3547.2	–
Earn Tot	95.923	3969.3	93.252	34.400	965.4	14.277	77.161	3560.9	77.459
Non-Earn	44.622	998.4	10.911	98.100	2032.7	85.726	60.930	1506.2	25.872
Rent	4.205	562.0	0.579	11.500	487.3	2.409	6.430	521.3	0.945
Int + Div	18.458	144.4	0.653	47.500	333.3	6.806	27.314	244.6	1.883
So. Sec.	10.507	1427.9	3.675	91.800	1395.2	55.062	35.298	1402.0	13.951
Pensions	7.386	1197.3	2.166	37.500	1060.4	17.095	16.570	1102.8	5.151
Benefits	12.294	499.5	1.504	0.500	137.6	0.030	8.697	493.1	1.209
Welfare	5.787	1100.1	1.559	9.000	995.9	3.853	6.767	1057.8	2.018
Oth. Inc.	3.333	926.5	0.756	3.600	559.6	0.866	3.414	808.5	0.778

				Poverty Class = 4				
CPS Inc.	–		–	–		–	–		–
Earn Tot	99.893	9540.2	91.789	62.500	6725.0	49.252	95.595	9216.6	88.222
Non-Earn	67.939	8766.2	6.536	96.600	5299.5	50.782	71.234	8505.7	10.247
Rent	8.342	917.9	0.914	20.800	3535.3	8.912	9.774	1325.9	1.165
Int + Div	56.022	1045.0	2.447	72.000	1264.8	9.656	57.859	1098.8	3.051
So. Sec.	5.995	416.6	0.682	82.300	901.9	20.057	14.766	486.1	2.307
Pensions	7.739	1084.7	1.250	45.400	1638.9	11.878	12.069	1439.7	2.141
Benefits	9.411	1540.6	0.445	3.400	1759.4	0.287	8.720	1635.2	0.432
Welfare	1.227	451.5	0.114	2.000	568.1	0.337	1.316	456.8	0.132
Oth. Inc.	3.597	883.4	0.656	5.200	1132.0	1.289	3.781	926.8	0.709
		1738.9			1666.7			1727.5	

Table 8-2
A Profile of Income Sources for Female-Headed Units

Sex = Female Poverty Class = 2

Source	Nonaged Non-Z	Nonaged Mean(N-Z)	Nonaged /CPS	Aged Non-Z	Aged Mean(N-Z)	Aged /CPS	Total Non-Z	Total Mean(N-Z)	Total /CPS
CPS Inc.	—	1552.8	—	—	1076.7	—	—	1324.1	—
Earn Tot	59.314	1035.1	39.539	13.400	497.5	6.192	37.259	942.3	26.514
Non-Earn	77.155	1218.9	60.566	98.900	1020.7	93.756	87.600	1111.4	73.529
Rent	4.552	524.4	1.537	10.800	376.8	3.780	7.553	423.0	2.413
Int + Div	18.760	200.7	2.424	36.900	224.7	7.701	27.474	216.2	4.485
So. Sec.	18.728	927.5	11.187	79.400	780.1	57.528	47.871	810.1	29.287
Pensions	7.715	728.6	3.620	8.400	680.7	5.311	8.044	704.6	4.280
Benefits	4.404	488.1	1.394	0.100	291.1	0.027	2.337	484.0	0.854
Welfare	35.285	1418.1	32.223	24.400	760.6	17.237	30.057	1161.7	26.370
Oth. Inc.	15.505	822.7	8.215	5.600	456.8	2.376	10.747	731.1	5.934

Poverty Class = 3

Source	Nonaged Non-Z	Nonaged Mean(N-Z)	Nonaged /CPS	Non-Z	Mean(N-Z)	/CPS	Total Non-Z	Total Mean(N-Z)	Total /CPS
CPS Inc.	—	2742.8	—	—	1946.5	—	—	2364.8	—
Earn Tot	72.789	2108.6	55.960	25.800	1219.8	16.168	50.483	1893.0	40.411
Non-Earn	76.119	1592.8	44.205	98.700	1652.1	83.772	86.838	1624.8	59.665
Rent	9.004	620.9	2.038	21.200	538.7	5.867	14.793	565.0	3.534
Int + Div	24.757	226.4	2.043	53.700	346.3	9.554	38.496	305.8	4.978
So. Sec.	36.468	1202.6	15.990	88.200	1034.5	46.875	61.025	1087.3	28.058
Pensions	14.463	1007.8	5.314	30.800	832.1	13.167	22.218	892.2	8.382
Benefits	7.549	438.9	1.208	2.400	458.8	0.566	5.105	443.3	0.957
Welfare	18.454	1632.9	10.987	11.300	1075.6	6.244	15.058	1434.4	9.134
Oth. Inc.	11.794	1534.3	6.597	4.500	694.6	1.606	8.331	1319.0	4.647

				Poverty Class = 4				
CPS Inc.	–	6011.7	–	–	5090.9	–	–	5750.6	–
Earn Tot	93.811	5051.2	78.823	53.600	4777.0	50.295	82.410	5000.6	71.662
Non-Earn	75.726	1689.3	21.279	97.600	2592.7	49.706	81.928	1994.4	28.414
Rent	9.648	1168.1	1.875	25.200	1055.7	5.226	14.058	1111.0	2.716
Int + Div	54.396	485.9	4.397	75.200	883.1	13.045	60.295	626.4	6.568
So. Sec.	23.345	1437.2	5.581	81.100	1045.4	16.654	39.721	1210.4	8.360
Pensions	11.370	1328.1	2.512	34.000	1497.8	10.003	17.787	1420.1	4.392
Benefits	8.582	529.8	0.756	2.400	614.3	0.290	6.829	538.2	0.639
Welfare	3.575	1157.9	0.689	6.400	1235.4	1.553	4.376	1190.0	0.906
Oth. Inc.	13.489	2404.6	5.395	9.900	1337.5	2.601	12.471	2164.4	4.694

Table 8-3
A Profile of Income Sources for All Units

Both Sexes		Poverty Class = 2	
Source	Non-Z	Nonaged Mean(N-Z)	/CPS
CPS Inc.	—	1973.2	—
Earn Tot	75.956	1783.6	68.658
Non-Earn	59.223	1059.6	31.804
Rent	3.799	493.2	0.949
Int + Div	16.806	174.1	1.483
So. Sec.	14.001	961.2	6.820
Pensions	6.007	802.2	2.442
Benefits	6.691	475.4	1.612
Welfare	21.716	1376.6	15.150
Oth. Inc.	8.619	762.8	3.332

Both Sexes		Poverty Class = 3	
Source	Non-Z	Nonaged Mean(N-Z)	/CPS
CPS Inc.	—	3804.3	—
Earn Tot	91.113	3660.2	87.662
Non-Earn	51.170	1182.2	15.901
Rent	5.203	583.2	0.798
Int + Div	19.767	165.7	0.661
So. Sec.	15.905	1320.5	5.521
Pensions	8.858	1132.9	2.638
Benefits	11.308	491.1	1.460
Welfare	8.421	1342.8	2.972
Oth. Inc.	5.092	1219.1	1.632

Both Sexes		Poverty Class = 4	
Source	Non-Z	Nonaged Mean(N-Z)	/CPS
CPS Inc.	—	9150.4	—
Earn Tot	99.221	8378.2	90.848
Non-Earn	68.800	1011.7	7.606
Rent	8.486	1060.5	0.984
Int + Div	55.842	424.1	2.588
So. Sec.	7.912	1199.6	1.037
Pensions	8.140	1507.8	1.341
Benefits	9.320	459.5	0.468
Welfare	1.487	956.3	0.155
Oth. Inc.	4.689	1950.4	1.000

An examination of Tables 8-1, 8-2, and 8-3 yields, among others, the following significant observations:[3]

1. Earned income is very important to the nonaged poor. Approximately three fourths of all units report income from this source, and it comprises about two thirds of all income received by the nonaged poor. Male units are well above these average figures, female below.
2. The most marked difference in the income profile of the nonaged poor and nonaged near-poor is the increase for the latter of the percentage of people reporting nonzero earned income and the relative importance of this source of income coupled together with a decrease in the importance of various public transfer payments. This same phenomenon also serves greatly to distinguish poverty class 4 from 3.

These facts are not unexpected. They indicate the crucial way in which the majority of the nonaged poor are dependent upon labor-market activity for their income and its future improvement, thus emphasizing the importance to them of the high levels of economic activity that we discussed in the context of the redistributional bias of various aggregate unemployment rates in Chapter 6.

3. Various types of transfer payments from the public sector (social security and welfare) are by far the most important source of income for the aged-poor and near-poor. For the nonaged they are second to earned income in importance but are still quite significant, especially for female headed units.

The effect that inflation may have on the welfare of the poor through the erosion of the real value of these sources of income is therefore potentially large. For this reason, we explore this subject in some detail in the next section.

4. Rent is a fairly inconsequential source of income for the poor, and is distributed rather evenly across income groups.

This would indicate that, to the extent to which this component of income might lag behind price increases in an inflationary period (as was suggested in Chapter 5), the absolute loss to the poor is minimal, and the redistributive bias negligible.

5. Contrary to popular belief, only a small percentage of the aged-poor (probably under 10 percent) receive income from pensions, annuities, and other forms of fixed (in nominal terms) value income. Also, the data suggest that such sources account for considerably less than 10 percent of the annual income of all the poor.[4] However, for those who do receive income of this type, it is likely to be of considerable importance.[5]

This suggests that the aged-poor as a whole are not particularly adversely affected by inflation by the erosion of the real value of these forms of fixed income.[6] There will be a small subset of this population, however, for whom the detrimental effects of inflation are substantial—primarily those who are subsisting principally upon fixed income from a private pension. The rapid increase of the investment of private pension plans in stocks rather than bonds and in the provision of escalator clauses should serve to greatly reduce the magnitude of this problem over time.[7]

Social Security and Other Public Assistance

Since the items under "So. Sec." and "Welfare" are such an important source of income to the poor, particularly the aged, it is useful to the purposes of this study to examine the behavior of these sources of income during inflationary periods. Accordingly, we have graphed in Figures 8-1 and 8-2 indices (reported in Table 8-4) of average payments for many of the various types of public transfers that comprise "Welfare" for the period 1947-69 along with an index of disposable income per capita deflated by the CPI as a rough indicator of changes in the standard of living. Deterioration of real income from a given source occurs only when the slope of a portion of the curve for that source in Figure 8-1 or 8-2 is actually negative. With the exception of "General Assistance," there are very few negatively sloped portions on any of the curves (except for the 1950-51 period). Thus there have been surprisingly few cases in which for a given year rises in average payments have lagged behind rises in the price level.

Since the trend in payments as represented by the overall slopes of the curves is positive, and since these are all in constant dollar terms, this means that in the longer run the real value of these payments has been increasing. In addition, many of the slopes of the payments curves are as great as, or greater than, that of the disposable income per capita curve, indicating that in the longer run these payments have been a force working toward the raising of the relative income position of the recipients. To be sure, rises in particular types of payments do lag behind price index changes in particular years; thus some recipients groups are hurt in those years—but these lags seem to be much less widespread and longer lasting than is generally supposed and are offset by other periods in which payment levels increase considerably more than the CPI.

In attempting to assess the effects of changes in the price level on the economic well-being of recipients of public transfer payments, care must be taken in selecting the standard upon which such an assessment is to be based. In evaluating the effects of price level changes over a given period, it certainly is not enough to look at a single year to see whether the payment rose in that year by as much as the price index. It has often been the practice to make an assessment by looking at the value of the payment at the end of the period, deflating it by

Table 8-4
Various Forms of Public Assistance (1966 Dollars)

Year	1	2	3	4	5	6	7	8
1947	52.50	25.85			29.58	70.76	29.87	1,513
1948	57.40	28.55			27.81	67.23	30.24	1,567
1949	62.35	30.25			28.29	68.54	28.90	1,547
1950	56.70	27.45		28.03	49.28	126.77	30.04	1,646
1951	55.40	27.35	86.5		45.00	117.25	28.63	1,657
1952	60.20	28.90	88.0		49.65	129.32	28.43	1,678
1953	59.95	28.45	92.2		49.49	135.40	26.68	1,726
1954	59.95	28.60	90.8		56.02	157.91	27.65	1,714
1955	61.40	28.85		30.30	58.93	163.83	28.19	1,795
1956	63.50	29.55	92.7	32.15	56.62	167.79	27.91	1,839
1957	64.25	29.40	96.5	32.40			26.11	1,844
1958	64.80	30.35	100.1	34.25	58.13	169.90	26.94	1,831
1959	63.55	30.60	103.5	33.76	62.94	197.25	27.81	1,881
1960	65.05	31.30	103.4	36.16	63.47	206.80	27.34	1,883
1961	63.20	32.30		36.84	70.74	206.34	28.50	1,909
1962	66.75	31.75	107.1	36.98	70.51	204.05	28.14	1,958
1963	66.95	31.65	110.0	37.40	70.91	204.05	29.10	2,013
1964	67.10	33.20	110.5	37.76	71.30	203.07	32.03	2,123
1965	65.20	33.95	118.1	38.31	75.12	226.39	32.60	2,232
1966	68.05	36.25	125.1	39.76	74.30	221.90	36.20	2,317
1967	70.15	39.50	143.3				39.40	2,398
1968	69.55	42.05	153.5				44.70	2,480
1969	73.95	45.15					50.05	2,517
1970	75.45	48.15					54.85	2,579

Note:

1 = Old age assistance per recipient—average monthly payment.
2 = Aid to families with dependent children—average monthly payment.
3 = Aid to persons totally disabled—average monthly payment (1957/59 = 100).
4 = Unemployment insurance, state summary—average monthly for total unemployed.
5 = Survival families, aged widow only—average monthly payment.
6 = Survival families, widow with two children—average monthly payment.
7 = General assistance per recipient.
8 = Per capita disposable income (1958 dollars).

the price index rise over the period, and then comparing it to the value at the beginning of the period. We would argue that even this is a somewhat biased standard for it weights very heavily the position at the end of the period and ignores what may have transpired at other points in the period. While there are some years in which the price level rises while the money amount of the transfer

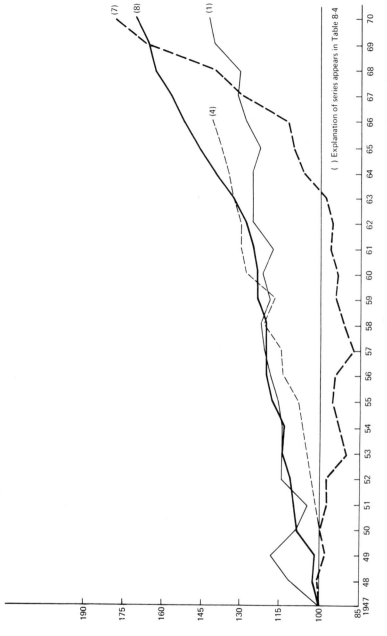

Figure 8-1. Indices of the Real Value of Various Forms of Public Assistance and Per Capita Disposable Income

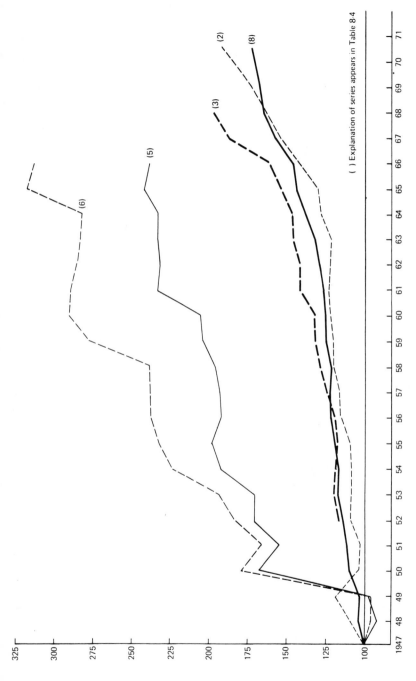

Figure 8-2. Indices of the Real Value of Various Forms of Public Assistance and Per Capita Disposable Income

( ) Explanation of series appears in Table 8-4

remains constant, so are there other years in which the money value of the payment rises by considerably more than the price level. Thus a standard which balances years of real income gains against those of real income losses would more accurately reflect the effects of inflation on the well-being of the recipient.

With respect to most of the types of transfer payments reported in Table 8-4 and Figures 8-1 and 8-2, this choice among standards of assessment is not of crucial importance. As we have already noted, for most of the payments there are very few single years in which there was real income loss, and in most cases real income gains have exceeded increases in per capita income.[8] However, for Social Security retirement benefits, data of the type presented in Table 8-4 could be seriously misleading. In this case, changes in average monthly payments reflect not only changes in the level of benefits received by particular groups of retirees, but also the higher benefit levels for new retirees with higher past-earnings records. Once drawing Social Security, the beneficiary received increases in benefits only through specific amendments in the Social Security legislation. In the past twenty years the record of such legislation has been as follows: benefits were approximately doubled in 1950, increased by 15 percent in 1952, 15 percent in 1954, 7 percent in 1958, 7 percent in 1965, 13 percent in 1968, 15 percent in 1970, 10 percent in 1971, and 20 percent in 1973. Thus, while by 1971 a pre-1958 retiree had received benefit increases more than sufficient to offset increases in the CPI, there were a number of interim years in which he suffered real income losses. On the other hand, a 1965 retiree has had higher real benefits than in 1965 in all but one year and his position relative to disposable income per capita was even increased by the end of 1971.

To make a precise estimate of the net overall effect of amendments raising benefit levels, of changes in the price index, and of growth in disposable income per capita on the relative position of Social Security recipients as a group would require taking into account the distribution of retirees according to their year of retirement, their survival rates, and the cumulative value of each cohort's survivors' yearly real gains and real losses from this source. The results of one study,[9] which is nearly this comprehensive, indicate that, at the worst, some cohorts of retirees experienced a loss of real income over what it would have been in the absence of inflation of up to 4 percent on the average over an inflation period. Most cohorts, however, have increased their real benefits and many have even outstripped the rising standard of living.[10]

We can conclude from this evidence that the real benefits of most recipients of public assistance and Social Security have not been eroded by inflation over the past twenty years. In fact, in many cases the relative income positions of the recipients have been raised by the payments increases. In the minority of instances where there has been a decrease in real benefits due to price level increases, the amount of the loss was not very appreciable. Recent increases in Social Security benefits have been particularly favorable; and finally in 1972 Congress voted to institute an automatic cost-of-living increase into Social

Security benefits, indicating an even greater sensitivity on the part of Congress to the necessity of protecting the aged from real income losses.[11] In any event, it is important to be clear about the fact that regardless of the historical relationship between these transfer payments and the price level, public transfer payments are policy variables which can be quickly and directly altered. If the objective is to protect low-income transfer recipients from the real income losses of inflation, a policy decision can be made to do so. As was done with OASDI, legislation simply can be passed to tie the payment levels of the benefits to an appropriate price index—although, again, we must be aware of the consequences of such an action in promoting inflationary expectations and inflation in our economy.

9

The Effects of Inflation on Net Worth: Some Empirical Evidence

One of the oft-cited evils of inflation relates to the undesirable redistribution of wealth that it is presumed to cause. Of particular concern are the aged poor—the stereotype being of an individual or couple living on a meager (fixed) income derived from accumulated fixed value assets. We saw in the previous chapter that the importance of fixed income to the poor has been greatly overemphasized. However, in order to assess more comprehensively the impact of inflation on the economic welfare of the poor, we do need to examine the magnitude and distribution of the various types of assets and liabilities that they hold and to ascertain the increase or decrease in their real net worth that is likely to occur in an inflationary period.

We can express the real value of the net worth (NW) of a consumer unit at time 1 as

$$\frac{NW_1}{P_1} = \sum_{i=o}^{m} A_{1i} + \sum_{i=o}^{n} C_{1i} - \sum_{i=o}^{s} D_{1i} \qquad (9.1)$$

where

P_1 = the price level of time 1, which we will choose as the numeraire.
A = the current dollar value of a nonclaim asset (of which the consumer unit has m) of the consumer unit.
C = the current dollar value of claims (of which the consumer unit has n) of the consumer unit against other units or institutions.
D = the current dollar value of the debts (of which the consumer unit has s) owed by the consumer unit.

Correspondingly, for some later time, 2, after a period of inflation

$$\frac{NW_2}{P_2} = \sum_{i=o}^{m} A_{1i}\left(\frac{1+a_i}{1+p}\right) + \sum_{i=o}^{n} C_{1i}\left(\frac{1+c_i}{1+p}\right) - \sum_{i=o}^{s} D_{1i}\left(\frac{1+d_i}{1+p}\right) \qquad (9.2)$$

where $p = (P_2 - P_1)/P_1$, the proportionate change in the general level of prices, and a, c, and d are the proportionate change in the current dollar value of A, C, and D that are associated with the change in P. Thus the change in real net worth that takes place between time 1 and time 2 is

$$\Delta NW = \frac{NW_2}{P_2} - \frac{NW_1}{P_2} = \sum_{i=o}^{m} A_{1i}(\frac{a_i - p}{1 + p}) + \sum_{i=o}^{n} C_{1i}(\frac{c_i - p}{1 + p}) +$$
$$\sum_{i=o}^{s} D_{1i}(\frac{p - d_i}{1 + p}). \qquad (9.3)$$

Now, in order to estimate ΔNW from (9.3) for a particular unit or group of units, given the distribution and magnitude of its assets and liabilities by type, it is necessary to have knowledge of their c_i, d_i, and a_i. Table 9-1 shows the distribution of total net worth of poor families and the median value by age and race of head. In Table 9-2 we present some data which, coupled together with some extremely simplifying assumptions, enable us to approximate the possible detrimental effects that an inflation would have had on the real net worth of the poor in 1961. We have separate data for the aged and the nonaged since there is considerable difference in the magnitude of their holdings. The distribution of net worth is quite skewed with the median value being less than half of the mean, so we choose the median value as being more representative of the population.

Some simplifying assumptions that we make here are that the c_i and d_i are equal to zero and the a_i equal to p in inflationary periods.[1] Equation (9.3) then reduces to

$$\Delta NW = (\frac{p}{1 + p})(\sum_{i=o}^{n} D_{1i} - \sum_{i=o}^{m} C_{1i}) = \frac{p}{1 + p}(D' - C') \qquad (9.4)$$

where

$$C' = \sum_{i=o}^{n} C_{1i} \text{ and } D' = \sum_{i=o}^{m} D_{1i}.^2$$

Row (5) of Table 9-2 reports the mean and median ($C' - D'$) of aged, nonaged, and all poor units. As one can see by focusing on the medians, the amounts vulnerable to inflation for both the aged and nonaged are quite small. Under our assumptions, the net worth of the nonaged poor would be reduced by between $3 and $4 and the aged poor by about $5 per annum for each 1 percent rise in P.[3] Notice also that for the aged this loss in net worth is a considerably smaller proportion of their total net worth than it is for the nonaged.

It is probably most reasonable to think of the loss in real net worth as reflected in (9.4) as an upper bound on the actual loss (given our assumption concerning the c_i, a_i, and d_i). This is because, if the increases in P are anticipated, consumer units will shift the composition of their assets and liabilities in order to reduce the detrimental consequences of the inflation.[4] Since our data are for the year 1961, we are relatively safe in assuming that expectations of inflation

Table 9-1
Net Worth of Families with Income Below the Poverty Line (and Net Worth Below $50,000) in 1961

Net Worth			Distribution					
	Negative	0-999	1,000-4,999	5,000-9,999	10,000-19,999	20,000-49,999	Mean	Median
Percentage	12.3	26.5	22.5	19.3	13.0	6.4	$5,845	$2,594

Median Values by Age and Race of Head

Nonaged white	2,356
Nonaged nonwhite	1,474
Aged white	4,083
Aged nonwhite	5,014
All poor	2,434

Table 9-2
Value of Types of Assets for Families with Income Below the Poverty Line (and Net Worth Below $50,000) in 1961

	Median Values			Mean Values		
	Nonaged Head	Aged Head	All Heads	Nonaged Heads	Aged Heads	All Heads
(1) Net Worth	1,823	5,121	2,434	5,539	6,418	5,845
(2) Fixed Value Assets	790	607	743	2,932	2,224	2,686
(3) Nonfixed Value Assets	317	2,384	611	3,516	4,570	3,883
(4) Fixed Value Debt	58	17	23	910	376	724
(5) Amount Vulnerable to Inflation	366	501	422	2,023	1,849	1,962
(6) Income	1,336	1,059	1,164	1,660	1,149	1,482
(7) (5) as a percentage of (1)	20	9.8		36.5	28.8	

Source: *Survey of Financial Characteristics of Consumers*, 1961.

were minimal, so we most probably are examining folios that are not adjusted in anticipation of general price level increases.[5]

Again, as in the previous chapter, we should point out that these aggregate results do not indicate that there are no consumer units whose economic welfare is severely impaired by inflation—in this case by decreasing the real value of their net worth. We are dealing with means and medians of populations, not individual observations. However, the data do suggest that, taken as a group, the poor, and particularly the aged-poor, do not suffer substantial losses in their real wealth due to inflation.[6]

In addition to estimating the absolute effects of inflation on the real net worth of the poor, we are also interested in discovering the possible redistributional consequences for real net worth of inflations. We have no direct evidence of this by income groups, but there is a study in which the redistribution of real net worth of consumer units classified by real net worth was examined.[7] Since, at least for the broad groupings of family income classes in Table 9-3, the median net worth of consumer units increases as the CPS income increases, changes in the distribution of real net worth of consumer units classified by net worth will be highly indicative of changes in the real net worth of consumer units classified by income.

Data are displayed in Table 9-4 reflecting the effects of a 2 and 5 percent annual rate of inflation. The underlying analysis here is considerably more sophisticated than ours since the a_i were each estimated separately (rather than the value of each equated to p) based upon the experience of different

Table 9-3

Median Net Worth by Income Class for Families, 1962

Income Size Class	Median Net Worth
Under $3,000	2,250
3,000-4,999	2,330
5,000-7,499	5,560
7,500-9,999	11,290
10,000-14,999	18,320
15,000-24,999	37,020

Source: SFCC

Table 9-4

Effect of Simulated Inflation on Value of, and Shares in, Real Net Worth for Quantile Groups[a]

Quantile (Percentile Units)	Relative Share	% Change in Shares		% Change in Real Value	
		p = 0.05	p = 0.02	p = 0.05	p = 0.02
1-10	−0.214	10.546	4.386	10.485	4.340
11-30	0.247	11.048	4.614	11.099	4.593
31-40	0.997	5.026	2.087	5.084	2.104
41-50	2.245	3.688	1.528	3.742	1.548
51-60	3.729	1.523	0.631	1.578	0.653
61-70	5.648	0.754	0.312	0.809	0.335
71-80	8.427	0.189	0.079	0.245	0.101
81-90	13.845	−0.406	−0.168	−0.349	−0.145
91-95	11.755	−0.413	−0.170	−0.356	−0.148
96-100	53.530	−0.361	−0.150	−0.303	−0.128

[a]Ranked by size of initial net worth.

Source: This table appeared as Table 3 in Edward Budd and David Seiders, "The Impact of Inflation on the Distribution of Income and Wealth," *American Economic Review*, Papers and Proceedings (May 1971).

inflationary periods in the post-World War II era. The data are for the year 1962 (another year when one would probably expect little or no inflation). The results are rather striking. Not only is the inflation-engendered redistribution of real net worth a significant force in promoting greater equality in the net worth distribution, but also the lower quantiles (1-10 and 11-30) make considerable absolute gains in their real net worth.[8] This further substantiates our earlier conclusion that the net worth of the poor as a group is not likely to be affected in a detrimental manner by an inflation, and also suggests that a considerable relative gain in their real net worth position might accrue to the poor as a result of general price increases.

10 The Phillips Curve, Expected Prices, and Monetary-Fiscal Policy

Repeatedly throughout this study our analysis has indicated the necessity for consideration of inflation and unemployment in a more general equilibrium context (rather than in the limited context that is characteristic of the Phillips curve literature—see below) and one which gives explicit recognition to the role of expectations and incorporates those instruments through which policymakers hope to manipulate the economy in a desirable manner. The specification and estimation of a model of the nature that would be useful for detailed policy prescriptions could be (and has been) the subject of many studies considerably more time-consuming than this one; however, in this chapter, we discuss some theoretical considerations and supporting evidence from a fairly simple aggregate model which we believe helps to illuminate some issues of controversy in this area.

The literature on the Phillips curve is now so voluminous and diverse as to render dubious any statement claiming application to all of it. Nonetheless we will hazard one: in the empirical work on the Phillips curve, unemployment is always treated as an exogenous variable and the wage rate as endogenous.[1] That is, it is assumed implicitly either that (1) the unemployment percentage (U) is a random variable or (2) that U may be chosen by a policymaker without altering the structural relation between U and the rate of change of the money wage rate ($\dot{w}$). However, neither assumption is acceptable; for example, no one would contend that shifting U by shifting aggregate demand will affect $\dot{w}$ to the same degree as (say) raising (and/or more vigorously enforcing) minimum wage laws.

If this is granted, both U and $\dot{w}$ become endogenous variables depending (*inter alia*) upon policy variables which themselves may or may not be exogenous. It then follows that one cannot properly estimate a tradeoff between U and $\dot{w}$ from an ordinary least squares (OLS) regression of $\dot{w}$ upon U and (perhaps) other variables. Such a tradeoff, if it exists, can be inferred only from a structural relation between the two variables. But such a structural relationship is not what policy-oriented students of Phillips curves (should) seek. Their purposes do not require knowing the effect of a *ceteris paribus* change in U on $\dot{w}$, but rather the effect of a specific change in monetary-fiscal policy on both U and $\dot{w}$; this can be ascertained only from the coefficients of parameters representing policy variables in the reduced forms of U and $\dot{w}$. The tradeoff relevant to a specific policy choice will not usually be given by a structural coefficient of $\dot{w}$ upon U because the policy change itself may have direct effects upon $\dot{w}$ or may otherwise act upon $\dot{w}$ through channels unrelated to U.

Consider an illustrative example; suppose the size of the Full Employment Surplus (FES) is the policy variable in question. Let the effect of a $1 billion per annum decrease in FES upon $\dot{w}$ via the (allegedly) associated reduction in U be 0.1 percent per annum; e.g., assume that the effect of a $1 billion decrease in FES is to lower U by 0.5 percent and that the effect of a 1 percent reduction of U is to increase $\dot{w}$ by 0.2 percent (+0.002) per year. But suppose the effect of FES upon $\dot{w}$ via increases in expected prices is 0.4 percent per annum per $1 billion decrease in FES. Then the "cost" of a $1 billion decrease in FES will be a 0.5 percent per annum increase in $\dot{w}$, though only one-fifth of it is associated with the change in U.

In this chapter we argue that the alleged inverse association between $\dot{w}$ and U is largely spurious and arises mainly from a correlation of both variables with unanticipated changes in aggregate demand. Our point of departure is a neoclassical competitive model of product and factor markets and the quantity theory of money. While we are far from having exhaustively tested the implications of this model in the present context, we claim to have made a *prima facie* case that during our sample period (the 1960s) one can reasonably account for wage and price behavior without utilitzing the unemployment percentage.

The Theoretical Framework

Our point of departure is the assumption that a neoclassical model provides a reasonable first approximation to the real world. That is, we assume that prices and wages act so as to clear all product and factor markets and that none of the transactors entertain money illusions. In our version of a long-run neoclassical model, actual and expected money prices vary through time at the same rate as increasing functions of the growth rate in the money stock. Real quantities are independent of the (uniform) rate of change of nominal factor and product prices, and the nominal rate of interest equals the real rate plus the rate of change of expected prices.[2]

Because of search and transaction costs, optimal planning of purchases and sales of productive services implies that there will normally be a positive quantum of unused productive capacity that will serve as a reserve or inventory of productive services. This quantum does not reflect excess supply and should be thought of as an equilibrium inventory.[3] The size of the *equilibrium* inventory for each type of productive capacity is assumed independent of the rate of price change; that is, when the rates of change of all prices—current and expected—are equal, the equilibrium or desired stock of each type of productive capacity will be independent of the rate of inflation. As will be seen, the only type of productive capacity to which we shall pay much attention is labor.

A model (Model I) satisfying these conditions is set forth in equation Set I. Equation Set II differs from Set I in that it posits the existence of a divergence between actual (realized) and expected rates of price change at some moment in the past (see Table 10-1); this divergence is assumed to cause an alteration of the rate of actual present price changes ($\dot{p}$). Set II assumes further that a divergence between actual and expected prices will cause not only a change in $\dot{p}$, but also a divergence of actual from equilibrium rates of utilization of productive capacity.[4]

All variables with a dot refer to rates of change; for example,

$$\dot{w} = \frac{dw}{dt}$$

Table 10-1
Specification of Models I and II

Model I			
$\dot{p}_c$	$=$	$\ddot{p}_c + e_1$	(10.1)
$\dot{p}_o$	$=$	$\ddot{p}_o + e_2$	(10.2)
$\dot{w}$	$=$	$\ddot{w} + e_3$	(10.3)
U	$=$	$(\dot{w}, \dot{p}_c, \dot{p}_o, e_4)$	(10.4)

$\dot{M}$ is exogenous; $\dfrac{\partial \ddot{p}_c}{\partial \dot{M}} = \dfrac{\partial \ddot{p}_o}{\partial \dot{M}} = \dfrac{\partial \ddot{w}}{\partial \dot{M}} > 0$

Model II	
$\dot{p}_c = f_1(\ddot{p}_c, \dot{p}_{c',-t}, \ddot{p}_{c',-t}, \dot{p}_{o',-t}, \ddot{p}_{o',-t}, X_c, \dot{w}, \dot{w}_{-t}, \epsilon_1)$	(10.5)
$\dot{p}_o = f_2(\ddot{p}_o, \dot{p}_{o',-t}, \ddot{p}_{o',-t}, \dot{w}_{-t}, X_o, \epsilon_2)$	(10.6)
$\dot{w} = f_3(\ddot{w}, \dot{w}_{-t}, \dot{p}_{c',-t}, \ddot{p}_{c',-t}, U, U_{-t}, \epsilon_4)$	(10.7)
$U^* + \theta = U = f_4(\dot{w}, \ddot{w}. \dot{p}_c, \dot{p}_o, \ddot{p}_o, D_{-t}, \epsilon_4)$	(10.8)
$\ddot{p}_c = f_5(\dot{M}_{-t}, F_{-v}, \epsilon_5)$	(10.9)
$\ddot{p}_o = f_6(\dot{M}_{-t}, F_{-v}, \epsilon_6)$	(10.10)
$\ddot{w} = f_7(\dot{M}_{-t}, F_{-v}, \epsilon_7)$	(10.11)
$X_c = f_8(----)$	(10.12)
$X_o = f_9(---)$	(10.13)

$\dot{M}$ and F exogenous

t and $v = 1, 2 \ldots n$

These variables are measured as the percentage change from one quarter to the next; for example, $\dot{w}$ is measured as

$$\frac{w_{quarter\ 2}\ -\ w_{quarter\ 1}}{w_{quarter}}$$

Variables with a bar refer to anticipated or expected values; for example, $\bar{\dot{w}}$ is the anticipated value of $\dot{w}$. Variables with the subscript $-t$ refer to lagged values of the variables; for example, $\bar{\dot{w}}_{-t}$ is the anticipated value of $\dot{w}$ t quarters prior to that of the left-side variable in the equation. (All lagged variables are predetermined.)

List of Variables

$\dot{p}_c$ = rate of change of price level of consumption goods.
$\dot{p}_o$ = rate of change of price level of all goods other than consumption.
$\dot{w}$ = rate of change of the wage rate.
X_c = excess capacity in the consumption goods sector.
X_o = excess capacity in the sector other than consumption goods.
U = unemployment percentage.
U^* = equilibrium unemployment percentage.
$\theta = U - U^*$
$(\ )_{-t}$ = variable lagged t periods.
$(\ )_{-v}$ = variable lagged v periods.
D = investment tax credit dummy.
$\dot{M}$ = rate of change of money stock.
F = fiscal policy variable.
$e_1, \ldots, e_4$ = disturbances.
$\epsilon_1, \ldots, \epsilon_9$ = disturbances.

Model I does not specify how $\dot{M}$ affects any of its endogenous variables. We assume that all e's are normally distributed with zero means and uncorrelated with $\dot{M}$, with U, with any actual or expected price, and with one another. Given these assumptions it follows that

$$\frac{\partial\ [E\ (\dot{P}_c)]}{\partial\ \dot{M}}\ =\ \frac{\partial\ [E\ (\dot{p}_o)]}{\partial\ \dot{M}}\ =\ \frac{\partial\ [E\ (\dot{w}\ )]}{\partial\ \dot{M}}$$

when $E\ (\ )$ is the expected value of $(\ )$. Since U^* is the long-run equilibrium value (the "natural rate") of U, the unemployment percentage

$$\frac{dU^*}{d\dot{M}} = \frac{\partial U^*}{\partial \dot{M}} = 0$$

and f_4 is homogeneous of zero degree in $\dot{p}_c$, $\dot{p}_O$ and $\dot{w}$. (F is not included for reasons of brevity.)

In Model II, $\dot{M}$ and/or F operate upon the endogenous variables as in I. We also assume as in Model II that the ϵ's are normally distributed random variables with zero means, independent of one another or of any other variable in the model. If all changes in prices and wages were completely foreseen, Model II would collapse into Model I. However, as in the real world, in Model II deviations of actual from past expected (rates of change in) prices and wages affect present rates of change in wages and prices. In the real world, no doubt, changes in $\dot{M}$ and F cause such deviations; in our model, however, these deviations

$$[(\dot{p}_c - \bar{\dot{p}}_c), (\dot{p}_O - \bar{\dot{p}}_O) \text{ and } (\dot{w} - \bar{\dot{w}})]$$

are attributed to the effect of disturbances. Also, deviations of actual from (long-run) equilibrium quantities such as θ, X_c, and X_O also result from disturbances.[5]

$$(\dot{p}_c - \bar{\dot{p}}_c) X_c + (\dot{p}_O - \bar{\dot{p}}_O) X_O = f_{10}(\dot{M} - M^*) \qquad (10.14)$$

$\dot{M}^*$ is a steady growth rate in the nominal money stock that everyone would anticipate perfectly if it were maintained for a sufficiently long time. ($\dot{M} - \dot{M}^*$) reflects the vagaries of monetary policy and is assumed to be exogenous.

When $\dot{M} - \dot{M}^* = 0$, both terms on the left hand side of (10.14) vanish. f'_{10} > 0, so that if $\dot{M} > \dot{M}^*$, aggregate payments for output exceed long-run equilibrium values, and vice versa. We assume that each term on the left-hand side has the same sign as f'_{10} so that the signs of the product terms are always positive. But we also assume that $f_{10} < 0$ when $\dot{M} - \dot{M}^* < 0$; therefore, the left-hand side of (10.14) must be multiplied by (-1) when $M - M^* < 0$.

Put differently, when $\dot{M} = M^*$, GNP is at its balanced growth path value. $f_{10}(\dot{M} - M^*)$ is the difference between actual and "growth path GNP." (10.15) expresses the same *aggregate* relation as (10.14) viewed from the side of factor payments (including taxes). G is a measure of the deviation of nonhuman factor utilization (including services of publicly owned nonhuman capital); $\dot{p}_g$ and $\bar{\dot{p}}_g$ are defined analogously to $\dot{w}$ and $\bar{\dot{w}}$ and refer to nonhuman factors.

$$(\dot{w} - \bar{\dot{w}}) \theta + (\dot{p}_g - \bar{\dot{p}}_g) G = f_{11}(\dot{M} - \dot{M}^*) \qquad (10.15)$$

Nothing is specified about the relation between any individual price term and its corresponding quantity term in either (10.14) or (10.15). Indeed nothing is said about the relation between either f_{10} or f_{11} and a weighted average of all prices or all quantities on the left side.[6] Clearly, a full discussion of our subject would require an investigation of this relation but this would take us far beyond our limited objectives.

A Word on the Measurement of Price Expectations

In view of the central role assigned to "expected prices" in our models—and in those of many other writers—it is in order to discuss briefly their definition and measurement. In our models, expected prices are defined as the prices that would be observed if all commodities (including labor services) were actively traded in futures markets such as those that function for various agricultural staples. Since such markets do not generally exist, most investigators have found it impossible to observe expected prices directly and have resorted to makeshifts. We believe that it is possible to construct a series of directly observed expected prices, but have not yet been able to do so.[7] *Faute de mieux*, we have resorted to estimating expected prices from a weighted average of past actual prices and movements thereof.[8]

$$\dot{\bar{p}}_{t+1} - \dot{\bar{p}}_t = \alpha (\dot{p}_t - \dot{\bar{p}}_t) \qquad (10.16)$$

$$\dot{\bar{p}} = \sum_{i=1}^{n} \alpha (1 - \alpha)^{i-1} p_{t-i} \qquad (10.17)$$

We estimated $\dot{\bar{p}}_t$, the rate of change in the expected future price at moment t, from (10.17) on the assumption that $\alpha = 0.4$; experimentation with values of α between 0.2 and 0.7 did not produce "important" differences in our estimates of $\dot{\bar{p}}_t$.[9] (10.16) expresses the hypothesis of "adaptive expectations"; that is, the hypothesis that the change in the expected rate of price change between moments t and $t + 1$ is a proper fraction of the discrepancy between the actual change experienced at t and the change expected.[10]

Yet another way of estimating expected prices is to make use of the equilibrium condition that the equilibrium money rate of interest is equal to the real rate of interest plus the expected rate of change in the price level. This may be done by regressing the money rate of interest on all of its various determinants, including an estimate of the real rate, and using the coefficient on the rate of change of the price level (appropriately lagged) as an estimate of the expected rate of price change ($\dot{\bar{p}}$). This procedure has been carried out by Eckstein and Feldstein[11] whose results we have used in several of our regressions. In general, their estimate of $\dot{\bar{p}}$ behaves much like our own. Another estimate of this same general character, though differing in details, has been made by R.J. Gordon.[12]

$\dot{\overline{w}}_t$ was estimated from $\dot{w}_{t-1}$ in a manner analogous to (10.17). However, the rationale for doing so is slightly different than in the case of output prices. Our hypothesis is the $\dot{\overline{w}}$ is expected to vary in proportion to changes in $\dot{\overline{p}}_c$ plus on appropriate weighted, lagged average growth in the real wage rate. When the past growth in the real wage rate is constant, our measure of $\dot{\overline{w}}$ becomes equal to the expected change in consumer prices plus this constant (expected) growth in the real wage rate.

The estimating equation for $\dot{\overline{w}}$ is

$$\dot{\overline{w}}_{(t)} = \dot{\overline{p}}_{c(t)} + \sum_{i=1}^{n} \lambda \, (\dot{w} - \dot{p}_c)_{t-i} \text{ where } \lambda_i = \alpha \, (1-\alpha)^i$$

Here, again α was put equal to 0.4. The expansion of this expression is

$$\dot{\overline{w}}_{(t)} = \alpha \sum_{i=1}^{n} (1-\alpha)^{i-1} \, \dot{p}_{c\,(t-i)} + \alpha \sum^{n} (1-\alpha)^{i-1} (\dot{w} - \dot{p}_c)_{t-i}$$

$$= \alpha \sum_{i=1}^{n} (1-\alpha)^{\lambda-1} \, \dot{w}_{t-i} \quad [13]$$

It should be noted that this particular specification of the wage adjustment equation requires disaggregation between wage and nonwage goods and is the reason for our distinction between p_c and p_o.

Price and Wage Equations:
Ordinary Least Squares (OLS) Estimates

(10.18)-(10.20) report the results of our attempts to fit Model I to the decade from the fourth quarter of 1959 to the fourth quarter of 1969.[14]

$$\dot{p}_c = \underset{(-1.26)\ (22.2)}{0.13 + 1.17\,\dot{\overline{p}}_c} \qquad R^2 = .93 \qquad \text{D.W.} = 1.10 \qquad (10.18)$$

$$\dot{p}_o = \underset{(-.47)\ (13.7)}{0.09 + 1.12\,\dot{\overline{p}}_o} \qquad R^2 = .83 \qquad \text{D.W.} = .73 \qquad (10.19)$$

$$\dot{w} = \underset{(.13)\ (10.7)}{+0.06 + 1.02\,\dot{\overline{w}}} \qquad R^2 = .75 \qquad \text{D.W.} = .99 \qquad (10.20)$$

The numbers between the parentheses are the t-values. In none of the equations does the constant term differ significantly from zero; the coefficient of $\dot{\overline{p}}_c$ in (10.18) differs significantly from unity, but the analogous coefficients in (10.19) and (10.20) are compatible with the hypothesis that their true values are one.[15] However, the Durbin-Watson statistics (D.W.) indicate that in none of the equations would we be justified in rejecting the hypothesis that the disturbances are serially correlated.

If the neoclassical hypothesis applied to our data, $\dot{p}_c \cong \dot{\bar{p}}_c$, $\dot{p}_O \cong \dot{\bar{p}}_O$, $\dot{w} \cong \dot{\bar{w}}$ and all constant terms would approximate zero. That is, prices and wage rates would move at about the same speed as their expected value; the only clear rejection of the hypothesis comes in (10.18). However, the low values of the D.W. statistics suggest that the formulae used to construct expected prices and wages do not permit rapid enough "adaption" to prevent correlated disturbances.

Accordingly, we experimented with expectations variables that permitted wage rates and prices to adjust more rapidly to divergences between actual and expected values. This led to (10.21)-(10.23) which furnish considerable support for the neoclassical hypothesis. In all three of these equations

$$\dot{p}_c = \begin{array}{c} -0.01 \\ (-.12) \end{array} + \begin{array}{c} 1.05\dot{\bar{p}}_c \\ (17.4) \end{array} + \begin{array}{c} .50\,(\dot{p}_c - \dot{\bar{p}}_c)_{-1} \\ (3.05) \end{array} \qquad \begin{array}{l} R^2 = .94 \\ D.W. = 2.07 \end{array} \qquad (10.21)$$

$$\dot{p}_O = \begin{array}{c} .08 \\ (.59) \end{array} + \begin{array}{c} .98\dot{\bar{p}}_O \\ (13.8) \end{array} + \begin{array}{c} .66\,(\dot{p}_O - \dot{\bar{p}}_O)_{-1} \\ (4.8) \end{array} \qquad \begin{array}{l} R^2 = .89 \\ D.W. = 1.90 \end{array} \qquad (10.22)$$

$$\dot{w} = \begin{array}{c} .46 \\ (-1.15) \end{array} + \begin{array}{c} .91\dot{\bar{w}} \\ (10.4) \end{array} + \begin{array}{c} .24\,(\dot{w} - \dot{\bar{w}})_{-1} \\ (3.7) \end{array} \qquad \begin{array}{l} R^2 = .81 \\ D.W. = 1.95 \end{array} \qquad (10.23)$$

the constant term is insignificantly different from zero and all coefficients on current expectations differ insignificantly from unity. Moreover, the coefficients on the lagged adjustment terms are significantly different from both zero and one (and are below unity), while the D.W. statistics are well above the minimum levels compatible with rejecting the hypothesis of serial correlation of the residuals.

In effect (10.21)-(10.23) amend (10.18)-(10.20) by redistributing the weights among the various lags on the right-hand sides. However, with the new distribution of weights, the values of $\dot{\bar{p}}_c$, $\dot{\bar{p}}_O$, and $\dot{\bar{w}}$ will steadily approach their corresponding actual values if the actual values grow or decline at a steady rate, and this without obvious serial correlation among the residuals.

If we were to accept (10.21)-(10.23) as an adequate explanation of wage rate and price behavior, there would be neither need nor room for U in the wage equation (10.23). Clearly, this would not satisfy devotees of the Phillips curve; nor should it. The structures of all of the equations (10.18)-(10.23) are autoregressive which also biases upward the coefficient on the lagged variables. If the errors are serially correlated, our estimates will be inconsistent as well as biased.

The D.W. statistics provide some testimony in favor of the hypothesis of no serial correlation among the disturbances. But these should not be taken literally where the structure of the equation is autoregressive; in this case the D.W.

statistic is biased toward 2 and our confidence that serial correlation is absent from the residuals of (10.22) and (10.23) must be deflated somewhat. These considerations certainly do not justify ignoring the above results whose statistical flaws are shared by most other work in this field; but they do suggest restraint in claims about what has been discovered.

(10.21)-(10.23) may surprise some readers because they appear to make the course of (percentage) changes in wage rates and prices depend solely upon their own lagged values. As we shall see, this is a misleading interpretation, but before discussing this point, it will be helpful to consider some further results.

$$\dot{p}_c = -0.00 + 1.04\dot{\bar{p}}_c + .46\,(\dot{p}_c - \dot{\bar{p}}_c) + .18\,(\dot{p}_o - \dot{\bar{p}}_o)_{-2}$$
$$(-0.02)\quad (18.3)\qquad (3.00)\qquad\qquad (2.61)$$
$$R^2 = .95$$
$$\text{D.W.} = 2.07 \qquad (10.24)$$

$$\dot{p}_o = 0.08 + .97\dot{\bar{p}}_o + .57\,(\dot{p}_o - \dot{\bar{p}}_o)_{-1} + .21\,(\dot{w} - \dot{\bar{w}})_{-1}$$
$$(.58)\quad (13.9)\qquad (4.09)\qquad\qquad (.75)$$
$$R^2 = .90$$
$$\text{D.W.} = 1.77 \qquad (10.25)$$

$$\dot{w} = .95 + .78\dot{\bar{w}} + .55\,(\dot{w} - \dot{\bar{w}})_{-1} + .80\,(\dot{p}_c - \dot{\bar{p}}_c)_{-2}$$
$$(2.31)\quad (8.4)\qquad (3.92)\qquad\qquad (2.78)$$
$$R^2 = .85$$
$$\text{D.W.} = 1.67 \qquad (10.26)$$

$$\dot{w} = 1.29 + .69\dot{\bar{w}} + .47\,(\dot{w} - \dot{\bar{w}})_{-1} + .95\,(\dot{p}_c - \dot{\bar{p}}_c)_{-2}$$
$$(3.24)\quad (7.5)\qquad (3.57)\qquad\qquad (3.51)$$
$$+ .42\,(\dot{p}_o - \dot{\bar{p}}\,'_o)_{-2}$$
$$(2.74)\qquad\qquad\qquad R^2 = .87$$
$$\text{D.W.} = 1.35 \qquad (10.27)$$

$$\dot{p}_c = .01 + 1.09\dot{\bar{p}}\,'_c + .55\,(\dot{p}_c - \dot{\bar{p}}\,'_c)_{-1} + .18\,(\dot{p}_o - \dot{\bar{p}}\,'_o)_{-2}$$
$$(.09)\quad (10.5)\qquad (6.3)\qquad\qquad (3.77)$$
$$R^2 = .96$$
$$\text{D.W.} = 2.11 \qquad (10.24')$$

$$\dot{p}_o = .40 + .77\dot{\bar{p}}\,'_o + .81\,(\dot{p}_o - \dot{\bar{p}}\,'_o)_{-1} + .27\,(\dot{w} - \dot{\bar{w}}\,')_{-1}$$
$$(2.09)\ (8.0)\qquad (11.4)\qquad\qquad (2.69)$$
$$R^2 = .91$$
$$\text{D.W.} = 1.76 \qquad (10.25')$$

$$\dot{w} = 2.11 + .50\dot{\bar{w}}\,' + .56\,(\dot{w} - \dot{\bar{w}}\,')_{-1} + .72\,(\dot{p}_c - \dot{\bar{p}}\,'_c)$$
$$(3.38)\quad (3.25)\qquad (4.39)\qquad\qquad (4.13)$$
$$R^2 = .85$$
$$\text{D.W.} = 1.75 \qquad (10.26')$$

(10.24) is similar to (10.21) save for the addition of a lagged term reflecting a lagged adjustment to accelerations of the rate of price change of nonconsumption goods. Although this term is significant, it has little effect on the other coefficients in (10.21)—slightly lowering the coefficient on ($\dot{p}_c - \bar{\dot{p}}_c$)—or the R^2 or D.W. of the entire equation. (10.25) is obtained from (10.22) by including ($\dot{w} - \bar{\dot{w}}$)$_{-1}$ as a regressor, and as in the equation for $\dot{p}_c$, the added term had little effect on the other coefficients, R^2 or D.W. Although the sign of the added term is "correct" its size is a bit too small for significance at the 5 percent level.

Putting ($\dot{p}_c - \bar{\dot{p}}_c$)$_{-2}$ into (10.23) gives us (10.26), an equation incompatible with the neoclassical hypothesis. This is because the constant term is significantly higher than zero and the coefficient on $\bar{\dot{w}}$ is significantly below unity. The strong coefficients on $(\dot{p}_c - \bar{\dot{p}}_c)_{-2}$—not significantly differing from one—in both (10.26) and (10.27) are worth noting.

(10.27) amends (10.26) by adding ($\dot{p}_o - \bar{\dot{p}}_o$)$_{-2}$ as a regressor. The coefficient on this term is positive and significant, but including it raises the constant term above its level in (10.26) and increases the deviation from unity of the coefficient on $\bar{\dot{w}}$; it also sharply lowers the D.W. statistic.

(10.24')-(10.26') are analogues to (10.24)-(10.26) respectively, except that the measurements of expected prices is made from the Eckstein-Feldstein regressions instead of our own calculations. The "qualitative" characteristics of these equations are very similar to those of (10.24)-(10.26). (10.25') is not as good a regression as (10.25) in that its constant is significantly higher than zero and its coefficient on $\bar{p}_o$ is significantly below one; (10.26') shares the faults of (10.26).

To the Phillips curve devotee, any acceptable regression explaining $\dot{w}$ must include U with a significantly negative coefficient. However, our attempts to produce such a relationship met with very limited success. (10.28)-(10.31) are the four "best" regressions (i.e., most favorable to the Phillips curve hypothesis) we could produce involving the unemployment percentage. In all of them the inverse of the unemployment percentage has a (correct) positive sign, and in one case (10.29) its coefficient is 2.0 times its standard error.[16] In all other cases the coefficient on variables involving the unemployment inverse is less than twice its standard error. In none of these equations is the coefficient on $\bar{\dot{w}}$ large enough to be free of the suspicion that its true value differs from one, though in (10.28) and (10.29) one minus the coefficient is a little less than twice its standard error. The constants do not differ significantly from zero except in (10.30). The D.W.'s are "respectable" in (10.30) and (10.31), but in (10.28) and (10.29) are much too low to be compatible with the hypothesis of zero serial correlation among the residuals. In short, we submit that (10.23) (without U) is at least as good a wage equation as any of those from (10.28) to (10.31) inclusive (all of which include U).

$$\dot{w} = \begin{matrix} .42 \\ (.95) \end{matrix} + \begin{matrix} .64\dot{\overline{w}} \\ (3.3) \end{matrix} + \begin{matrix} 3.35U^{-1} \\ (1.90) \end{matrix} + \begin{matrix} 17.5\,(U_p^{-1} - (U_p^{-1})_{-1} \\ (1.86) \end{matrix}$$

$$R^2 = .81$$
$$D.W. = 1.12 \qquad (10.28)$$

$$\dot{w} = \begin{matrix} -.55 \\ (-1.12) \end{matrix} + \begin{matrix} .69\dot{\overline{w}} \\ (3.85) \end{matrix} + \begin{matrix} 9.32U^{-1} \\ (2.0) \end{matrix} + \begin{matrix} 31.1\,(U^{-1} - (U^{-1})_{-1}) \\ (1.68) \end{matrix}$$

$$R^2 = .80$$
$$D.W. = 1.04 \qquad (10.29)$$

$$\dot{w} = \begin{matrix} 1.07 \\ (2.67) \end{matrix} + \begin{matrix} .52\dot{\overline{w}} \\ (3.19) \end{matrix} + \begin{matrix} .52\,(\dot{w} - \dot{\overline{w}})_{-1} \\ (3.84) \end{matrix} + \begin{matrix} .50\,(\dot{p}_c - \dot{\overline{p}}_c)_{-2} \\ (1.57) \end{matrix}$$
$$+ \begin{matrix} 3.05U_p^{-1} \\ (1.92) \end{matrix}$$

$$R^2 = .86$$
$$D.W. = 1.75 \qquad (10.30)$$

$$\dot{w} = \begin{matrix} .40 \\ (.70) \end{matrix} + \begin{matrix} .62\dot{\overline{w}} \\ (3.99) \end{matrix} + \begin{matrix} .55\,(\dot{p}_c - \dot{\overline{p}}_c)_{-2} \\ (1.62) \end{matrix} + \begin{matrix} .52\,(\dot{w} - \dot{\overline{w}})_{-1} \\ (3.76) \end{matrix}$$
$$+ \begin{matrix} 6.36U^{-1} \\ (1.40) \end{matrix}$$

$$R^2 = .85$$
$$D.W. = 1.73 \qquad (10.31)$$

The usual rationalization of the Phillips curve is that the unemployment inverse varies with excess demand for labor and is therefore positively correlated with upward pressure on the wage rate (e.g., Gordon).[17] R.G. Bodkin concludes his extensive survey of the literature on empirical studies of wage and price determination by stating that, "with the exception of Andersen and Carlson's monetarist model of the U.S. economy, the models surveyed describe price formation as principally a matter of cost factors, with the direct influence of demand pressures entering secondarily or not at all."[18] To the extent that this argument is valid (see below) it should also apply to nonlabor factors; in particular to plant and equipment. That is, if (nonlabor) productive facilities are being used near capacity rates, this should drive up quasi rents per unit of utilization analogous to the (alleged) Phillips curve effect on wage rates. Such upward pressure would be partly reflected as ceteris paribus accelerations of the rates of price increase.

To test this hypothesis we tried several measures of capacity utilization as determinants of $\dot{p}_c$ or $\dot{p}_o$. The results are given below.[19]

$$\dot{p}_c = \begin{matrix} 1.13 \\ (-4.45) \end{matrix} + \begin{matrix} .94\dot{\overline{p}}_c \\ (11.1) \end{matrix} + \begin{matrix} 2.47\,\text{UNF} \\ (3.48) \end{matrix} + \begin{matrix} 6.08\,\text{NODEV} \\ (2.07) \end{matrix}$$

$$R^2 = .96$$
$$D.W. = 1.73 \qquad (10.32)$$

$$\dot{p}_c = \underset{(-3.9)}{.46} + \underset{(7.12)}{.86\dot{\bar{p}}_c} + \underset{(2.65)}{2.32U_p^{-1}} + \underset{(1.23)}{5.63\,[\,U_p^{-1} - (U_p^{-1})_{-1}\,]}$$

$$R^2 = .96$$
$$\text{D.W.} = 1.56 \qquad (10.33)$$

$$\dot{p}_c = \underset{(-1.21)}{.14} + \underset{(18.7)}{1.08\dot{p}_c} + \underset{(2.46)}{.38\,(\dot{p}_c - \dot{\bar{p}}_c)_{-1}} + \underset{(2.11)}{.15\,(\dot{p}_o - \dot{\bar{p}}_o)_{-2}}$$

$$+ \underset{(2.04)}{6.16\,\text{NODEV}} \qquad\qquad R^2 = .96$$
$$\text{D.W.} = 2.13 \qquad (10.34)$$

$$\dot{p}_o = \underset{(2.68)}{-1.37} + \underset{(6.25)}{.70\dot{\bar{p}}} + \underset{(3.98)}{.51\,(\dot{p}_o - \dot{\bar{p}}_o)_{-1}} + \underset{(1.04)}{.12\,(\dot{w} - \dot{\bar{w}})_{-1}}$$

$$+ \underset{(2.95)}{3.7\,\text{UNF}} \qquad\qquad R^2 = .92$$
$$\text{D.W.} = 1.88 \qquad (10.35)$$

(10.32) should be compared with (10.21); that is, UNF and NODEV function as the analogue of $(\dot{p}_c - \dot{\bar{p}}_c)_{-1}$. As in (10.21), the coefficient on $\dot{\bar{p}}_c$ in (10.32) does not differ significantly from unity, but (unlike (10.21)) the constant term is significantly above zero. The signs on both UNF and NODEV are positive and more than twice their standard errors.

(10.33) is (10.32) but with measures of the unemployment inverse replacing UNF and NODEV. There is not much ground for preferring (10.32) to (10.33) or vice versa. In both equations, the constants are significant, but the signs on the other coefficients are "correct," the R^2's are exactly equal and the D.W.'s roughly similar.

Replacing UNF in (10.32) by $(\dot{p}_o - \dot{\bar{p}}_o)_{-2} + (\dot{p}_c - \dot{\bar{p}}_c)_{-1}$ gives us (10.34) in which the constant is made insignificantly different from zero, and the D.W. raised to 2.13, without impairing the significance of the coefficients on NODEV and $\dot{\bar{p}}_c$. The lesson, if any, from comparing (10.32) and (10.34) is that $(\dot{p}_c - \dot{\bar{p}}_c)_{-1} + (\dot{p}_o - \dot{\bar{p}}_o)_{-2}$ has as great a predictive power as UNF.

(10.35) is (10.25) with UNF added. The effects are generally unsatisfactory: in (10.35) the constant differs significantly from zero and the coefficient on $\dot{\bar{p}}_o$ differs from unity, whereas the reverse was true in (10.25). Both the coefficient on $(\dot{w} - \dot{\bar{w}})_{-1}$ and its t value are substantially lower in (10.35) than in (10.25), although the R^2 and D.W. are increased somewhat. In short, the positive and significant coefficient on UNF is bought at the expense of worsening those on other variables.

Superficially our results would seem very different from those of economists who explicitly introduce behavior of wage (and other) costs per unit of output into the price equations of the model. However, correctly interpreted, the differences disappear. In our various price equations, we obtain substantial explanatory power from lagged price variables (interpreted as reflecting price expectations). Gordon,[20] for example, does more or less as well as we by using various aspects of labor costs per unit of output such as changes in wage rates per hour; changes in man-hour productivity (both at standard and actual levels of output), and so forth, instead of lagged prices. But though Gordon argues as though prices were set by a process involving cost-push with variable markup percentages (the markup fraction varying with the ratio of unfilled orders to capacity), his equations are equally compatible with one or more quite different interpretations.

Consider: the changes in wages per unit of output that push prices up (in Gordon's equation 20)[21] can be interpreted as resulting from the increases in product prices that employers expect to occur and that lead them to pay more to avoid or to settle strikes. Unions, knowing and sharing employer price and profit expectations, adjust their settlement terms accordingly so that movements in unit wage costs reflect product price expectations. An analogous statement might well apply to the reservation prices of nonunionized workers. Alternatively, the effect of expectations may go from unit costs to product prices. That is, employers anticipate the rate of cost increase (per unit of output) that their competitors will face and infer a rate of increase in expected product prices. In point of fact, the "price expectation generating mechanism" probably varies from one industry to another and may well vary from time to time with a given industry. Nothing is specified about this mechanism in economic theory and not much is known about it in fact. The climate of opinion that determines price (and wage) quotations at any moment reflects events and portents bearing upon the cost elements of products, and upon the prices of both substitutes and complements as well as those directly affecting the product market themselves.

One feature of our specification of the relation of actual and expected prices is worth explicit mention. We assume that past *deviations* of actual from expected input prices influence the behavior of current prices. For example, we write $\dot{p}_c = f\,[(\dot{p}_o - \dot{\bar{p}}_o)_{-t}, (\dot{w} - \dot{\bar{w}})_{-t}]$, but not $\dot{p}_c = f(\dot{\bar{p}}_o, \dot{\bar{w}})$. The rationale is that changes in input prices that are fully anticipated are assumed to have been taken fully into account in determining the rates of change in the expected prices of output and in expected wages.

It should also be noted that, in general, $\dot{\bar{p}}_o \neq \dot{\bar{p}}_c \neq \dot{\bar{w}}$. Secularly increasing man-hour productivity should make $\dot{\bar{w}}$ greater than either of the others, and *de facto* $\dot{\bar{p}}_c > \dot{\bar{p}}_o$. If our various equations for $\dot{p}_c$, $\dot{p}_o$, and $\dot{w}$ are even rough approximations to reality, $\triangle \bar{w} - \triangle \bar{p}_c$ should be roughly equal to changes in man-hour productivity in the production of consumption goods and $\triangle \bar{w} - \triangle \bar{p}_o$ roughly equal to changes in man-hour productivity in the production of other goods.[22] A calculation between actual and calculated changes in productivity indeed did show them to be of approximate value, thus offering weak corroboration of the general plausibility of our model. Unfortunately, there are no data available on changes in man-hour productivity for these two sectors separately, but our calculation for each sector bracketed nicely the actual change for the two sectors combined.[23]

To summarize: Gordon's wage and price equations (like those of most investigators) reflect essentially the same forces as ours—lagged response to previous wage and price changes that were partially anticipated. The critical difference between our views and theirs lies in the interpretation of the coefficient on the employment percentage. Let us now turn to this issue.

Unemployment and the Wage Rate

As stated at the outset, we believe it incorrect to treat U as exogenous. We believe that U, $\dot{w}$, $\dot{p}_o$, and $\dot{p}_c$ are determined jointly by the "whole system," with growth in the (nominal) money stock and fiscal policy operating as exogenous forces. Given this standpoint, there is no more reason to put U on the right side of a Phillips relation than on the left.

In principle, U depends upon the relative rates of change of wages and prices as well as upon deviations of actual from expected rates. However, the relationship of U to these variables is complicated and economic theory gives us no theoretical prior as to the effect of relative prices upon U. We do now know that the labor force participation rates and unemployment percentages of married prime-age males (20-44 years of age) vary less through time and are much less responsive to the level of economic activity than of other components of the labor force. Consequently, we exaggerate slightly and assume the natural or equilibrium rate of unemployment for prime age males, U_p, to be independent of $\dot{p}_c$, $\dot{p}_o$, and $\dot{w}$; that is,

$$U_p = \text{constant, when } (\dot{p}_c - \dot{\bar{p}}_c) = (\dot{p}_o - \dot{\bar{p}}_o) = (\dot{w} - \dot{\bar{w}}) = 0 .$$

As indicated above, we assume nothing about the coefficient of U upon $(\dot{w} - \dot{\bar{w}})$, $(\dot{p}_c - \dot{\bar{p}}_c)$, or $(\dot{p}_o - \dot{\bar{p}}_o)$; that is, all equations of this section are merely descriptive. This is as it should be. The determinants of the "natural rate" of U (U^*) are not considered here and we have no theoretical prior with which to interpret the coefficients of U on the price and wage deviation variables.

(10.36) and (10.36′) and two regressions relating U to differences between actual and expected rates of change in wage rates and product prices. Both equations show significant positive constants, significant negative coefficients on $(\dot{p}_c - \dot{\bar{p}}_c)$ and $(\dot{p} - \dot{\bar{p}}_o)$, and positive, but insignificant, coefficients on $(\dot{w} - \dot{\bar{w}})$. The equations differ only in the manner in which price and wage expectations are estimated: in (10.36), expected values are estimated from lagged values of the variable considered, but in (10.36′) they are estimated from the Eckstein-Feldstein interest-rate equation.

$$U_p = 3.6 - 2.26\,(\dot{p}_c - \dot{\tilde{p}}_c) - .58\,(\dot{p}_o - \dot{\tilde{p}}_o) + .15\,(\dot{w} - \dot{\tilde{w}})$$
$$\quad\;\;\;(27.4)\;\;(-7.12)\qquad\quad(-2.78)\qquad\quad(.79)$$

$$R^2 = .59$$
$$\text{D.W.} = 1.12 \qquad (10.36)$$

$$U_p = 3.6 - 1.07\,(\dot{p}_c - \dot{\tilde{p}}_c') - .24\,(\dot{p}_o - \dot{\tilde{p}}_o') + .08\,(\dot{w} - \dot{\tilde{w}}')$$
$$\quad\;\;\;(63.2)\;\;(-9.96)\qquad\quad(-4.4)\qquad\quad(1.05)$$

$$R^2 = .94$$
$$\text{D.W.} = 1.13 \qquad (10.36')$$

The significant negative coefficients on $(\dot{p}_c - \dot{\tilde{p}}_c)$ and $(\dot{p}_o - \dot{\tilde{p}}_o)$ have suggested (to some readers) the interpretation that unanticipated increases in aggregate demand simultaneously reduce unemployment and make prices rise faster than had been anticipated. This interpretation may be valid, though it will not always hold.[24]

The low values of the D.W. statistic in (10.36) and (10.36') indicate serial correlation of the residuals. In an attempt to eliminate this, we experimented with a dummy (D) reflecting the presence or absence of the investment tax credit; (in effect 1963-66) presented in (10.37) and (10.37').

$$U_p = 3.8 - 2.22\,(\dot{p}_c - \dot{\tilde{p}}_c) - .49\,(\dot{p}_o - \dot{\tilde{p}}_o) + .20\,(\dot{w} - \dot{\tilde{w}})$$
$$\quad\;\;\;(24.7)\;\;(-6.3)\qquad\quad(-2.38)\qquad\quad(1.08)$$
$$-\;.54\,D_{-2}$$
$$\;\;(-2.12)$$
$$R^2 = .69$$
$$\text{D.W.} = 1.09 \qquad (10.37)$$

$$U_p = 3.8 - 1.14\,(\dot{p}_c - \dot{\tilde{p}}_c') - .15\,(\dot{p}_o - \dot{\tilde{p}}_o') + .09\,(\dot{w} - \dot{\tilde{w}})$$
$$\quad\;\;\;(59.1)\;\;(-12.7)\qquad\quad(-2.86)\qquad\quad(1.58)$$
$$+\;.40\,D_{-2}$$
$$\;\;(-4.20)$$
$$R^2 = .96$$
$$\text{D.W.} = 1.64 \qquad (10.37')$$

The effect of this credit was presumably to increase demand for final output (and reduce U). Insertion of D with a zero or one-quarter lag did not generate a significant coefficient. However, with a two-quarter lag, the D coefficient became negative and more than twice its standard error. Entering D did not raise the D.W. of (10.36) but substantially raised that of (10.36'); it also (slightly) raised the $(\dot{w} - \dot{\tilde{w}})$ coefficients in both equations.

The constant terms in all of the above equations seem reasonable, *a priori*. A 3.6 to 3.8 percent natural or equilibrium unemployment rate (achieved when actual and expected rates of change in prices and wages coincide) for prime-age married males lies somewhere between the rates obtained during a boom period such as 1966-68 and a slump such as 1958-60. We present results for U_p only and not for U. The reason is that the natural rate for U_p is much steadier—more nearly constant—than that of U. The natural rate of U is sensitive to the effects of changes in the age composition of the labor force—especially important in the period covered—while that of U_p is much less so.

In fine, we have offered an account of the behavior of U in the 1960s as "explained" by a constant natural rate of unemployment and the predetermined unlagged deviations of actual from expected rates of change in prices and wages. The natural rate is, of course, determined by the equilibrium conditions of the system and hence varies over time, especially in response to the age-sex composition of the labor force. We have attempted to minimize the effect of changes in labor-force composition by defining our unemployment variable by U_p instead of U. Nonetheless, other forces affect the natural rate and our trouble with serial correlation in the residuals may reflect our misspecification of the natural rate as a constant. Despite this and other defects, we feel that our account of U_p in the equations of this section is not inferior to the (few) others presently available.

One shortcoming of our unemployment equation is that none of its arguments is influenced by monetary-fiscal or any other policy. The wage and price deviation terms are predetermined, though endogenous. In fact, they are surely influenced by various governmental policies; the question is how. It may be that an expansionary monetary-fiscal policy reduces unemployment by increasing the deviations between actual and expected product prices. But to estimate this impact from one of the equations of this section, it is necessary either to deny that the rate of monetary-fiscal expansion is itself influenced by these deviations (of U) or to specify the arguments and functional form of the relation.

Neither of these options is attractive: economic policy is affected by the level of unemployment as much as—or more than—it affects it. But economic theory offers no guidance in specifying the relation between U (or any of its correlates) with governmental activity. And attempting a usable *ad hoc* specification is far beyond our (immediate) aspirations or capacity. Accordingly, we have taken refuge from the dilemma by uncoupling the unemployment equation from the rest of the system. This makes it possible to estimate the unemployment-inflation tradeoff on a given policy. Such an estimate cannot be made from a time series until one can specify (and allow for) the feedback response of policy to economic variables.

Two-Stage Least Squares Estimates

Thus far we have treated price expectation as exogenous. However, the rationale of our entire discussion has been that price expectations are determined (*inter alia*) by the actions of the monetary and fiscal authorities and that there is no feedback. But it is not obvious that the actions of the monetary and fiscal authorities may properly be treated as exogenous. To do so implies denying that the professed stabilization objectives of these authorities has any predictive implications for their actual conduct. As indicated above, we are far from convinced that this assumption is appropriate, but some preliminary experiments have convinced us that the specification of either a nominal money supply function or a fiscal policy functions is well beyond anything we are prepared to undertake. Accordingly, for better or worse we have been compelled to consider the effects of monetary and/or fiscal policy as though they were determined exogenously. The spirit of neoclassical model such as ours accommodates a monetary variable more readily than a fiscal variable. In effect, fiscal policy is one—albeit a very important—determinant of velocity. However, for our immediate purpose we can introduce a fiscal policy variable along side, or even in place of, a monetary variable.

The operational question is how to quantify either monetary or fiscal variables for inclusion in a regression. The structure of our model makes the policy variables affect the endogenous ones through their effect upon price expectations. "Quantity of money" taken literally is best approximated by some measure of the means of payment such as demand deposits plus currency outside banks, M_1; or by M_1 plus time deposits, M_2. But both M_1 and M_2 are to some extent influenced by business activity which increases demand for loans and commercial banks use of their own lines of credit; that is, M_1 and M_2 are influenced by actual and expected prices, and hence are (to some extent) endogenous. M_3, the monetary base, is more directly under control of the Federal Reserve Board (Fed) and perhaps closer to being exogenous. Yet, to argue that the Fed's actions are independent of business conditions is surely inconsistent with its own rationalizations of its behavior. In any case, we eschewed assumption as to which version of M best suits our purpose and experimented with all of them.[25]

Specifying the fiscal policy variable (F) presents even greater problems than the monetary. The effect of business conditions upon tax-expenditure policy obviously is not nil, but specifying what the impact is, and the appropriate lags, is difficult in the extreme. Rather than attempt this specification, we posited that F was exogenous with an unknown distributed lag, measured by the ratio,

$$F = \frac{\text{Potential GNP} - \text{Full Employment Surplus (FES)}}{\text{Potential GNP}}$$

F is a well known and widely used measure of the impact of the federal budget upon GNP; and there is an existing quarterly series available.[26]

As a measured fiscal policy, F is heir to at least one shortcoming of FES; that is, FES reflects current federal payments to vendors while the effect of federal appropriations on economic activity is felt earlier. This discrepancy is particularly applicable to defense expenditures.[27] To offset this potential error, we followed Galper in adjusting federal expenditures to reflect changes in "Defense Goods in Process Inventory Adjustment."[28] This adjusted measurement of F we designate F_2, as distinguished from F_1, the unadjusted measurement.

In general, we assume

$$p = \phi(\dot{M},F) \text{ with } \frac{\partial \dot{p}}{\partial M} \text{ and } \frac{\partial \dot{p}}{\partial F} \geqslant 0$$

Since, in practice, F hovers around unity and never approaches zero, we would expect $F > h, h > 0$, and probably $h > 1/2$, where h is a positive constant. As indicated above, we do not assume that either F or $\dot{M}$ has the greater impact upon $\dot{p}$; only that they have positive coefficients.[29] We posit that both F and $\dot{M}$ affect $\dot{p}$ with unknown distributed lags. This lag is characterized by an Almon polynomial of the third degree.[30]

A further problem in estimating the impact of $\dot{M}$ and F on price expectations is whether to use "raw" observations of $\dot{M}$ and F or (seasonally corrected) smoothed ones. For each, we distinguish two cases: (1) *price expectations measured by lagged realized prices*. In this case (our main one), use of smoothed data yielded higher R^2's, but markedly lower D.W.'s than were obtained with the raw observations. With smoothed data, the D.W.'s were unacceptably low (less than 1), but with unsmoothed data they were all above 1.4. Accordingly, when price expectations are measured in this manner, $\dot{M}$ and F are used without seasonal adjustment. (2) *price expectations estimated from Eckstein-Feldstein equation*. In this case, the unsmoothed data yielded both higher R^2's and higher D.W.'s than the smoothed. However, smoothed or unsmoothed, the D.W.'s of regressions involving this measure of expected prices remain below 1.0, and regressions involving it are accordingly suspect. However, we shall present some results based on this measure; in these $\dot{M}$ and F will be—as in case (1)—unsmoothed.[31]

Table 10-2 contains a selection of our experiments in regressing $\dot{p}_c$ and $\dot{p}_o$ on $\dot{M}$ and F; in fact only a few of our "better" results.[32] The following three comments pertain to these results:

1. None of the equations in Table 10-2 includes $\dot{M}_2$. This is because almost invariably better results (higher R^2's, lower D.W. and higher t values on the coefficients) were obtained with either $\dot{M}_1$ or $\dot{M}_3$.

2. When F_1 is used the (sum of the) coefficients on the monetary variable is almost always less than twice their standard error and often has a negative (wrong) sign. But (with F_1 as its measure), fiscal policy has a consistently significant positive effect (as measured by the sum of coefficients) on price expectations. When F_2 is the measure of fiscal policy, the sum of the coefficients on $\dot{M}$ becomes consistently positive and significant while those on F decline sharply though remaining significant.

Table 10-2

Results of Monetary and Fiscal Variables Regressed on $\dot{p}$

$$\dot{p}_O = -107.3 + .06 \sum_{i=1}^{10} \dot{M_1}_{(t-i)} + 110.1 \sum_{i=1}^{10} F_1{}_{(t-i)}$$

$\quad (-13.2) \quad [.06] \; 14.3 \qquad\qquad [8.2] \; 4.5$

$R^2 = .96$

$D.W. = .66$

$$\dot{p}_c = -94.6 - .06 \sum_{i=1}^{10} \dot{M_1}_{(t-i)} + 97.3 \sum_{i=1}^{10} F_1{}_{(t-i)}$$

$\quad (-18.1) \quad [.30] \; 2.8 \qquad\qquad [5.3] \; 5.4$

$R^2 = .97$

$D.W. = .42$

$$\underline{\dot{p}_O} = -98.6 - .11 \sum_{i=1}^{10} \dot{M_1}_{(t-i)} + 101.0 \sum_{i=1}^{10} F_1{}_{(t-i)}$$

$\quad (-5.0) \quad [.14] \; .63 \qquad\qquad [20.2] \; 5.3$

$R^2 = .86$

$D.W. = 1.66$

$$\dot{p}_c = -81.2 - .01 \sum_{i=1}^{10} \dot{M_1}_{(t-i)} + 91.8 \sum_{i=1}^{10} F_1{}_{(t-i)}$$

$\quad (-8.4) \quad [.07] \; 2.4 \qquad\qquad [10.8] \; 5.8$

$R^2 = .94$

$D.W. = 2.02$

$$\dot{p}_O = -13.0 + .41 \sum_{i=1}^{10} \dot{M_3}_{(t-i)} + 14.1 \sum_{i=1}^{10} F_2{}_{(t-i)}$$

$\quad (-5.96) \quad [.04] \; 4.0 \qquad\qquad [2.2] \; 4.7$

$R^2 = .81$

$D.W. = .33$

$$\dot{p}_c = -11.4 + .32 \sum_{i=1}^{10} \dot{M_3}_{(t-i)} + 12.7 \sum_{i=1}^{10} F_2{}_{(t-i)}$$

$\quad (-8.3) \quad [.08] \; 5.1 \qquad\qquad [1.4] \; 4.0$

$R^2 = .88$

$D.W. = .25$

$$\underline{\dot{p}_O} = -8.1 + .47 \sum_{i=1}^{10} \dot{M_3}_{(t-i)} + 8.9 \sum_{i=1}^{10} F_2{}_{(t-i)}$$

$\quad (-2.1) \quad [.08] \; 5.7 \qquad\qquad [4.0] \; 6.0$

$R^2 = .84$

$D.W. = 1.75$

$$\underline{\dot{p}_c} = -7.3 + .37 \sum_{i=1}^{10} \dot{M_3}_{(t-i)} + 8.1 \sum_{i=1}^{10} F_2{}_{(t-i)}$$

$\quad (-2.4) \quad [.085] \; 3.7 \qquad\qquad [3.1] \; 4.1$

$R^2 = .92$

$D.W. = 2.51$

$$\dot{p}_O = -2.5 + .17 \sum_{i=5}^{20} \dot{M_3}_{(t-i)} + 4.4 \sum_{i=4}^{14} F_2{}_{(t-i)}$$

$\quad (-.73) \quad [.05] \; 11.0 \qquad\qquad [3.5] \; 5.0$

$R^2 = .57$

$D.W. = .11$

$$\dot{p}_c = -2.2 + .21 \sum_{i=5}^{20} \dot{M_3}_{(t-i)} + 3.5 \sum_{i=4}^{14} F_2{}_{(t-i)}$$

$\quad (-1.94) \quad [.02] \; 18.7 \qquad\qquad [1.2] \; 4.9$

$R^2 = .88$

$D.W. = .18$

$$\underline{\dot{p}_O} = -2.7 + .27 \sum_{i=5}^{20} \dot{M_3}_{(t-i)} + 3.7 \sum_{i=4}^{14} F_2{}_{(t-i)}$$

$\quad (-1.9) \quad [.07] \; 7.3 \qquad\qquad [1.3] \; 4.3$

$R^2 = .98$

$D.W. = .69$

$$\underline{\dot{p}_c} = -2.89 + .11 \sum_{i=5}^{20} \dot{M_3}_{(t-i)} + 1.5 \sum_{i=4}^{14} F_2{}_{(t-i)}$$

$\quad (-1.3) \quad [.06] \; 9.2 \qquad\qquad [.93] \; 4.3$

$R^2 = .98$

$D.W. = .92$

3. Where either $\dot{M}$ or F is used without the other, both the R^2's and D.W.'s become much lower than in most cases where both variables are included. For this reason, no regressions with $\dot{M}$ or F alone are reported.

The intent of these remarks is to warn the reader not to use our results to judge the relative impact of monetary and fiscal policy upon wages and prices. The inability of either $\dot{M}$ or F alone to effectively estimate $\dot{p}_c$ and $\dot{p}_o$ indicates the strong historical intercorrelation of these policy instruments and our consequent inability to obtain a reliable estimate of their individual contributions from a single decade of observations. This inability might be offset if we were able to specify a model of policymaking that would jointly determine $\dot{M}$ and F. Because such a model is unavailable, our results are necessarily limited and tentative.

The estimates of the impact of $\dot{M}$ and F upon $\dot{p}_c$, $\dot{p}_o$, $\dot{w}$, and U are presented below. They are estimated from the equations in Table 10-2 via two stage least squares. That is, the equations of Table 10-2 determine the effect of various pairs of values of $\dot{M}$ and F upon price expectations, and these expectations in turn enter the estimates of $\dot{p}_c$, $\dot{p}_o$, $\dot{w}$, and U. Where a variable in an equation is estimated via a relation in Table 10-2, it is designated by a $\wedge$; $\hat{\dot{w}}$ is estimated from the sum of the estimated value of $\hat{\dot{p}}$ and the lagged observations on $\dot{p}_c$ and $\dot{w}$ in accordance with the equation discussed in the earlier section on the measurement of price expectations.

The endogenous variables of our various models are $\dot{p}_c$, $\dot{p}_o$, $\dot{w}$, $\dot{\bar{p}}_c$, $\dot{\bar{p}}_o$, U, and $\dot{\bar{w}}$. The exogenous variables are D, $\dot{M}$, and F. As the latter two variables are used only in tandem, they are one variable. The predetermined endogenous variables are $(\dot{p}_c - \dot{\bar{p}}_c)$, $(\dot{p}_o - \dot{\bar{p}}_o)$, and $(\dot{w} - \dot{\bar{w}})$, all of which may be lagged. All equations are clearly overidentified. The system is recursive, and the equations are mutually independent. The linkage of U, $\dot{w}$, and $\dot{p}$ as in a Phillips curve is precluded by this specification, though we do report (what we consider relatively unsuccessful) experiments in which U is included in the wage equation and $\dot{w}$ in the unemployment equation.

For each specification of $\dot{M}$ and F we have a different equation system. Because the results with $(\dot{M}_3, F_1)$ were generally inferior to those with $(\dot{M}_3, F_2)$ we report only the latter. For a similar reason, we report only the results with $(\dot{M}_1, F_1)$ which are superior to those with $(\dot{M}_1, F_2)$; the omission of $\dot{M}_2$ was explained above. Of the results obtained with $(\dot{M}_1, F_1)$ and $(\dot{M}_3, F_2)$ only those where U_p is the left-hand variable differ appreciably when we switch from one system to the other. Accordingly, we present results for $(\dot{M}_3, F_2)$ only for the equations determining U_p. Despite the low D.W.'s for regressions of $\dot{\bar{p}}$ on $\dot{M}$ and F for the Eckstein-Feldstein measures of price expectations, we present (in System 3 of Table 10-3) a set of equations involving their use: as before when expected prices or wages are measured from the Eckstein-Feldstein regression, they are designated with primes.[33]

Table 10-3
Results of Two Stage Least Square Regressions

System 1   Expectations Measure: $\dot{\bar{p}} = f_1(\dot{M_1}, F_1)$

$$\dot{p}_c = -0.01 + 1.04\,\dot{\hat{\bar{p}}}_c + 0.18\,(\dot{p}_o - \dot{\hat{\bar{p}}}_o)_{-2} + 0.46\,(\dot{p}_c - \dot{\hat{\bar{p}}})_{-1}$$
$$(-0.05)\quad(16.4)\qquad(2.36)\qquad\qquad\qquad(2.68)$$

$R^2 = 0.94$
D.W. = 1.90
(10.38a.1)

$$\dot{p}_o = 0.04 + 0.99\,\dot{\hat{\bar{p}}}_o + 0.56\,(\dot{p}_o - \dot{\hat{\bar{p}}}_o)_{-1} + 0.20\,(\dot{w} - \dot{\hat{\bar{w}}})_{-2}$$
$$(0.29)\quad(15.6)\qquad(4.36)\qquad\qquad(1.89)$$

$R^2 = 0.92$
D.W. = 1.72
(10.38a.2)

$$\dot{w} = 0.74 + 0.83\,\dot{\hat{\bar{w}}} + 0.73\,(\dot{p}_c - \dot{\hat{\bar{p}}})_{-2} + 0.53\,(\dot{w} - \dot{\hat{\bar{w}}})_{-1}$$
$$(1.96)\quad(9.54)\qquad(2.75)\qquad\qquad(4.14)$$

$R^2 = 0.87$
D.W. = 1.75
(10.38a.3)

$$U_p = 3.80 - 3.47\,(\dot{p}_c - \dot{\hat{\bar{p}}}) - 0.88\,(\dot{p}_o - \dot{\hat{\bar{p}}}) + 0.61\,(\dot{w} - \dot{\hat{\bar{w}}})$$
$$(45.6)\quad(-12.1)\qquad\quad(-4.91)\qquad\qquad(3.77)$$

$R^2 = 0.85$
D.W. = 0.96
(10.38a.4)

$$U_p = 3.90 - 2.95\,(\dot{p}_c - \dot{\hat{\bar{p}}}_c) - 0.54\,(\dot{p}_o - \dot{\hat{\bar{p}}}_o) + 0.40\,(\dot{w} - \dot{\hat{\bar{w}}})$$
$$(31.1)\quad(-8.67)\qquad\qquad(-2.41)\qquad\qquad(2.06)$$
$$\quad - 0.52\,D_{-2}$$
$$\quad\;(-2.53)$$

$R^2 = 0.77$
D.W. = 0.95

(10.38a.5)

$$\dot{w} = 1.32 + 0.67\,(\dot{w} - \dot{\hat{\bar{w}}}) + 1.83\,U_{pd} + 0.51\,(\dot{w} - \dot{\hat{\bar{w}}})_{-1}$$
$$(2.10)\quad(4.09)\qquad\qquad(1.14)\qquad(4.01)$$
$$\quad + 0.55\,(\dot{p}_c - \dot{\hat{\bar{p}}})_{-2}$$
$$\quad\;(1.81)$$

$R^2 = 0.88$
D.W. = 1.82
(10.38b.3)

Regressions (10.38b.1-2) and (10.38b.4-5) are approximate to their 1a counterparts.

System 2   Expectations Measure: $\dot{\bar{p}} = f_2(\dot{M_3}, F_2)$

$$U_p = 3.76 - 3.06\,(\dot{p}_c - \dot{\hat{\bar{p}}}) - 0.68\,(\dot{p}_o - \dot{\hat{\bar{p}}}_o) + 0.22\,(\dot{w} - \dot{\hat{\bar{w}}})$$

$R^2 = 0.77$
(10.39a.4)

$$(36.2)\quad(-2.53)\qquad\qquad(3.33)\qquad\qquad(1.16)$$

D.W. = 1.04
(10.39a.4)

$$U_p = 3.86 - 2.76\,(\dot{p}_c - \dot{\hat{\bar{p}}}_c) - 0.58\,(\dot{p}_o - \dot{\hat{\bar{p}}}_o) + 0.14\,(\dot{w} - \dot{\hat{\bar{w}}})$$

$R^2 = 0.76$
(10.39a.5)

$$(30.2)\quad(-7.90)\qquad\qquad(-2.67)\qquad\qquad(0.75)$$

$$\quad + 0.45\,D_{-2}$$
$$\quad\;(-2.08)$$

D.W. = 1.02
(10.39b.5)

All other regressions in System 2 are approximate to their System 1 counterparts.

Table 10-3 (cont.)

System 3   Expectations Measure: $\hat{\dot{p}}_c' = f_3\,(\dot{M}_3, F_2)$

$$\dot{p}_c = \underset{(-0.50)}{-0.08} + \underset{(10.3)}{1.16\,\hat{\dot{p}}_c'} + \underset{(5.57)}{0.61\,(\dot{p}_o - \hat{\dot{p}}_o')_{-1}} + \underset{(3.93)}{0.19\,(\dot{p}_o - \hat{\dot{p}}_o')}$$

$R^2 = .94$
D.W. = 2.07
(10.40.1)

$$\dot{p}_o = \underset{(0.70)}{0.13} + \underset{(9.84)}{0.92\,\hat{\dot{p}}_o'} + \underset{(13.5)}{0.84\,(\dot{p}_o - \hat{\dot{p}}_o')_{-1}} + \underset{(2.68)}{0.29\,(\dot{w} - \hat{\dot{w}}')}$$

$R^2 = .94$
D.W. = 1.43
(10.40.2)

$$\dot{w} = \underset{(2.43)}{1.47} + \underset{(4.17)}{0.63\,\hat{\dot{w}}'} + \underset{(1.35)}{2.56\,U_{pd}} + \underset{(4.11)}{0.48\,(\dot{w} - \hat{\dot{w}}')_{-1}}$$
$$+ \underset{(0.92)}{0.28\,(\dot{p}_c - \hat{\dot{p}}_c')_{-2}}$$

$R^2 = .90$
D.W. = 2.03
(10.40.3)

$$U_p = \underset{(68.0)}{3.63} - \underset{(-8.54)}{1.07\,(\dot{p}_c - \hat{\dot{p}}_c')} - \underset{(-5.06)}{0.29\,(\dot{p}_o - \hat{\dot{p}}_o')} + \underset{(1.09)}{0.11\,(\dot{w} - \hat{\dot{w}}')}$$

$R^2 = .95$
D.W. = 0.47
(10.40.4)

$$U_p = \underset{(66.1)}{3.83} - \underset{(-12.3)}{1.28\,(\dot{p}_c - \hat{\dot{p}}_c')} - \underset{(-3.29)}{0.16\,(\dot{p}_o - \hat{\dot{p}}_o')} + \underset{(2.39)}{0.18\,(\dot{w} - \hat{\dot{w}}')}$$
$$- \underset{(-4.76)}{0.39\,D}$$

$R^2 = .97$
D.W. = 0.83
(10.40.5)

The common feature of all equations determining $\dot{p}_c$, $\dot{p}_o$, and $\dot{w}$ is their similarity to (10.24)-(10.26). Thus the coefficients, t values, R^2 and D.W. of (10.38a.1)—see Table 10-3—are virtually identical with (10.24) and the similarity between (10.40.1) and (10.24) is almost as close. The matches between (10.38a.3) and (10.25)—and (10.40.2) and (10.25′)—are about as close as those reported in the previous sentence. The similarity between (10.38a.3) and (10.26) is about as close as that between the other pairs, and so forth.

What this means is that the two stage estimates in this section are virtually identical with the OLS equations (for $\dot{p}_c$, $\dot{p}_o$ and $\dot{w}$) in the third section of this chapter, "Price and Wage Equations." This is not really surprising since the corresponding equations differ only in the method of measuring price (and wage) expectations. The two sets of measures both involve time-series regressions—one on past prices and the other on past values of $\dot{M}$ and F. Economic theory implies that past movements in (at least) $\dot{M}$ should parallel movements in $\dot{p}$ and $\dot{w}$ so that the regressions of $\hat{\dot{p}}$ on ($\dot{M}, F$) and on $\dot{p}$ lagged should be very similar.

The only difference between the equations in the fifth section of this chapter, "Two Stage Least Squares Estimates" and their analogues in the third section is that in the latter expected wages and prices are exogenous while in the former they are endogenous and determined by the expectation functions of

Table 10-2. Consequently, virtually all of the characteristics of the equations of the third section also inhere in those of the fifth section. Specifically, in the equations determining $\dot{p}_c$ and $\dot{p}_o$, the constants do not differ significantly from zero and the coefficients on expected prices from unity. Also, in System 1a, the constant term in the wage equation is close to being two standard deviations above zero and the coefficient on $\dot{w}$ is close to being two standard deviations below unity. In System 3, the constant term in the wage equation is significantly different from zero and the coefficient on $\hat{\dot{w}}$ is significantly below unity. The obvious corrective is to introduce $U_p{}^{-1}$. (b systems are differentiated from a systems by this addition in the $\dot{w}$ regression.) In (10.38b.3) U_{pd} has the correct (positive) sign, but the coefficient is only 1.1 times its standard error: Moreover, it raises the constant term to well over unity, and reduces the coefficient on $\hat{\dot{w}}$ without materially altering the R^2 or D.W. of the equation. Also it weakens the coefficient on $(\dot{p}_c - \hat{\dot{p}}_c)_{-2}$.[34] In short, our wage rate equation does about as well without the unemployment percentage as with it.

Whether $\dot{w}$ simply outran the expectations thereof during the 1960s (as suggested by the constant term in (10.38a.3) or whether the function for estimating expected wage rates is biased high (as suggested by the low coefficient on $\hat{\dot{w}}$) is anybody's guess. It is not hard to "correct" (10.38a.3) by *ad hoc* adjustments (see below) but the rationale for doing so is questionable. For example, equations (i)-(iii) in note 34 indicate that if $\dot{w}_m$ is substituted for $\dot{w}$, the wage rate equation will perform in a manner compatible with neoclassical theory. Wage data outside of the manufacturing sector are far less adequate than inside. It is, therefore, quite possible that measurement errors in nonmanufacturing wages or genuine shifts in relative wages between manufacturing and other sectors (i.e., specification error), or both, are responsible for the marginally acceptable performance of our wage equation. Another possible explanation is that our price expectation variables are arithmetic constructs and not direct observations, which might perform differently. Until these possibilities are explored, we feel it would be unproductive to experiment extensively with the lag structure of the model.

However, out of curiosity, we performed one (arbitrary) experiment. The residuals in the unemployment equation were consistently negative from the second quarter of 1961 to the second quarter of 1964, and positive in all but two quarters thereafter. Accordingly, we entered a dummy (zero for the period prior to the third quarter of 1964 and one thereafter) and reestimated equations (10.38a.1)-(10.38a.4) which are presented in notes 35 and 36.[35] Principal effects of the dummy on the wage equation are lower slightly the constant, raise the coefficient on $\hat{\dot{w}}$ and lower the t ratios on both. With the dummy entered, the constant is appreciably less than two standard errors from zero and the coefficient on $\hat{\dot{w}}$ is comfortably less than two standard errors from unity. (The effects on the unemployment equation are noted below.) While this adjustment makes the wage equation conform more closely to neoclassical theory, we do not wish to place any weight on this result because of the *ad hoc* nature of the adjustment.

Our theory is that U is independent of rates of change in (absolute) prices and wage rates when these are equal to expected rates. This theory is reflected in (10.36), (10.36'), (10.38a.4), (10.39a.4). The price deviations terms in those equations are contemporaneous (i.e., unlagged) with U_p because it is assumed that both reflect the same forces. That is, U_p minus the constant term, and the wage and price deviation terms, all reflect incompletely anticipated changes in $\dot{M}$ and/or F. The maintained hypothesis is that when $\dot{w} = \hat{\dot{w}}$ and $\dot{p}_i = \hat{\dot{p}}_i$, $U_p =$ constant. In all of these equations, the deviations of actual from expected wages and (actual from expected) prices give reasonably good explanations of U_p. That is, the constants are reasonable; the signs of the coefficients on the price deviations are negative and significantly different from zero, and the signs of the coefficients on the wage deviations are positive and (usually) significant. The trouble is that the D.W.'s are persistently low when expected prices are constructed from lagged price changes. When the Eckstein-Feldstein data are used and D_{-2} is introduced as in (10.37') the D.W. climbs to 1.64. However, (10.40.5) has a D.W. below 1.

Introducing the binary dummy for the periods before the third quarter of 1964 and the period thereafter into (10.40.4) yields a significant negative coefficient on the dummy, but a D.W. of 1.14. Adding $\dot{w}$ to the equation, raises the D.W. to 1.73, but $\dot{w}$ has a significant negative coefficient (its t value is 5.9).[36] With the Eckstein-Feldstein measure of expected prices and wages, the dummy is negative and significant and the D.W. is 1.50 or higher regardless of whether $\dot{w}$ is entered; moreover the coefficient of $\dot{w}$ is insignificant and positive. Despite these "favorable" results, our unemployment equation has a number of loose ends. Its major difficulty, the need for a dummy to curb serial correlation in the residuals, is probably due to changes in labor force characteristics that reduced the natural rate of unemployment during the latter 1960s. For example, the Vietnam war may easily have led to labor hoarding beyond what normally occurs in a business expansion of comparable impact on wage and price deviations (from expected levels). The fact that in some equations $\dot{w}$ has a significant negative coefficient is difficult to explain. (If anyone cares to argue that ceteris paribus—in particular $\dot{M}$ and F constant—an increase in $\dot{w}$ reduced U_p, he is free to do so.) In short, the U_p equation will bear much more work.

We decided in advance of our computer runs to end the period of analysis in the fourth quarter of 1969. Whether it is possible to massage the data or bend the equations to fit the 1970-71 experience is an open question.[37] We offer this piece as a contribution to the pre-1970 debate on the Phillips curve. As indicated earlier, we are discontented with the constructs that serve as measures of expected prices and wages, and it is largely for this reason that we refrain from further manipulation of these contrived measures.

The spirit of our model would be more fully satisfied if our exogenous variable was $\dot{M}$ and not an $(\dot{M},F)$ vector. Indeed, the neoclassical model on which the discussion of this chapter's first section rests makes M the determinant of $\dot{p}$ with no explicit place for F. F must somehow creep into our model as a backstage determinant of the relation between deviations of actual and expected prices and wages on the one hand, and the rate of capacity utilization (including the unemployment percentage) on the other. Clearly this part of our model is in need of further development.

A further and related need is a specification of the relation between fiscal policy (or behavior) and the behavior of $\dot{M}$. Such a model may well compel abandonment of the assumption that either $\dot{M}$ or F is exogenous. That is, we might be forced to treat the behavior of $\dot{M}$ and F as the constrained response of monetary-fiscal authorities to the relation between actual and desired behavior of various target variables.

All of the above findings tend to support the (neoclassical) conclusion that if actual prices and wages equalled expected prices and wages, the unemployment percentage would not affect the rate of increase in the wage rate ($\dot{w}$). Moreover, when actual wages and prices equal those expected, the unemployment percentage itself will be determined by (nonprice or wage) forces operating outside the model. We conjecture that these forces are responsible for the serial correlation among the residuals of the U_p equations. In short, the long-run Phillips curve is vertical. If expected prices and wages tend to their actual values in the "long run," it follows that in the same long run, there is no way for monetary or fiscal policy to influence U. Whether one accepts such a conclusion depends (*inter alia*) upon his confidence in our specification of the $(\dot{M},F)$ function. We have already indicated our own reservations about this specification. Nevertheless, we believe that equation set (10.38a.1-4) or (10.40.1-4) present as good an account of the wage-price-unemployment history of the 1960s as can be found.

If this account is substantially correct, it follows from the unemployment equation that monetary-fiscal policy can affect a reduction in the unemployment percentage only by creating a positive deviation between actual and expected prices and/or a negative deviation of actual from expected wage rates. Since the relation between actual and expected wages is assumed to be very nearly the same as that between actual and expected consumption prices (see above), the large coefficient on $(\dot{p}_c - \dot{\bar{p}}_c)$ relative to that on $(\dot{w} - \dot{\bar{w}})$ ensures that the effect of an increase in the $(\dot{M},F)$ variable on U will be dominated by the price deviation terms. [i.e., by $(\dot{p}_c - \dot{\bar{p}}_c)$ and $(\dot{p}_o - \dot{\bar{p}}_o)$].[38]

Let us focus attention upon those cases where an increase in $(\dot{M},F)$ is followed soon after by a (temporary) decrease in U_p.[39] (That is, assume the existence of a short-run Phillips curve tradeoff.) Suppose the increase in (M, F) to be permanent. Then it will push up $\dot{\bar{p}}_c$, $\dot{\bar{p}}_o$ and $\dot{w}$ and eventually eliminate the temporary decrease in U_p unless the gap between actual and expected rates of inflation is (somehow) reopened. Thus a permanent reduction in U_p requires an accelerating rate of inflation.

Some Policy Implications

The previous argument does not imply that it is necessarily unsound to attempt to reduce U_p below its natural rate for a time; it may be worth what it costs. The "cost" is that—barring an intervening decrease in price expectations—any subsequent attempts to reduce U_p will require a greater acceleration of inflation than what was required "this time." The main cost of attempting to move along an (imaginary) Phillips curve is that it involves trenching upon a valuable social asset.

This asset is the faith of the public in the currency as a store of value and a standard of deferred payment. It is this faith that permits temporary increases in the quantities of factor services supplied to occur contemporaneously with unexpected reductions in their real prices. It is these increases in factor supplies that enable a government quickly to mobilize resources by expanding the nominal money stock without first securing the real resources to pay for them. The value of the power to obtain additional (real) resources by inflating—the power to reallocate by inflation—is that of a contingency reserve for the public authorities which can be drawn upon more quickly than resources raised through taxes.

The importance of the government having access to inflationary methods of financing unanticipated expenditures will be judged differently depending upon attitudes toward government behavior. Those who distrust or otherwise disapprove of what governments usually do will value the loss of this asset lower than those who feel otherwise. Also, there is no ready consensus as to just what is lost when a government loses the ability to increase the real value of the resources it can command by an unanticipated increase in the nominal money stock. Clearly, the magnitude of the loss will depend upon access to loans of real assets from abroad or from private citizens; upon the ease of raising taxes, and so forth. But despite difficulties of calculation, loss of the "power to inflate further" is a major part of the welfare cost of generating a (fully anticipated) inflation.[40]

Granted the cost of a loss of influence over the real stock of payment media, the practical question is how much difference is made by the "incremental loss" requited to reduce the unemployment percentage by (say) 1 percent for one year. This question is hard to answer. If the cost of inflation is considered appreciable only if it becomes hyperinflation, then the problem becomes that of estimating the increase in the probability that the camel's back will eventually break because of the laying on a given feather that (it is agreed) will not of itself fracture the dromedary's spinal cord. Or, it becomes akin to the problem of determining the cost-benefit ratio of an additional official misstatement which improves tomorrow's headline but contributes to a collapse of public confidence in the trustworthiness of all official reports—or of an additional pound of detergent in a river that is not yet inimical to organic function.

We do not have any formula for solving such puzzles; nor do we believe that one exists. However, we recommend the wisdom of Keynes on this range of problems: "you cannot run a country on *transparent* humbug."

Conclusions

In this chapter we have developed and discussed the implications of a modified neoclassical theory of wages, prices, and unemployment used in this study. A simple aggregate model constructed in the neoclassical spirit was estimated by both ordinary and two-stage least squares procedures in an attempt to demonstrate its consistency with the theoretical expectations and to analyze further some properties of our economy.

The evidence is, for the most part, quite consistent with the implications of neoclassical price theory, which places considerable emphasis on expectations of rates of increase of prices and wages as major determinants of movements in the actual rates of increase. A further implication of neoclassical price theory is that short-run changes in quantity variables, particularly the unemployment rate, are associated primarily with disequilibrium in the sense that expectations of rates of increase of prices and wages are not being met. The various estimates of our unemployment equation offer considerable support for this view, although the prevalence of serial correlation is indicative of the need for further work on the specification of this equation.

A major conceptual point, which cannot be overemphasized in view of its implications for monetary-fiscal policy, is that a Phillips curve type relationship should not be inferred from the wage equation as has typically been done. For such a derivation, it is improper to consider the wage equation in isolation from a more general system in which the unemployment rate is explicitly recognized as an endogenous variable. Our results indicate that when this more general approach is taken, the relationship between $\dot{w}$ and U (or $\dot{p}$ and U) is by no means as straightforward or powerful as it previously appeared,[41] and, indeed, expectations of both prices and money wages do appear to play a crucial role in this regard.

Our attempt to enter explicitly the macroeconomic policy instruments into the model met with very limited success. A significant indirect influence of monetary and fiscal policy on actual rates of price and wage increase via altered expectations was indicated, but the lack of knowledge regarding the appropriate indicators of these policies is a serious obstacle to deeper analysis of the forces involved. However, another major conceptual point, also with important policy implications, is made explicit by this approach; the relationships between monetary and fiscal instruments and rates of inflation and unemployment can be seen to be both complex and imprecise, and one of the primary reasons for this relates to the role of expectations. It is not surprising that the efforts of policymakers in recent years to alleviate inflation have met with such undesirable results. Inflationary expectations were probably quite strong.

The ability of macroeconomic instruments to guide us along a predetermined inflation-unemployment time path is extremely limited. We neither have sufficient knowledge of the true relationship that exists in this area, nor even if we did is it likely that we would be able to manipulate (through the use of aggregate monetary-fiscal policies) the economy so as to achieve "acceptable" rates of inflation and unemployment simultaneously over a sustained period of time.

11 Implications for Policy and Research

Since the scope of this study is so broad, it would be tedious to undertake a summary. We did attempt to state our conclusions with as much emphasis as seemed warranted as the study proceeded. Rather than simply reiterate these here, we believe that it would be more useful if we briefly spell out a few of the more important implications of our analysis for both policy and further research. In doing so, we will build upon (and repeat) some of our results.

Economic research has always been at least two steps behind the dictates of necessity on the subject of macroeconomic policy. Economic policymakers are confronted daily with the need to make decisions utilizing a knowledge base that is insufficient to permit confidence that they will, or indeed are, able to achieve a desired result. But, as we mentioned in our introduction, policies must still be implemented, if only on a best-guess basis.[1] It is our belief that many aspects of our analysis make an incremental contribution to the aforementioned knowledge base. It is for this reason that we follow through to policy recommendations in many areas where our discussion of research implication indicates that considerable advances in the theory are still desirable.

We chose to deal with policy implications first, then research ones. This is because in the first section we will make recommendations concerning policy in some of those areas in which there is inadequate knowledge. If we were to reverse the order of discussion, we might find ourselves too weakhearted to make any such policy recommendations.

Implications for Policy

One of our most important findings was that actual and potential low-wage earners, particularly the young, and their families derive considerably more benefit than higher wage and salary earners from high levels of economic activity and low rates of aggregate unemployment. This was not a surprising result—indeed many studies have indicated the high positive correlation between low unemployment rates and rapid reductions in the incidence of poverty[2]—but, unlike ours, these past analyses have not examined this issue in the context of a specific model of labor-market activity. Our model permits us to assert with more confidence that these short-run reductions in poverty incidence are indicative of long-run welfare gains to this part of the population relative to the remainder.

115

This fact, coupled together with our finding that the redistributional consequences of inflation for relative costs-of-living, nonearned income, and value of assets are, if not neutral, probably favorable to the poor as a group, argues for a macroeconomic policy that aims for a point fairly high on the Phillips curve if it is significantly nonvertical in the longer run.[3] We believe this view should only be tempered moderately when efficiency of allocation considerations are also introduced, in light of our argument that the resource misallocations caused by moderate rates of inflation and somewhat lower-than-price-stable rates of aggregate unemployment are not as severe as generally believed. Choosing such a point on the Phillips curve is going to have detrimental effects on some subgroups of the poor, particularly the aged with no labor-force attachment, but those adversely affected are not so numerous. Building escalator clauses into private pensions and public transfers is one way of alleviating detrimental impact of inflation on this subgroup of the poor, but it must be recognized that such policies, however humane, increase the tendency toward inflation of an economy already too prone in this direction for most people's tastes.

We emphasize that we are referring in the above discussion to a situation in which inflation and unemployment can be traded off to some extent even in the longer run. Whether this is so for our economy is, of course, a critical distinction that lies at the heart of much of our analysis. Just as we have become convinced in the course of this study that for the welfare of the poor as a group it is worthwhile, *if possible*, to trade lower rates of aggregate unemployment for higher rates of inflation (over most ranges of the two), so have we been persuaded that in the longer run it becomes considerably less possible to affect any such tradeoff.

The reasons for this are twofold. The first is that people tend to anticipate inflation and adjust their behavior accordingly when they have reason to believe it will occur. They are given such reason primarily because: (1) inflation has occurred in the recent past, and/or (2) they believe the policies being pursued by other economic actors, particularly the government, are inflationary in nature. This, as we have seen, causes the Phillips curve to be unstable and to tend to the vertical in the longer run. As partial evidence in favor of this we submit: (1) the results of the analysis we performed in Chapter 10, and (2) the United States economic experience of the early 1970s.[4]

The second difficulty that presents itself to policymakers who may be trying to achieve the best time path of inflation and unemployment under conditions of a shifting (short-run) Phillips curve is that knowledge is inadequate to permit more than a guess as to its exact shape and location at any point in time. Further compounding the difficulty is the fact that, even if one were to guess correctly, we lack the knowledge to utilize macroeconomic policy instruments to guide the economy to the Phillips curve, let alone to a particular point on it.[5] We have sufficient problems in simply identifying the appropriate dimensions of monetary and fiscal policy to treat as independent variables, not to mention specifying the structural relationship between them and our dependent variables (rates of inflation and unemployment).

In short, the Phillips curve is a weak reed, indeed, for policy purposes. Throughout the sixties it seemed a sensible idea, but it obviously is not.[6] Policymakers who are concerned about utilizing macroeconomic policies to benefit the low-income population should remain very concerned about aggregate rates of unemployment—and not so concerned about inflation—but not have high expectations of being able to continuously trade them off against each other. In fact, if the empirical results of Chapter 10 have any validity, it may be difficult to maintain an aggregate rate of unemployment much below 5 percent with incurring a significant and gradually increasing rate of inflation.[7]

This is not a particularly optimistic view of our economic prospects. It leads us to the conclusion that only major alterations in certain structural aspects of our economy (or, in the very short run, extensive controls such as are now being imposed by the Nixon administration)[8] will permit us to achieve a "reasonable" balance of inflation and unemployment. But desirability of such measures as reducing the ability of unions to restrict labor supply to certain industries and trades, vigorously enforcing antitrust laws against large corporations, abolishing the minimum wage, promoting the reliance of employers on credentials as screening devices that bear a closer relationship to ability to perform on the job, promoting the possibilities for low-wage earners to progress up job ladders, and increasing the flow and accuracy of labor-market information available to both workers and employers[9] alike do not depend upon whether or not one believes that there is a long-run, downward sloping Phillips curve. Measures which would serve to reduce the natural rate of unemployment, for any or all demographic groups, also would shift downward to the left of the (imaginary) Phillips curve(s) (or increase the acceptability of any given rate of aggregate unemployment), thus making possible a more appealing set of inflation-unemployment time paths.

The greatest mileage to be gotten in this direction should be through attempts to reduce through structural alterations the relatively high rates of unemployment among particular demographic groups, and thus distribute unemployment more equally across the labor force. However, we should be forewarned that the "natural" rates of unemployment are probably very high for such subgroups—it is partially for this reason that their actual unemployment rates are so high. This suggests that policies and programs ought to focus more on other dimensions of unemployment[10] (and employment) than just its rate, such as its duration, the intensity of job search of unemployed persons, and the behavior of employers with respect to their vacancies and upgrading procedures where these groups are concerned. The potential role for public-service employment and other job creation activities that do not rely upon expansionary monetary-fiscal policies also need to be explored fully.

Implications for Research

Many of the important implications of this study for further research flow from our efforts in the previous chapter. A primary point is that, despite the volume of the research throughout the sixties and early seventies on the Phillips curve, there is still a poor understanding of the relationship between inflation and unemployment. For reasons we have stated earlier, we believe that the approach taken by most researchers on this subject is unfruitful; and that a model along the general lines of the one we constructed in Chapter 10 is a more appropriate context in which to explore this subject. However, there are a number of topics which require further research if such efforts are to be successful.

First, more work needs to be done on the theory of the formation of expectations. We have shown that expectations play a crucial role in the relationship between inflation and unemployment, but, until we can be more confident of how expectations are formed and how they can be measured, we will be unable to fully understand this role—and, therefore, the relationship. We experimented with two different methods of measuring price expectations—Cagan's adaptive mechanism and Feldstein and Eckstein's interest-rate measure—and two ways of measuring wage expectations—a one-quarter lag of the CPI and the measure we constructed. In the former case, using one formulation as opposed to the other did not greatly alter the results,[11] but in the latter it did. The relationship between inflation and unemployment depicted in the usual Phillips curve model (our wage equation) is quite sensitive to the way expectations of the rate of increase in money wages are measured.

A second subject which requires more attention, as should be obvious from our discussion in Chapter 10 and the first section in this chapter, is the specification of the appropriate dimensions of monetary and fiscal policy to enter into a model such as ours. This is particularly critical since for policy purposes it is ultimately the relationships among the policy instruments which are truly exogenous and those endogenous variables which we are trying to affect that must be explicitly understood. This necessitates knowledge not only of how changes in policy instruments might influence the actual value of certain economic variables, but also how they might influence the expected value of these same variables. This was the aspect of our analysis that was least successful.

Thirdly, if the type of modified neoclassical theory with which we dealt is going to continue to be the basis of such empirical models (as we believe it should be), more effort should be expended to arrive at a useful empirical counterpart of the theoretical notion of a natural rate of unemployment. In our case, this would require making more appropriate adjustments to the aggregate unemployment rate or that of some subgroup of the population (such as prime-age males) in such a way as to account for structural changes that take place over time in the economy. Not until we have an empirical measure that satisfies as nearly as possible theoretical dictates can estimates of an equation like our unemployment one provide a reasonable test of the theory.

Finally, there are two other important subjects for further research which did not arise directly from our analysis in Chapter 10. We refer here to the primary issue of ascertaining with greater confidence the implications of various rates of aggregate unemployment and inflation for the efficiency of allocation of economic resources and the distribution of economic benefits over time, and the subsidiary issue of better understanding the causes and cures of the unequal burden that is borne across various age, education, sex, race, income, and so forth, cohorts of the population at different rates of aggregate unemployment and levels of economic activity.

We believe that it is not nearly as important for policy purposes to examine further the implications of inflation for distribution and efficiency as it is to examine the same implications of unemployment (or of different kinds of economic activity). Our analysis of the former was fairly conclusive in indicating the degree and directions of the redistributional consequences of inflation. In addition, it was also shown that the efficiency effects of moderate inflation are not likely to be severe. On the other hand, while we believe that we have been able to shed some additional light on the implications for efficiency and distribution of the level of economic activity and the aggregate unemployment rate, it is evident that this is still relatively unmapped territory.

In the first section of Chapter 6, we sketched the basic elements of a model which permitted us to draw some conclusions about the relationships among the level of economic activity, the aggregate unemployment rate, and distribution and efficiency. Such conclusions should only be drawn in the context of such a model of the workings of the labor market. While we believe that the one we presented is a useful one in this regard, as it stands now, more research on the implications for efficiency and distribution of a fuller version of this model, and alternative models, needs to be done. From a Pareto optimality viewpoint, the aggregate unemployment rate can be too low as well as too high; less unemployment is not necessarily a good thing, but we lack the information (and to some extent the theory) to enable us to know when and to what extent it is good.

The types of neoclassical models which we analyzed in this study and which view unemployment as an investment activity in information accumulation provide interesting and, hopefully, fruitful opportunities for further research. Use of these models is likely to offer more insight than the usual Keynesian deficient demand or structural unemployment models into the analysis of the duration of unemployment (of individuals), into its incidence across different groups of labor-force participants at all levels of economic activity, and into general unemployment at rates which correspond to high levels of economic activity. However, such analyses will require data not now readily available that measure many dimensions of unemployment (such as the intensity of job search) and not just its rate. In addition, greater attention has to be paid to the demand side of the labor market, in particular, examining the determinants of job vacancies, their duration, and upgrading procedures for unskilled and semiskilled laborers.

Notes

Notes

Chapter 1
Introduction

1. And, throughout much of the fifties, that the federal budget be nearly balanced—which, of course, reduced an important degree of freedom.

2. In his American Economic Association presidential address ["Inflation and Unemployment," *American Economic Review* 62 (March 1972), pp. 1-18] James Tobin presents a most thoughtful discussion of the profession's "understanding" of these issues. His speech, although written well after most of this study was completed, provides a blueprint for the analyses it undertakes.

3. Granted, this may entail a naive assumption concerning the consciousness of the decision-making process in Washington with regard to economic policy.

4. "The Perils of Inflation," *Tax Review* 29, no. 5 (May 1968), p. 21.

5. We have in mind here (and will define as poor throughout this study) that subset of the population whose income and demographic characteristics are such that they are (or would be) designated as poor according to the official U.S. government standards. For a description of this definition and its rationale, see Mollie Orshansky, "Counting the Poor: Another Look at the Poverty Profile," and "Who's Who Among the Poor: A Demographic View of Poverty," *Social Security Bulletin*, January and July, 1965.

6. Time did not permit us to mine more fully the Survey of Economic Opportunity (SEO) data which became available in the course of our study. This data, together with the soon-to-be-available five-year longitudinal study sponsored by the Survey Research Center at Michigan University, will make possible detailed empirical estimation of the magnitude of the effects of various rates of aggregate unemployment and inflation across income groups.

Chapter 2
The Concept and Measurement of Inflation

1. An example of the type of thing we have in mind here could result from an increase in many states' sales taxes within the same year.

2. This situation, which is particularly characteristic of a wartime economy, is treated extensively by Harold K. Charlesworth in *Economics of Repressed Inflation* (London, 1956).

3. The emphasis here is on "normally" and "permitted." This is to acknowledge that there are a great number of instances in our economy where factors other than prices are utilized to ration, even though prices are not prevented by law from fulfilling this function, and that there is also considerable

government regulation of prices that does have the effect of causing other criteria to be utilized for rationing, although this may not be the primary purpose of the regulation. An example of the first instance would be a public library system, of the latter, minimum wage laws.

4. Our construction of aggregate supply and demand curves follows that of John Lindauer in his text, *Macroeconomics* (New York: Wiley, 1968).

5. A shift of the savings function induced by a change in P occurs because of the effect of P on wealth holdings of consumers. This is the well-known "Pigou Effect." The outward shift in the LM function due to the decrease in P operating through a decreased transactions demand for money is the "Keynes Effect." The overall model is, of course, very Keynesian in its approach. However, one could obtain a similarly shaped aggregate demand function using the quantity theory of money as a basis. Since $MV \equiv PY$, for a given nominal supply of money and relatively stable demand for money as a function of P and Y, P, and Y must be inversely related to one another. We will be analyzing exogenous causes of increases in P in the context of the Keynesian model, but we could just as easily do it in the quantity theory model. In the first section of Chapter 3, we will describe more fully the basic assumptions and differences of the two approaches as they relate to dynamic inflationary processes.

6. By a turning out of the labor-supply function, we mean that after a point labor supply becomes a very steeply sloped function of the real wage. This would presumably be true at some point for Ns in our figures (see the dashed extension of Ns in Figure 2-4), just as it is usually presumed to be the case in a Keynesian model as reflected in the inverted L-shaped labor-supply function.

7. Thus full employment in the Keynesian sense means that little, if any, additional labor will be supplied even though money and real wages are increased significantly. It is a concept related to capacity. In contrast, full employment occurs in the standard neoclassical model at the point where Ns intersects Nd even though at a higher real wage (if it could be obtained) more labor would be supplied. This concept of full employment corresponds to the "natural rate of unemployment," which we discuss in Chapter 4.

Note that while the neoclassical model with wages inflexible on the downside and the Keynesian model can both yield the similar aggregate supply curves, movements up along the vertical portion of the neoclassical supply curve reflect a constant real wage while this is not necessarily true in the Keynesian case.

8. Variables that are exogenous in one model can, of course, be endogenous in another. We shall argue in Chapter 3 that the insistence by many economists that certain variables always be treated as exogenous in a model of inflationary processes is crucial to the understanding of many of the conflicting and limited views on the subject.

9. We have in mind here primarily such things as affect the structure of credit institutions and various other aspects of financial markets in the economy.

10. Expectations of future prices may be just one element that enters into the determination of the "climate of opinion." How the government is likely to respond to inflation is an example of another consideration.

Note that a quantity-theory-of-money approach would indicate that exogenous upward shifts in the aggregate demand curve could be brought about by an increase in M or an increase in V (corresponding to a decrease in the demand for money), thus causes of price increases can be categorized in this manner. Of course, many of the same exogenous influences that can cause shifts in the component curves underlying our demand curves are presumed to influence V.

11. Martin R. Gainsborough and Jules Blackman, *Inflation and the Price Indexes*, The National Industrial Conference Board Studies in Business Economics, no. 94 (New York: National Industrial Conference Board, 1966), p. 1.

12. A complete discussion of these problems is contained in Nissan Litavian and Don Patinkin, "On the Economic Theory of Price Indexes," *Economic Development and Cultural Change*, 1961.

13. Some empirical analysis in this direction is performed in Chapter 8 with emphasis on various low-income subgroups of the consumer population.

14. As opposed to the CPI and the WPI which are fixed quantity weight price indices (Lespeyres) in which the contents of the "market basket" are kept constant for a longer period of time.

15. These arguments have been made many times by many different people. One source of items 1-3 is Albert E. Rees, "Price Level Stability and Economic Policy," in *Compendium on the Relationship of Prices to Economic Stability and Growth*, JEC, 86th Congress (Washington, D.C.: G.P.O., 1958), p. 656. For "4" see the testimony of R. Bowman, Ass't. Director for Statistical Standards, Bureau of the Budget, *Hearings, Part 2, Government Price Statistics*, before a JEC subcommittee on Economic Statistics, 87th Cong., 1st sess., May 1-5, 1961, pp. 766-67.

16. An example of an alteration of the structure of the economy is a change in tax rates which affects the three indices differentially, or a sudden increase in the proportion of GNP allocated to the public sector as in wartime. For instance, if the nature of the inflation and the prevailing government policy toward it are such that interest rates are very high, this would bias the CPI upward more than the WPI or IPI due to the fact that mortgage rates are an important component of homeowners' costs in the CPI even though most mortgages are not refinanced.

17. Early in 1964 Evan Clague reported that: "A few years ago, a survey of users of the WPI produced the estimate that upward of $14 billion of contracts had provisions for adjustment of prices on the basis of WPI data." (U.S. Senate, Subcommittee of the Committee on Appropriations, *Hearings* on labor, health, welfare and education appropriations for 1965, 88th Cong., 2nd sess., 1964, p. 57.) This was during a time of relative price stability. Once inflation became more prevalent we would expect the proportion of contracts with such provisions to increase.

18. Gainsborough and Blackman, *Inflation*, p. 17.

Chapter 3
Traditional Views of Inflation

1. That is, in terms of yielding the "best" theory of inflation. Also note that these models are dealing with a P that reflects only the transactions market for goods and services in the economy. The securities market does not enter into these analyses directly, although the influence of the nature of the demand for money does have implications for equilibrium in the Keynesian and quantity theory models. The relationship between P, Y, and security prices, however, is by no means clear in any of these analyses, nor is it something that we will deal with in any substantial way, except to make some simple assumptions in order to estimate the wealth redistributional effects of inflation in a later chapter.

2. Changes in PY have three components: $\Delta P \cdot Y$, $\Delta Y \cdot P$, and the interaction term $\Delta P \cdot \Delta Y$. In a demand-pull inflation, all three of the components and, thus, $\Delta (P \cdot Y)$ must be nonnegative; where the economy is on its aggregate supply curve will determine how the increase in $P \cdot Y$ is divided between P and Y. ΔY is zero on the vertical portion of the aggregate supply curve. In a cost-push inflation the components are mixed in sign and even the net result with regard to $\Delta (P \cdot Y)$ is uncertain. We shall see in the next three sections what each of the theories of inflation derived from the three models has to say about ΔY during inflationary periods.

3. In Chapter 2, note 6, we indicated how an aggregate demand function could be directly derived from a quantity theory formulation.

4. Friedman's ideas on this subject have been presented in numerous publications. To mention just one that is a fairly complete treatment of the material we discuss here: "The Quantity Theory of Money: A Restatement," in *Studies in the Quantity Theory of Money*, ed. by Milton Friedman (Chicago: University of Chicago Press, 1956), pp. 3-21.

5. The view of labor-market activity that underlies disequilibrium adjustment in this model is very simplistic. In Chapter 4 we will be focusing our attention on a more sophisticated theory that is consistent with neoclassical postulates.

6. The "older school" reaches well into the twentieth century. For a comprehensive and representative view of the quantity theory of money, particularly as contrasted to Keynes' views in the 1930s, see Arthur Margret, *The Theory of Prices* (New York: Prentice Hall, 1938).

7. This is an empirical finding, not an implication of the theory.

8. Recall that full employment in this context refers not to a capacity concept, but to the level of employment determined by the intersection of labor supply and demand as functions of the real wage in a neoclassical model.

9. We are emphasizing the role of M in a demand-pull inflation here. The more passive role of M in a cost-push inflation will be dealt with later.

10. The particular statement of his views that we are summarizing here is to

be found in *Growth Without Inflation* (New Delhi: National Council of Applied Economic Research, 1965).

11. Melvin W. Reder, "Alternative Theories of Labor's Share," in *The Allocation of Economic Resources*, Moses Abramovitz, ed. (Stanford University Press), p. 187.

12. The short-run profit maximizing position is given by marginal revenue = marginal cost $(MC) = \dfrac{p \, \Delta q + q \, \Delta p}{q} = p(1 + 1/e)$ where q is the output of the firm. We are focusing on the marginal cost of labor since for most firms labor comprises the bulk of variable costs. Other costs are assumed to be marked up in a similar way so we need not consider them explicitly here.

Equation (3.4) is not intended to convey any behavioral assumption concerning the mechanism by which a firm arrives at the position of profit maximization, but only to describe the relationship that holds between certain variables in such a position.

13. U.S. Steel is often cited as a price leader among steel companies. Note that if other firms follow with price increases, this does not imply that they were not previously profit-maximizing because of the interdependence of their demand functions, but it does imply that as an industry, steel producers had unexercised market power.

14. For instance, the price of steel, which is a "key cost" item, might increase, thus affecting the marginal costs of many other firms in the economy.

15. As is the case in the automobile industry, whenever a wage increase is negotiated between the UAW and one of the big three.

16. This was first discussed by Charles Schultze in: U.S. Congress, JEC, *Recent Inflation in the United States*, Study Paper 1, prepared in connection with the study of employment, growth and price levels (Washington, D.C.: G.P.O., 1959).

17. C, I, G, and F are in money terms in this identity. When we derived our aggregate demand curve in the second section of Chapter 2, these variables were defined in real terms (C', I', G', and F') where at first approximation we can consider $C' = C/P$, $I' = I/P$, etc. Presently we shall discuss the implications of defining these aggregate demand components in real as opposed to monetary terms and the choice of the P by which to inflate G.

18. This is the disaggregation used in the Wharton Econometric Forecasting Unit as described by Michael K. Evans in his *Macroeconomic Activity* (New York: Harper and Row, 1969). The determinants of demand for consumer durables mentioned in the next sentence are also those used in this model.

19. Where full employment is defined in relation to a capacity concept.

20. It is the inflationary processes at, or near, full employment output that are primarily dealt with in the neo-Keynesian literature. At lower levels of real output, shifts in aggregate demand cause similar one-time price increases which are not, presumably, of great concern.

21. A brief, but illuminating, typology of income distribution theories is contained in Reder, "Labor's Share." The theory that we have in mind here is the Widow's Cruse Theory which first appeared in Keynes' *Treatise on Money*. At less than full employment, labor's share is determined in the context of a markup model as we have already discussed. Under conditions of full employment, assuming constant marginal propensities to consume out of labor and nonlabor income, with the latter MPC less than the former, a decrease in the savings ratio must be accompanied by an increase in labor's share.

22. It may be even more appropriate when making this kind of distinction to think in terms of three categories of expenditures: (1) those consciously planned or desired only in money terms, such that in the face of inflation no effort is made to increase money expenditure in order to achieve some given level of real expenditures; (2) those planned or desired in real terms, but which have to be revised downwards (in real terms) by some or all of the percentage of the price increase due to the inability of the spending agent to meet its real target; and (3) those planned and desired in real terms which are carried out despite the inflation because the spending agent has the ability to achieve this target.

23. It is also true that once an inflation is underway, it is often anticipated to continue (although usually the estimates are too low) by governmental budgetary planners and an upward adjustment of monetary expenditures is made in some areas based upon some estimate of the expected inflation.

24. It is not sufficient that budgetary planners correctly predict what the relevant fiscal year's increase in the CPI or IPI is going to be for many reasons: (1) Estimates on costs for many contracts have been so unrealistically low that simply adjusting for some general price increase may not begin to cover the cost overruns; (2) in any event, the relevant inflator is not the expected rate of general price increase but of price increases of those goods and services that are being purchased by the government. These are often likely to far exceed any general price increase because: (a) the lack of free-market operation in these areas encourages overcharging, inefficiency, etc.; (b) the goods and services purchased are fixed in real terms and the government can usually insure that this target is met simply by paying a sufficient amount; thus the greatest upward pressure on prices is likely to be put in just these areas because of the government competition with the private sector for relatively scarce resources. Health care is an example of the 1960s that embodies both situations (a) and (b) and the price index for medical services increased nearly 100 percent over this period.

25. In the case of the regulated industries, it is clear that they are not profit maximizing and can increase revenues by raising prices; however, for our point to be valid with regard to nonregulated industries, there has to be unexploited market power present. One reason why we might expect this to be the case is because of the effect of government pressure (either moral suasion or legal

threat) on these industries. See Arthur M. Okun, "Inflation: The Problems and Prospects Before Us," Reprint 182 (The Brookings Institution: Washington, D.C., 1970) for an argument with empirical support that this indeed was the situation for many industries in the period from 1960 to 1968.

26. This section is similar to Martin Bronfenbrenner and Franklyn D. Holtzman's treatment in their survey article; however, they consider only Keynesian aggregate supply and demand curves: "Survey of Inflation Theory," *American Economic Review* 53, no. 4, (September 1963), pp. 595-97.

27. In this case we need not distinguish among our various aggregate supply curves. They all have a vertical portion and what we are about to say is true, whichever curve is assumed to be the most appropriate one.

28. This process would most likely come into play after increases in M have led to some continuing inflation since it is believed that expectations of future price increases are based primarily on past price performance. See Phillip Cagan, "The Monetary Dynamics of Hyperinflation," in *Studies in the Quantity Theory of Money*, pp. 25-117.

29. It can be argued from a Keynesian point of view that this aggregate demand curve will continue to shift upward with the money wage increases since this will increase desired C even though M is held constant. However, short of widespread expectations of a sustained rapid inflation there is presumably an upper limit on the ability of V to increase so that increases in M are probably necessary to perpetuate this type of inflationary process for any but the very short run.

30. It makes sense to talk of this type of inflationary process only in the context of a Keynesian aggregate supply curve.

31. Ralph Turvey, "Some Aspects of Inflation in a Closed Economy," *Economic Journal* 61 (September 1951), pp. 532-43.

32. This quote is taken from Bronfenbrenner and Holtzmann, "Inflation Theory," p. 623, but appears to have been cited almost verbatim from Melvin W. Reder, "The Theoretical Problems of a National Wage-Price Policy," *Canadian Journal of Economics* 14 (February 1948), pp. 46-61.

33. We will continue to talk of changes in PY here. Of course the degree to which changes in P or Y occur depends upon how the aggregate supply and demand functions are shaped over their relevant portions.

34. Our use of "best understood" is a generous interpretation of these views. Causality is usually implied either explicitly or implicitly. In fact, this desire to discover causality in an inflationary process is probably a primary contributor to the prevalence of incomplete specification. This is understandable since the formulation of effective antiinflationary policy would be greatly furthered by the isolation of a cause of inflationary processes, but such partial analysis may ignore important interdependencies that can be analyzed only in the context of a more general equilibrium model. We discuss this later in this section.

Chapter 4
The Relationship between Inflation and
Unemployment: Its Nature and Implications

1. Under present institutional arrangements, such as hiring and dismissal procedures as embodied in union contracts, variations in the unemployment rate usually imply parallel variations in employment and output. Thus we will generally assume that, in the short run, increases in output are accompanied by increases in employment and a decrease in the unemployment rate (and conversely).

2. Lord William Beveridge, *Full Employment in a Free Society* (London: George Allen and Unwin, 1944), pp. 18-20.

3. See Abba Lerner, *The Economics of Employment* (New York: McGraw-Hill, 1951), p. 191, and Bertil Ohlin, *The Problem of Economic Stabilization* (New York: Columbia University Press, 1949), p. 6. Lerner and Ohlin more explicitly incorporated the aspect of price stability into their definition of full employment even though they conceptualized employment in a capacity-billet framework. Lerner's low-full employment and Ohlin's full employment were consistent with the maintenance of price stability in their views.

4. This curve shows the (presumed) relationship between the rate of change of money wages and the unemployment rate for a given economy at a given time. See A.W. Phillips, "The Relationship Between Unemployment and the Rate of Change of Money Wages in the United Kingdom, 1862-1957," *Economica* 25, (November 1958), pp. 283-99.

5. Richard G. Lipsey, "The Relation between Unemployment and the Rate of Change of Money Wage Rates: A Further Analysis," *Economica* 27 (February 1960), pp. 1-31.

6. The relevant literature here is too voluminous to list. Bibliographies can be found in most of the journal articles that we will cite in the next section of this chapter.

7. Most of these theories owe a debt to the ideas presented by George Stigler in "Information in the Labor Market," *Journal of Political Economy, Supplement* 5, pt. 2 (October 1962), pp. 94-105.

8. Most of the papers that reflect this approach to labor markets are collected in E.S. Phelps et al., *Microeconomic Foundations of Employment and Inflation Theory* (New York: W.W. Norton and Co., 1970). Robert Hall provides an interesting interpretation of various unemployment and income data consistent with this view of labor markets in "Why is the Unemployment Rate So High at Full Employment?" in Okun et al. (eds.), *Brookings Papers on Economic Activity*, vol. 3 (Washington, D.C.: The Brookings Institution, 1970), pp. 369-411. Phelps' introduction provides an excellent summary and overview of the various works. When we wrote this chapter Phelps had a manuscript in progress entitled "Rational Inflation Policy and the Consequences of Unemploy-

ment." (The final version was published in 1972 by Norton as *Inflation Policy and Unemployment Theory, the Cost-Benefit Approach to Monetary Planning*.) The opportunity that we had to read a draft of this manuscript and to talk with Phelps has improved our understanding and (hopefully) discussion of these topics.

9. "Continuously clearing" here means in the spirit of our neoclassical model of Chapter 2, which yielded a perfectly vertical aggregate supply curve, *Snf*.

10. This is the term coined by Milton Friedman which seems to have won the popularity contest with Phelps' "warranted rate." Other contenders were the "normal" and "optimal" unemployment rates. These two authors are most associated with this current revival of an older concept. See Friedman, "Comments," in *Guidelines, Information Controls, and the Market Place*, G.P. Schultz and R.Z. Aliber, eds. (Chicago: University of Chicago Press, 1966), and Phelps, "Phillips Curves, Expectations of Inflation and Optimal Unemployment Over Time," *Economica* 34 (August 1967), pp. 254-81.

This concept can be traced back to earlier writings of Henry Wallich and William Fellner in this country and has its roots in the writings of the earlier neoclassical economists. It is very much akin to other concepts such as the "natural" rate of interest, whose determination was believed to be solely dependent upon "real" factors in the economy. On a balanced growth path, changes in monetary variables are discounted and do not affect these natural values.

11. In the strictest sense, an inflation is "anticipated" or "fully anticipated" if the prevailing rate of inflation is equal to the current expected rate, and if the current prevailing rate was expected so long ago as to precede all currently existing money wage contracts outstanding. Thus a prevailing inflation may be "expected," but may not be "anticipated." Where this distinction is relevant, we will designate it by our choice of "expected" or "anticipated."

12. It will make more sense to talk of "speculative" employment rather than unemployment, given the way we have chosen to describe it.

13. An example of precautionary unemployment would be that of a movie star who rejects current scripts and wages so that he will be free to accept a potentially better situation in the future. The existence of this type of unemployment to a significant degree assumes the lack of a certain kind of market in which a non-risk-loving worker, whose profession is such that his future opportunities, wages, etc., are so uncertain that he would consider precautionary unemployment, can sell his services to a labor dealer in exchange for a guaranteed income stream.

14. This requires incomplete adjustment of the nominal interest rate to workers' expectations. It is interesting to note the similarity of these three motivations for unemployment in a neoclassical model with the Keynesian motivations for holding cash balances (transactions, precautionary, speculative).

This is essentially an inventory approach to unemployment. All of these types of motivations for holding inventories have been discussed at length in the literature on inventory theory. This approach is valid to the extent that workers can be separated into relatively distinct, but homogeneous, categories according to these motivations rather than spread out in some kind of continuum. The criticisms of the Keynesian approach to money demand levied by the modern quantity theorists for similar reasons are equally applicable to this modern neoclassical approach to labor supply.

15. If expectations of inflation are formulated symmetrically, then a greater-than-natural rate of unemployment would be necessary to reduce them.

16. An arbitrary assumption with regard to whether the worker or the firm is the wage setter is necessary unless a more general equilibrium model is going to be attempted.

17. Phelps, *Rational Inflation Policy and the Consequences of Unemployment*, draft, April 1970. Notice that this treatment of the demand side is assymetrical with respect to the treatment of the supply side. Presumably, one should address employers' motivations for having unfilled vacancies or hoarding labor and there would be a corresponding natural rate of vacancies. It is not in our interest, however, to pursue these weaknesses of this approach to labor-market activity. The crucial dimension of expectations in the unemployment-inflation relationship is well brought out in these treatments and this is the reason for our dealing with them.

18. Although, under the assumption that the employers do the hiring and set the wages, there will always be some job rationing even if all unemployment is of the search variety, since employers offer only a finite class of jobs.

19. This is the situation when the aggregate demand curve intersects *Sni* of Figure 2-4 on its upward sloping portion. People are involuntarily unemployed in the sense that they are willing to work for the same or lower real wage than is presently prevailing but cannot find employment.

20. In an extreme situation, the primary additional labor forthcoming at the same money wage may only be at low and unskilled levels, but other, more skilled positions can be filled by upgrading, overtime, and relaxing of retirement conditions (or recalling the retired).

21. In a strictly neoclassical world, if money wage increases in excess of mean expectations were not required to attract the additional labor, then this can occur only under the strong assumption that there is a shift inwards of labor supply as a function of the real wage. Once we introduce downward rigid money wages and involuntary unemployment into the model, then the concept of the natural rate of unemployment becomes less useful since, at any given rate of unemployment, people may be both voluntarily and involuntarily unemployed.

22. We assume for the moment that people are able to adjust immediately and costlessly to their expectations. Our mathematical formulation of these matters in this section was suggested by that of Robert Solow in his *Price*

Expectations and the Behavior of the Price Level (Manchester: Manchester University Press, 1969).

23. This assumes that the expected rate of inflation is a geometrically decaying weighted sum of past actual rates of inflation. The nearer is b to 1, the more weight is put on the recent past relative to the distant past.

24. For instance, it may be that as long as $\dot{p}$ does not exceed some critical threshold, $\dot{p}'$, people do not perceive the inflation at all. The type of exogenous variables that are likely to be relevant here are the proclamations of various academic and administrative soothsayers with regard to their $\dot{p}$.

25. $\dot{p}_{t+1} = \dot{p}_t - b\dot{p}_t + bg\dot{p}_t + bf(X_t)$. As $t \to \infty, \dot{p}_t \to \dot{p}_{t+1}$, so that at the limit this reduces to $bf(X) = b\dot{p} - bg\dot{p}$, which implies that $\dot{p} = f(X)/(1-g)$.

26. For example, see: Robert J. Gordon, "The Recent Acceleration of Inflation and Its Lessons for the Future," *Brookings Papers on Economic Activity*, vol. 1 (Washington, D.C.: The Brookings Institution, 1970), pp. 8-47; George Perry, "Inflation and Unemployment," mimeo (Washington, D.C.: The Brookings Institution, 1970); Albert Rees, "The Phillips Curve as a Menu for Policy Choice," *Economica* (August 1970); Charles Holt, "Improving the Labor Market Trade-off between Inflation and Unemployment," *AER Papers and Proceedings* (May 1969).

27. This is not inconsistent with an adaptive expectations hypothesis.

28. Given such a view, it is no longer as useful to talk in terms of a less-than-natural rate of unemployment. What they have in mind is, therefore, a less-than-price-stable (given flat expectations) rate of unemployment.

29. We have already talked about various possibilities in relation to b. As far as g goes, if an inflation is expected but not fully anticipated, then there may be costs to wage and price changes that do not warrant the adjustment in the short run, or it may simply not be possible to make such an adjustment due to, say, contractual arrangements. Rees ("Phillips Curve as a Menu") discusses such a situation and elaborates on the nature of the costs that might exist. In this article, though, he seems to assert that g might remain permanently less than one due to such costs: "If changing wage rates frequently involves costs to both employers and unions, then the labor market will not be in a state of continuous equilibrium. A moderate inflation can, even if anticipated, produce a higher level of employment than [the] price stability [level] and therefore the Phillips curve will have a negative slope to the left of a point corresponding to price stability."

We would maintain, to the contrary, that if a fully anticipated moderate rate of inflation persisted, the costs of adjusting to it would tend to zero. Only expectations of systematic jolts of a particular bias would lead to a g that is permanently less than one because of such adjustment costs.

30. See Rees, "Phillips Curve as a Menu," for arguments that depend upon such postulates and are made with regard to situations in which it is no longer assumed that there are no productivity increases or movements in relative wages and prices.

31. We should also point out that in the past year and one-half (January 1972-June 1973), since a great deal of the discussion and analyses comprising this study were completed, the already voluminous body of literature within the economics profession on price and wage determination and its relationship to unemployment has increased at a geometric rate. We refer here to such things (among others) as the recently published proceedings of a conference sponsored by the Federal Reserve System [Otto Eckstein (ed.), *The Econometrics of Price Determination* (Washington, D.C.: Board of Governors of the Federal Reserve System, 1972)], the many papers in the continuing Brookings Papers on Economic Activity, and the yet-to-be-published proceedings of a recent (April 1973) conference on Phillips curve held at the University of Rochester. To the reader who is quite familiar with all these new works, it will be obvious that these areas of Chapters 4 and 10 which deal with Phillips curves do not fully reflect their valuable addition to the profession's knowledge and treatment of this subject; however, we do not believe that it was necessary to incorporate discussion of but a few of the most relevant of these works into this study in order to preserve its timeliness. This we have done as best we could.

32. For ease of exposition from here on, we will assume that $g(Z) = 1$ at all times. The reader is encouraged to keep in mind, however, that movements in the disequilibrium aggregate supply curve SS only occur when adjustments are made to expectations.

33. After a point, SS could well become backward bending due to negative marginal productivity of additional workers.

34. Recall our discussion of the various price indices used to measure P. Expectations of, and adjustment to, inflation are often dictated by the value of these indices.

Chapter 5
Theoretical Aspects of the Effects of
Inflation on Distribution and the
Efficiency of Allocation

1. Here we are discussing a partial analysis, holding constant (in particular) the rate of unemployment. The primary emphasis is on distributional aspects of inflation.

2. When we discuss the distributional and efficiency implications of unemployment in Chapter 6, we will maintain that other dimensions than the aggregate rate (such as its distribution among income groups) are important to an understanding of its welfare implications. However, we shall also argue that these other characteristics of unemployment are highly correlated with its rate, given the present structure of the labor market.

3. To a very limited extent, we will also examine some empirical aspects of

redistributional consequences of inflation which are not pursued in Chapters 7, 8, and 9.

4. Albert Ando and G.L. Bach, "The Redistributional Effects of Inflation," *The Review of Economics and Statistics* 39, no. 1 (February 1957). In this article, Ando and Bach are primarily interested in effects on different sectors of the economy rather than within the household sector as we are.

5. Ibid., p. 2.

6. A.A. Alchian and R.A. Kessell in "Effects of Inflation," *The Journal of Political Economy* 70, no. 6 (December 1962), pp. 521-37, also discuss from an entirely theoretical viewpoint the effects of inflation. They stress the role of anticipations and accordingly analyze the consequences of inflation under three categories: (1) an unanticipated inflation; (2) during the transition to a fully anticipated inflation; and (3) a fully anticipated inflation.

7. See the introduction in Thomas Cargill's "An Empirical Investigation of the Wage-Lag Hypothesis," *American Economic Review* 59, no. 5 (December 1969), for the relevant references.

8. See for instance Cargill, "Wage-Lag Hypothesis"; A.A. Alchian and R.A. Kessell, "The Meaning and Validity of the Inflation Induced Lag of Wages Behind Prices," *American Economic Review* 50 (March 1960), pp. 43-66; E. Budd and D. Seiders, "The Impact of Inflation on the Distribution of Income and Wealth," *American Economic Review, Papers and Proceedings* (May 1971).

9. For some evidence indicating that wages and profits gain relative to interest and rent income during (presumably unanticipated) inflationary periods, see R.M.H. Hashmi, "Studies in Functional Income Distribution," Occasional Paper no. 3, Bureau of Business and Economic Research, Michigan State University, 1960.

10. Certainly the same structural imbalances that might have initially caused an inflation, if severe and continuing, could lead to a hyperinflation; however, there is little indication that a moderate inflation might tend to feed upon itself through adaptive expectations until a hyperinflation results. See Phillip Cagan, "The Monetary Dynamics of Hyperinflation," in *Studies in the Quantity Theory of Money*.

11. Alchian and Kessell, "Effects of Inflation," p. 532.

12. The relevant literature here is fairly small. The most central articles are: Martin J. Bailey, "The Welfare Costs of Inflationary Finance," *Journal of Political Economy* 64 (April 1956), pp. 93-110; Alvin L. Marty, "Money in a Theory of Finance," *Journal of Finance* (January 1964) and "Growth and the Welfare Cost of Inflationary Finance," *Journal of Political Economy* 75 (February 1967), pp. 71-76; Robert A. Mundell, "Inflation and Real Interest," *Journal of Political Economy* 71 (June 1963), pp. 280-83, and "Growth, Stability, and Inflationary Finance," *Journal of Political Economy* 73 (April 1965), pp. 97-109; Edmund S. Phelps, "Anticipated Inflation and Economic Welfare," *Journal of Political Economy* 73 (February 1965), pp. 1-17. Phelps

also discusses this topic in his unpublished manuscript, "Rational Inflation Policy."

13. It is necessary to specify assumptions with regard to a myriad of issues. Particularly crucial ones are how the government utilizes the resources that are transferred to it under inflationary finance and the alternative methods (and their costs) available to the government for obtaining control over real resources.

14. This effect may have redistributive consequences. For instance, wealthier people may have better knowledge and/or better access to financial markets which permit them to speculate more profitably. On the other hand, the opportunity cost of time is likely to be less for many poor people, thus giving them a relative advantage in certain activities like shopping.

15. To quote G.L. Bach, *Inflation: A Study in Economics, Ethics and Politics* (Providence, R.I.: Brown University Press, 1958), pp. 12-13: "The evidence on milder inflations is reasonably clear: history shows output generally rising in periods of inflation. . . . These facts, of course, do not prove that the inflation was not exerting a downward pressure on output that was persistently overcome by other expansive forces in these instances. But they do indicate that if this was the situation [sic], the output depressive force of inflation has generally been a relatively mild one." The problem here, of course, is one of general vs. partial equilibrium analysis. Most mild inflations for the United States and non-Communist Europe in the thirty years prior to 1968 were accompanied by relatively tight labor markets.

Chapter 6
The Implications of the Aggregate Unemployment Rate for Distribution and the Efficiency of Allocation

1. Note 1 of Chapter 4 is important enough in this context that it bears repeating at this point. "Under present institutional arrangements, such as hiring and dismissal procedures as embodied in union contracts, variations in the [aggregative] unemployment rate usually imply parallel variations in unemployment and output."

2. And which, as we have seen, may be inescapable if the given rate of unemployment is to be achieved and maintained.

3. Melvin W. Reder, "Social Mobility and Labor Market Structure" (Stanford: unpublished mimeo, 1971), p. 2. This mimeo is a summary statement of a theory that is contained in many, mostly unpublished, papers by Reder. This section draws heavily upon this summary statement.

4. This analysis is focused upon nonrural labor markets.

5. We realize that to some economists the concept of job ladders may seem an unnecessary and oversimplified apparatus for discussing the topics of this

section. Nevertheless, we find it useful for our exposition and do not believe that the important implications of the model are dependent upon the device.

One objection that is certain to be raised concerning this concept is that if it does reflect reality, then why do we not find that workers are able to advance at a more rapid pace up a ladder by offering to work at lower wages in return for a greater investment in their human capital on the part of employers. Briefly, it would appear that the absence of this practice is due to the difficulties involved in designing and enforcing the type of contract that would be necessary. Employers would be unwilling to make this investment in training the workers at lower wages unless they could be guaranteed that the workers would remain with the firm for a sufficient length of time to make such investment profitable. Under present institutional arrangements, such a guarantee is not possible.

6. In an earlier article, "The Theory of Occupational Wage Differentials," *American Economic Review* 95 (December 1955), pp. 833-52, Reder discusses more fully the kind of considerations that would lead employers to alter hiring standards in response to changes in labor-market conditions instead of, or in conjunction with, altering wage rates.

7. To quote Reder ("Social Mobility and Labor Market Structure"), "Not all jobs with these characteristics are unskilled but all unskilled jobs have these characteristics; moreover, it is only unskilled jobs for which potential bottom rung job candidates can hope to qualify. Therefore, for the present purpose, let us identify nonladder and unskilled jobs."

8. Although there are theoretical arguments that have led some authors to speculate that quit rates are higher among nonladder employees, we are told by John Pencavel that there is no reliable empirical evidence to support this notion. This suggests that the high turnover rate is due to the empirically verified higher layoff rate experienced by this group which would tend to support the argument concerning lack of anticipation of job separation.

9. In addition for this to be true, wages for unskilled workers must be sticky on the downside. Such a proposition is briefly argued with recourse to a social minimum concept further on. A full exposition of this issue can be found in Reder's, "The Theory of Occupational Wage Differentials."

10. Some empirical evidence that supports the view of a pool of nonladder workers which is characterized by young, unskilled, uneducated, low-wage workers is to be found in Melvin W. Reder, "Unemployment Among New Labor Market Entrants," (Stanford: unpublished mimeo, 1970) and Robert E. Hall, "Why is the Unemployment Rate so High at Full Employment?" Consider the following facts or propositions which are established in these two papers, and which are totally consistent with the arguments of this section:

1. In 1968, nearly half of the unemployed in the U.S. were new entrants or new entrants after a long absence from the labor force.

2. Labor turnover (layoffs) decreases with age as does the probability of being unemployed.

3. Age constant, new entrants have higher unemployment rates than older (in time) members of the labor force.

4. Among the unemployed in 1966, over one-third had experienced two or more spells of unemployment.

5. In 1966, skill levels were inversely correlated with the unemployment rates by skill grouping.

6. Also in 1966, unemployment rates by wage rate were inversely correlated with the level of the wage rate grouping.

Other empirical evidence which lends support to the views in this section can be found in Peter B. Doeringer and Michael J. Piore, *Internal Labor Markets and Manpower Analysis* (Lexington, Massachusetts: D.C. Heath and Company, 1971), although these authors' theory of labor-market structure is somewhat different than the one in this section.

11. The normal rate of growth in ladder-associated jobs reflects the primary long run determinants of economic growth such as costs, production techniques, etc. Differences between actual and normal growth rates of ladder-associated jobs are reflected in differences in the actual and normal levels of economic activity. Finally, the growth rate of the labor force depends upon demographic factors, net immigration rates, and certain institutional arrangements, such as conventions determining the school-leaving age.

12. M.W. Reder, "Social Mobility and Labor Market Structure," p. 7.

13. "Concepts of Full Employment," *American Economic Review* (May 1957).

14. Three references for such discussions are: B. Ohlin, *The Problem of Economic Stabilization*; H.K. Charlesworth, *Economics of Repressed Inflation*; and F.W. Paish, *Studies in an Inflationary Economy* (London: Macmillan Press, 1962).

15. The latter two of these costs are particularly characteristic of a repressed inflation where rationing is achieved through queues or other nonpricing means. A wartime economy such as the United States in WWII where various controls were imposed is a prime example. However, any economy in which the adjustment of prices to excess demand does not take place instantaneously can be thought of as incurring a repressed (suppressed) inflation to some degree. Victor Zarnowitz in his article, "Unfilled Business Orders, Price Changes and Business Fluctuations," *Review of Economics and Statistics* 44, no. 4 (November 1962), pp. 352-94, argues that in many manufacturing industries, particularly the durable goods, the rational response for a profit maximizing firm which faces uncertain future demand for its output is a policy which increases both prices and unfilled commitments (i.e., accumulating a backlog of orders) in some combination in response to an increase in demand for its product.

16. Where costs are broadly defined to include queueing time and are infinite for an unavailable input.

17. In fact, under these conditions the concept of a natural rate of capacity utilization becomes far less meaningful and we should substitute the PSR in our discussion.

18. The hypothesis here is that maintaining the economy at a less-than-PSR will actually have the effect of lowering that PSR (or shifting the Phillips curve to the left if you will). There are two main areas of externalities that may develop at these higher rates of economic activity as more nonladder workers find it possible to obtain ladder employment than would otherwise be possible:

1. As a result of the more steady employment, on-the-job training, advancement possibilities, etc., these workers become more integrated into the labor force. They may begin to acquire certain social skills and attitudes that were previously lacking and which are important to maintaining and upgrading their position in the labor market. They may find the opportunity to accept lower financial remuneration in order to invest further in their human capital—an opportunity which would not exist for them in a looser labor market under present institutional arrangements.

2. Because of the inducement for employers to hire and train more nonladder workers, there may be externalities in the form of increased knowledge on the employers' part of many different varieties. Most importantly, employers may acquire valuable expertise concerning the process of successfully filling vacancies for low and unskilled workers, in training these workers, and in reducing their turnover rates by a better accommodation of their firms to these workers. Secondly, employers could have certain unjustified prejudices overthrown. Finally, employers will have the incentive to gain more knowledge of their actual and potential employees which will enable them to make more efficient use of their labor force in the future.

These are some of the more obvious possibilities that could be explored. However, it is questionable how significant for efficiency in the longer run such effects might be, granted that they occur. Those that alter supply characteristics would reach directly just those relevant cohorts of workers (particularly the new entrants to the labor force) during the higher-than-natural level of economic activity. Transmission effects would be necessary to influence future workers. Alterations in demand characteristics probably would have more potential for longer lasting benefits.

19. There is also considerable evidence to suggest that certain broader measures of unemployment, such as one which would take into account people who indicate that they are interested in employment but have dropped out of the labor force because they were discouraged over their prospects of finding a suitable job, or those who are "underemployed," would reflect as high or higher a degree of concentration.

20. There has been considerable casual evidence and analysis presented in support of this contention. Perhaps the most often cited discussion is James Tobin's, "On Improving the Economic Status of the Negro," in *The Negro American*, T. Parsons and K. Clark, eds. (Boston: Beacon Press, 1966), pp. 451-72. Another prime example is Andrew Brimmer, "Inflation and Income Distribution in the United States," *The Review of Economics and Statistics 53*, no. 1 (February 1971), pp. 37-49.

21. Charles M. Beach, "Cyclical Impacts on the Distribution of Income," Working Paper (Department of Economics, Queens University, 1973). Edward D. Budd, "Postwar Changes in the Size Distribution of Income in the United States," *American Economic Review* (May 1970), pp. 247-60. Charles E. Metcalf, *An Econometric Model of the Income Distribution*, Institute for Research on Poverty Monograph Series (Chicago, 1972). Thad W. Mirer, "The Effects of Macroeconomic Fluctuations in the Distribution of Income," Institute for Research on Poverty Discussion Paper 110-72 (Madison, Wisconsin, 1972). T. Paul Schultz, "Secular Trends and Cyclical Behavior in Income Distribution in the United States: 1944-1965," in *Six Papers on the Size Distribution of Wealth and Income*, Lee Soltow (ed.), (New York, November 1969). Lester C. Thurow, "Analyzing the American Income Distribution," *American Economic Review* (May 1970), pp. 261-70.

22. Mirer's results are generally consistent with the viewpoint in his first discussion paper. However, in a later paper ["The Distribution Impact of the 1970 Recession," Institute for Research on Poverty Discussion Paper 136-72 Madison, Wisconsin, 1972] in which he applies the general methodology he developed in the earlier one to the 1970 recession, his analysis indicates "that, on average, families with low incomes improved their positions relative to the rest of the population—despite the fact that 1970 witnessed an increase in the poverty population." One possible explanation for this finding might lie in the peculiar nature of the 1970 recession. It was largely generated by cutbacks in government expenditures in the defense area, particularly aerospace-related. As a result of this, a much higher proportion of the increased unemployment fell on white-collar workers than would generally be the case in an across-the-board tax increase or cutback in government expenditure. Mirer did find that in this recession, the best-paying occupations (professional-technical and managerial classifications) suffered a greater loss of potential income than did some low-paying ones (service workers, general nonfarm workers and farm workers).

23. Beach, "Cyclical Impacts," p. 41.

24. See Locke Anderson, "Trickling Down: The Relationship between Economic Growth and the Extent of Poverty Among American Families," *Quarterly Journal of Economics* 78 (November 1964), pp. 511-24; Lowell Galloway, "The Foundations of the War on Poverty," *American Economic Review* 55 (March 1965), pp. 122-35; Henry Aaron, "The Foundations of the War on Poverty Re-examined," *American Economic Review* 57 (December

1967), pp. 1229-45, and "Reply" by Galloway, pp. 1241-43; Lester Thurow, *Poverty and Discrimination* (Washington, D.C.: The Brookings Institution, 1969), pp. 26-46; and Robinson Hollister and John Palmer, "The Impact of Inflation on the Poor," in M. Pfaff and K. Boulding, eds., *Redistribution to the Rich and Poor: The Grants Economics of Income Redistribution* (Belmont, Calif.: Wadsworth Publishing Co., 1972).

25. We take a movement toward greater equality of the lower tail of the income distribution with the rest to be favorable.

26. Previous authors who have discussed this question of the redistributional bias of changes in the aggregate unemployment rate have failed to do so in the context of an analytical framework which would permit them to infer long-run welfare conseqeunces. They have simply assumed that increases in current income necessarily signaled increases in longer run welfare. The primary reason for our developing the model of this chapter's first section was so that we could properly (and briefly) deal with this difficulty.

27. Much of employer discrimination is probably of a "statistical" or "Bayesian" nature, i.e., the result of uncertainty about the qualities of potential employees. If there are substantial costs to ascertaining information about the productive capabilities of any individual job applicant, then employers may find it rational (profitable) to estimate instead the probability of satisfactory performance on the part of various groups of applicants, the groups being defined by the employer, and to choose individual employees on this basis. Thus this kind of discrimination may be viewed as directed toward searchers, not employees. As the level of economic activity increases, the costs (such as unfilled vacancies) to the employer of this type of screening increase and the individual searcher finds himself in a more favorable position vis-á-vis employment possibilities.

28. We referred in note 18 of this chapter to the possibility for workers who have obtained ladder employment to increase their human capital by accepting lower remuneration than they might otherwise. One of the strong possibilities, of course, is that during sustained periods of less-than-natural (or PSR) unemployment, an employer might be "fooled" into investing more into the training of a worker than is optimally profitable for him to do so. This will be to the workers' advantage, however—especially if the training is of a general nature.

Another benefit of the more steady ladder employment as opposed to the more sporadic nonladder which will only become evident in the longer run is the increased probability of old-age security payments and/or participation in a pension plan.

29. This is the case, although we did not discuss it there. For a fuller development of this phenomenon, see Reder's "Occupational Wage Differentials."

30. Brimmer ("Inflation and Income Distribution," p. 43) attributes the continuing trend toward greater equality in the income distribution during the

1965-69 period (when the increase in the level of economic activity was not nearly so dramatic as between 1961 and 1965) to the more rapid upgrading of the already employed (as well as the increase in multiple earner, lower income families).

31. How much higher would depend, of course, upon the exact nature of the welfare function in question. (We are still observing the ground rules of partial analysis here—allowing only the unemployment rate and not the rate of inflation to vary.)

We have primarily framed our analysis in this chapter in the context of an economy that can be characterized appropriately in the neoclassical spirit (i.e., the concept of a natural rate of unemployment has relevance), although the model of this chapter's first section is an attempt to integrate this approach with a (hopefully) realistic view of the present institutional aspects of nonrural labor markets. We have taken this tack because we believe it constitutes the most severe test for the case regarding the desirability on distributional grounds of a less-than-PSR (given the present institutional environment).

One possible weakness of the argument leading to this conclusion relates to our assumption concerning the association between the level of economic activity and the aggregate rate of unemployment (see note 1, this chapter). A neoclassical-search-unemployment model presumably implies a weak link between the two—this association may just be a temporary, disequilibrium phenomenon. In this case what of our analysis? A major implication of institutional aspects of the first section's model is that this link is not weak in the short run. If it proves weak in the longer run for reasons implicit in a neoclassical model, then it would presumably be because the dichotomy between ladder and nonladder jobs has been broken down. The distribution of unemployment across income groups should, then, be more even (although there would still be different natural rates of unemployment for different demographic groups of workers) and we would be less concerned on distributional grounds about higher levels of aggregate unemployment.

Chapter 7
Inflation and the Relative Cost of Living

1. Refer back to Chapter 2's "The Measurement of the General Price Level" for our discussion of the nature of the CPI.

2. "Curious" in the sense that this issue has not been adequately considered, but, as we shall see, given the nature of the available data, it is not surprising that little previous empirical work has been done on the subject.

3. In this sense, this is a very partial analysis, with the focus on one aspect of the distributional effects of inflation (*ceteris paribus*), which was mentioned in the first section of Chapter 5.

4. Whenever possible, our references to theoretical analyses of price indices will be confined to the notes of this chapter—although a basic knowledge of this subject on the part of the reader is assumed in our discussion. A good source for the theoretical foundations of index numbers is Latavian and Patinkin, "Economic Theory of Price Indexes."

5. For an attempt to develop a poverty measure that takes into account the fact that low current income may reflect only "temporary poverty," see W. Lee Hansen and Burton Weisbrod, "An Income-Net Worth Approach to Measuring Economic Welfare," *American Economic Review* 58 (December 1968).

6. This group contains consumer units which have both income and expenditures for the year below the relevant poverty threshold.

7. These cutoffs were chosen primarily because the population density fell off rather sharply beyond these points.

8. The CPI from 1947 to 1958 is the Bureau of Labor Statistics series and reflects adjustments made by the BLS for shifting expenditure weights over that period. Since we could only estimate expenditure weights for the other indices based upon the SCE of 1960-61, those indices are fixed weight indices. Thus, in the 1947-58 period, comparisons between the CPI and the other indices are less reliable due to differences in weighting procedures. We return to this point later.

9. For this approximation, we simply followed Saul Waldman, "OASDI Benefits, Prices and Wages: 1966 Experience," *Social Security Bulletin*, June 1967, pp. 9-12, and cut the medical series weight by 40 percent to approximate effects of Medicare.

10. When price information was not available to correspond with a detailed expenditure weight, we applied the price index of the broader expenditure category to the detailed expenditure weight.

11. The effects of Medicare provisions began to appear in June 1966. Private per capita health expenditures on various types of services were estimated for the fiscal years 1966 and 1967 in D. Rice, Anderson, and Cooper, "Personal Health Care Expenditures of the Aged and Non-Aged, Fiscal Years 1966 and 1967," *Research and Statistical Note No. 11*, Social Security Administration, HEW, June 1968. From Table 2 of that publication, it was possible to estimate the decline from fiscal year 1966 to fiscal year 1967 in private per capita expenditures for those sixty-five and over. These figures indicate that there was an approximate decline in private per capita expenditures of 80 percent for hospital care and 31 percent for physician's service. These effects were taken into account by changing the expenditure weights for these two categories in the aged price indices by the following fashion:

$$\frac{(\text{A.P.I.} - W_H I_H - W_p I_p) + 1 - .8) W_H I_H + (1 - .31) W_p I_p}{1 - .8 W_H - .31 W_p} = \text{A.P.I.}^{a}$$

where   A.P.I. is the original Aged Price Index,

API[a] is the Aged Price Index adjusted for Medicare effects,

W_H is the expenditure weight for hospital care in the original index,

W_p is the expenditure weight for physician's services in the original index.

Effectively, this procedure reduces the weights for hospital care and physician's services and then redistributes the surplus over all other categories according to their original relative weights.

This procedure is used to calculate the index for 1967. Since Medicare became effective in the middle of the calendar year 1966, we adjusted the 1966 index with the same procedure and then averaged the adjusted and the unadjusted indices to reflect half a year with Medicare in effect. In using the data for all persons sixty-five and over given in the table, we have, of course, ignored any differences in the relative weight (percentage) reductions of private expenditures at different income levels. We have no grounds for conjecturing the direction of the bias which might thereby be introduced, although it seems evident that it must be of relatively small magnitude.

12. The CPI slides back and forth between being a Paasche and Laspeyre index and a bastardized combination of the two, depending upon how and when new expenditure weights are entered into its base.

13. The word *estimate* is used to indicate that the true index is not a measure of the partial compensation due to the rising price levels, but is a deflator for the total compensation when money income is changing. See Latavian and Patinkin, "Economic Theory of Price Indexes."

14. Recently the federal government has started to develop such data.

15. For instance (to invent an extreme case to make a point), even if both within the food and nonfood areas those specific items that were more important to the poor were inflating faster, a nonpoor index could increase more than a poor index if the poor spent 75 percent of their income on food, which in general was inflating considerably less than nonfood on which the nonpoor spent 75 percent of their total expenditures.

16. For instance, over a wide range of income, the lower is the real income of a consumer unit, the greater the proportion it tends to spend on "necessities" such as food and shelter.

Chapter 8
Inflation and the Redistribution of Income: Some Empirical Evidence

1. The thresholds here are somewhat more sophisticated than those applied in Chapter 7 in that they take into account age of head and children as well as family size and geographic location. Units reporting negative income are not

included in class 2. The data in the tables are from the Survey of Economic Opportunity.

2. The thresholds of this group are approximately one-third greater than for class 2. For instance, to qualify for class 2, a nonfarm family of four with two children below eighteen and a nonaged father has to have received less than $3,171 income in 1966, whereas to qualify for class 3 the income would have to be between $3,171 and $4,113.

3. Of course these data are for one particular year, 1966, which was a time of relatively full employment (3.8 percent). Although it is not reported here, we have similar data for 1960 and 1965. A comparison of 1966 with these years indicates that the observations that we make in this section based upon the 1966 data are equally true for other years.

4. This is not entirely evident from the data in Tables 8-1, 8-2, and 8-3, but can be surmised with one additional fact. Our attention here should be focused upon the three categories Int + Div, Pensions, and Oth. Inc. Each of these can be comprised of various types of income which may be fixed or not in nominal terms. Let us make the most conservative assumption—that all of Oth. Inc. is fixed and that much of Int + Div is in the form of fixed interest payments. Now Pensions can be military, civilian government, or private. The former two have escalator clauses; only private pensions do not—and only some proportion of these. We do not have data for 1966 that indicates the breakdown for the aged-poor of pensions into these finer categories, but in 1960, the mean private pension income for those reporting nonzero from the source was less than half that for military and government and the former source of income was barely one-third as important for all units as was the latter. Unless these percentages shifted dramatically between 1960 and 1966, then we would appear to be safe in assuming that the two 10 percents mentioned in "5." are fairly conservative upper limits.

5. We base this statement upon the information in Tables 8-1, 8-2, and 8-3 concerning the mean of these sources of income for those reporting nonzero income from the sources.

6. It is not surprising that the vast majority of the aged receive no income from pensions, particularly private, since their past employment history is often unlikely to have had the type of continuity necessary for eligibility for such benefits. Among the aged of poverty class four, pensions are much more prevalent, although not so important in terms of the overall income picture since its members still receive considerable earnings income. The data suggest to us that it is the aged near-poor and less wealthy members of poverty class 4 (a group corresponding loosely, perhaps, to the American conception of a lower middle class) who are most likely to bear the brunt of detrimental redistributional consequences of inflation through erosion of the real value of private pension benefits and interest payments.

7. Although the more extensive is the use of such clauses, the more likely it

is that inflationary expectations and inflation will become prevalent in our economy. This will further aggravate the problem for those who do not have the proper protection.

Recall also that our earlier analysis indicated that the redistributional consequences of any given inflation are reduced in proportion to the degree of its anticipation. In particular, during anticipated inflations nominal interest rates will increase and there will be more pressure for upward adjustment of pension payments.

8. It would be possible for steadily rising average payments in the country to be consistent with recipients in each individual state getting only infrequent changes in income. In his dissertation, "Inflation and the Distribution of Income," Department of Economics, University of Pennsylvania, 1969, Neil Swan did a study of APTD (Aid to Persons Totally Disabled) payments between 1951 and 1968 in the ten states with the largest number of such cases. On pp. 379-80, he concludes (based upon the most pessimistic assumptions regarding the erosion of the real value of the payments through inflation, wherever assumptions were necessary):

If the states studied are reasonably representative of the whole—and a brief scanning of the others suggests that this is so—we may infer that about three quarters of APTD recipients were at least as well protected as recipients of OASDI benefits, in the sense that the maximum erosion of benefits in any period has never exceeded 7%, meaning that the average loss over the period when erosion took place has not exceeded 3-1/2% of the income that would have accrued without inflation. For the remaining one quarter, periods have existed by the end of which benefits have dropped in real terms between 7.2% and 13.9%, i.e., during which, on average, real payments were between about 4% and 7% below what they might have been in real terms without inflation.

If the behavior of APTD payments is reasonably typical of the other general types of assistance payments, then we can be confident that the conclusions we have drawn from our country-wide averages are reasonably accurate.

9. Swan, "Inflation and the Distribution of Income."

10. We should note the relevance of our discussion of price indices in Chapter 7. The Aged-Poor Index results suggest that the relative position (however measured) of poor Social Security recipients may have been less detrimentally affected by rises in prices than has previously been believed.

11. It is not surprising that Congress has been more sensitive to this issue since the mid-sixties than before because throughout the fifties and early sixties there were rapid increases in the percentage of the aged who were Social Security recipients. In earlier years, there would not have been nearly so much pressure due to the smaller constituency. Congress had often considered the automatic cost of living escalator for OASDI in the past but never passed it. A cynic (or realist?) might be tempted to observe that this was largely because incumbents appreciated the periodic opportunity that this provided for pleasing

a constituency of considerable influence on the outcome of their efforts for reelection.

Chapter 9
The Effects of Inflation on Net Worth:
Some Empirical Evidence

1. Setting the c_i and d_i equal to zero is unlikely to cause any significant bias in the results we report below. Most debts held by the poor are fixed in dollar terms. The claims that they tend to have, primarily cash, bonds, and savings and checking accounts, are also of the same nature. In assuming the a_i equal to p, we were less confident about the possible bias that may result. However, the evidence we report from another study later in this chapter indicates that, if anything, the bias is likely to be unfavorable to the poor, thus reinforcing the conclusions that we draw below.

2. Recall again our discussion in Chapter 8 on changes in the relative cost of living for various consumer groups. Insofar as we are concerned about changes in real net worth as indications of changes in the command over real resources of the consumer unit in question, the correct p to enter into Equation (9.4) is the one that is relevant to the cost of living for this consumer unit.

3. We can also surmise something about fixed income from some asset sources for the poor from this data. If we assume that an average return of 5 percent is being earned on the full value of their fixed value assets, this amounts to only about $40 per annum for the nonaged (for the medium figures) and about $30 for the aged. Thus the value of their real income from such sources would be eroded at the rate of 40¢ and 30¢, respectively, per 1 percent increase in P per annum.

4. Changes in the composition of financial assets and/or a reduction in the total wealth tied up in such assets is likely, with a movement in the direction of less liquidity. (We touched upon the efficiency aspects of this inflation induced illiquidity in Chapter 5.)

5. Except insofar as previous inflations had caused a shift in wealth composition that is not yet altered in anticipation of steady prices.

6. Our definition of poverty based only upon current income is a limited one. What one generally desires is a more comprehensive index of economic welfare that presumably would take into account net worth as well as (perhaps) human capital. (This is why we excluded units with net worth in excess of $50,000 in Tables 9-1 and 9-2.) Hansen and Weisbrod, "Measuring Economic Welfare," have taken a step in this direction by annuitizing net worth and adding it to current income for families in the U.S. in 1962. When doing this, they find that poverty is considerably less a problem for the aged than is indicated by only a current income measure.

7. Edward Budd and David Seiders, "The Impact of Inflation on the Distribution of Income and Wealth," *American Economic Review*, Papers and Proceedings (May 1971).

8. The same qualification regarding adjustments of wealth composition due to inflationary expectations has to be made here. Budd and Seiders interpret their results as indicative of the first year's change in real net worth when an inflation of the indicated magnitude begins.

Chapter 10
The Phillips Curve, Expected Prices, and Monetary-Fiscal Policy

1. Of course there is an exception; the excellent paper of R.E. Lucas, Jr., and L.A. Rapping, "Real Wages, Employment, and Inflation," in E.S. Phelps (ed.) *Microeconomic Foundation of Employment and Inflation Theory*, pp. 257-305. In R.E. Lucas, Jr., and L.A. Rapping, "Price Expectations and the Phillips Curve," *American Economic Review* 59 (June 1969), pp. 342-50, these same authors discuss the Phillips curve in much the same spirit as we, but without explicitly considering the question of which variables are exogenous.

The reader is also reminded of note 31, Chapter 4 at this point.

2. We abstract from the real cash balance effects of the rate of inflation, because consideration of them would greatly complicate the discussion without improving our empirical results.

3. The "equilibrium size" of an inventory is a target value and not one normally achieved in a stochastic model. However, it will approach the limiting value of the average of actual values as the time increases during which the system is continuously in equilibrium.

4. We make no attempt to analyze the determinants of (disequilibrium) rates of utilization of productive capacity except of labor (via unemployment).

5. $X_c = X_c^a - X^*$ and $X_o = X_o^a - X_o^*$ where X_c^* and X_o^* are desired rates of capacity utilization in the two sectors and X_c and X_o are the actual rates of utilization.

6. This silence is due to the fact that as yet, the allocation of the effect of an increase in M as between prices and output is not satisfactorily explained by the quantity theory of money. On this point, see M. Friedman, "A Theoretical Framework for Monetary Analysis," National Bureau of Economic Research, Occasional Paper 112, 1971, pp. 48 ff.

7. Such a series might consist of weighted observations of transactions in commodity futures on organized exchanges, employment contracts (collectively bargained and otherwise) for fixed time periods and price observations on contracts for industrial commodities covering deliveries at a fixed price over given time intervals where there is no provision for escalation or other forms of recontracting during the contract period. Professor G.J. Stigler believes such

contracts to be quite common, but has thus far gathered data for only six commodities. Yet another alternative to devices such as are used here is to use surveys of opinions about future prices—or price movements—such as those conducted by J.A. Livingstone as surrogates for direct observations. Unfortunately, it is not clear what relation these answers to opinion surveys have to actual commitments to buy, sell, hire, and so forth.

R.J. Gordon, "Inflation in Recession and Recovery," *Brookings Papers on Economic Activity* 2, no. 1 (Washington, D.C.: The Brookings Institution, 1971), pp. 105-58, experimented with the data generated by the Livingston surveys and found that this measure of price expectations performed less well in his wage equation than the distributed lag estimators similar to those used here. S. Turnovsky and M. Wachter ["A Test of the 'Expectations Hypothesis' Using Directly Observed Wage and Price Expectations," *Review of Economics and Statistics* 54, no. 1 (February 1972)] use the Livingston data with more success. However, their theoretical framework embodies a more or less conventional Phillips curve.

8. The future price whose expected value is being estimated by (3.2) is a price index one quarter in advance of the present. That is, it is the average price that would be generated by a set of future markets quoting prices for transactions to be executed one quarter forward.

9. Not "important" in the sense that the results they led to in the regressions yet to be reported were generally the same for different values of within the range of .2 to .7.

The derivation of (3.2) from (3.1) is as follows:

rewrite (3.1) as $\dot{\bar{p}}_{t+1} = \alpha \dot{p}_t + (1 - \alpha)\dot{\bar{p}}$.

Substitute for $\dot{\bar{p}}_t$ from (3.1) to obtain

$$\dot{\bar{p}}_{t+1} = \alpha \dot{p}_t + (1 - \alpha) [\alpha \dot{p}_{t-1} + (1 - \alpha)\dot{\bar{p}}_{t-1}] =$$
$$\alpha \dot{p}_t + \alpha (1 - \alpha)\dot{p}_{t-1} + (1 - \alpha)^2 \dot{\bar{p}}_{t-1}.$$

Substituting for $\dot{\bar{p}}_{t-1}$,

$$\alpha \dot{p}_t + \alpha (1 - \alpha)\dot{p}_{t-1} + (1 - \alpha)^2 [\alpha \dot{p}_{t-2} + (1 - \alpha)\dot{\bar{p}}_{t-2}] =$$
$$\alpha \dot{p}_t + \alpha (1 - \alpha)\dot{p}_{t-1} + \alpha (1 - \alpha)^2 \dot{p}_{t-2} + (1 - \alpha)^3 \dot{\bar{p}}_{t-2}.$$

By induction,

$$\dot{\bar{p}}_t = \sum_{i-1}^{n} (1 - \alpha)^{i-1} \dot{p}_{t-1} + (1 - \alpha)^{i-1} \dot{\bar{p}}_{t-i} (1 - \alpha)^{i-1},$$

the latter term $\to$ 0 as $i \to \infty$ provided $0 < \alpha \leqslant 1$.   Q.E.D.

10. The hypothesis of adaptive expectations is discussed in P. Cagan, "The Monetary Dynamics of Hyperinflation," in *Studies in the Quantity Theory of Money*, p. 54 and Chapter 4's section, "Some Clarification of the Natural Rate of Unemployment Hypothesis."

11. M. Feldstein and O. Eckstein, "The Fundamental Determinants of the Interest Rate," mimeo.

12. Gordon, "Inflation in Recession and Recovery."

13. When the Eckstein-Feldstein measure of price expectations is used, $\dot{w}$ no longer equals $\lambda \dot{w}_{t-1}$ because we continued to apply the weights described in the text rather than those strictly appropriate to the Eckstein-Feldstein measure.

14. p_c is the implicit price deflator for the consumption sector of the National Accounts. It is taken from the *Survey of Current Business (SCB)*, Census Bureau, Department of Commerce.

p_o is the implicit price deflator for fixed business investment, used on the presumption that it is fairly representative of the private portion of the nonconsumption sector. It is also taken from the *SCB*.

w is compensation per man hour in the private nonfarm economy as reported in the *Monthly Labor Review (MLR)* of the Bureau of Labor Statistics, Department of Labor. It includes fringe benefits as well as the money wage.

15. That is, the difference between their estimated values and unity is less than twice the standard errors of the coefficients. Throughout the study, when we speak of a coefficient as significant, or the reverse, we refer to a one-tailed test at the 5 percent level.

16. In these equations we use the inverse of the variable measuring unemployment (the unemployment inverse). This has the effect of reversing the sign of the coefficient on the unemployment variable, but affects nothing else. Where the unemployment variable is the unemployment percentage, the unemployment inverse is its reciprocal. U_p is the unemployment percentage for prime-age males; the rationale for using U_p instead of U is discussed below.

17. Gordon, "Inflation in Recession and Recovery."

18. R.G. Bodkin, "Wage and Price Formation in Selected Econometric Models," Research Report 7023 (London, Canada: Department of Economics, University of Western Ontario; September 1970), pp. 101-102.

19. UNF is based upon the percentage of manufacturers unfilled orders (durable goods) as reported in series no. 26 of the *Business Conditions Digest* (BCD). If UN represents the observation of this series for quarter t, then

$$UNF = 1/4 \left(\frac{UN_t}{P_{o(t)}} + \frac{UN_{(t-1)}}{P_{o(t-1)}} + \frac{UN_{(t-2)}}{P_{o(t-2)}} + \frac{UN_{(t-3)}}{P_{o(t-3)}} \right)$$

NODEV is the deviation of new orders of manufacturing industries from a trend value. It is based upon series no. 16 of the BCD.

$$NODEV_t = NOAV_t - NOEX_t \text{ where}$$

$$NOAV_t = 1/4 \left(\frac{NO_t}{P_{o(t)}} + \frac{NO_{(t-1)}}{P_{o(t-1)}} + \frac{NO_{(t-2)}}{P_{o(t-2)}} + \frac{NO_{(t-3)}}{P_{o(t-3)}} \right)$$

$$NOEX_t = \sum_{i=1}^{10} \alpha^i \frac{NO_{(t-i)}}{P_{o(t-i)}} \text{ and } \alpha = .5.$$

20. Gordon, "Inflation in Recession and Recovery."

21. Ibid., p. 129.

22. This statement would hold exactly (apart from random disturbances) if $w/p_o = w/p_c =$ the marginal productivity of labor. This would be true, if the production functions of both consumer goods and other goods were CES. We assume for this particular purpose that this assumption is satisfied. In this context, the difference operator, Δ, refers to the percentage change in the variable in question.

23. From the wage equation, we made an estimate of the rate of change of output per man-hour in each sector:

$$\frac{\dot{w}}{w} = \frac{\dot{p}_o}{p_o} + \frac{\dot{H}_o}{H_o} \qquad \text{where } H_o \text{ is the output per man-hour in the nonconsumption goods sector.}$$

In the same way:

$$\frac{\dot{w}}{w} = \frac{\dot{p}_o}{p_c} + \frac{\dot{H}_c}{H_c}.$$

Depending upon the estimated trend values of wage and price variables, our estimates of the trend of the output per man-hour are the following:

$$2.43 \leqslant \frac{\dot{H}_c}{H_c} \leqslant 3.14$$

$$2.53 \leqslant \frac{\dot{H}_o}{H_o} \leqslant 3.26$$

These values are quite comparable to the trend of the overall output per man-hour for the same period as reported by the BLS, i.e., 2.85.

24. If the (unspecified) association of a current excess of actual over desired

(equilibrium) rates of output and utilization of the labor force is an immediate reduction in $\dot{p}_i$, then algebraically high values of ($\dot{p}_i - \dot{\bar{p}}_i$) will survive (appear) only in conjunction with low values of U and the coefficients on ($\dot{p}_i - \dot{\bar{p}}_i$) will be negative (as observed). But if actual prices are insensitive to current rates of output and factor utilization, then high values of ($\dot{p}_i - \dot{\bar{p}}_i$) can reflect only an unanticipated cost-push which will (level of effective demand the same) tend to reduce equilibrium output and employment. In this case, the coefficient of U on ($\dot{p}_i - \dot{\bar{p}}_i$) might well be negative.

In fact, the coefficients of U on ($\dot{p}_c - \dot{\bar{p}}_c$) and ($\dot{p}_o - \dot{\bar{p}}_o$) are negative and significant while the coefficient on ($w - \bar{w}$) is insignificantly positive. This suggests that prices in product markets tend to be relatively responsible to the state of demand while wage rates reflect primarily the lagged impact of past wage and price behavior (perhaps because of past contracts) and are insensitive to current labor-market conditions. Such a result is far from inconsistent with general appearances, but it is in no sense a proposition that can be derived from economic theory. Hence, we treat the coefficients of the equations in this section as interesting results to be replicated by further research before making serious efforts at interpreting them.

25. The above three concepts of M are described in L.C. Anderson, "Three Approaches to Monetary Stock Determination," *Review of the Federal Reserve Bank of St. Louis* 49, no. 10 (October 1967), pp. 6-13.

26. This concept is discussed by N. Teeters and A. Okun, "The Full Employment Surplus Revisited," *Brookings Papers on Economic Activity* 1, no. 1 (Washington, D.C.: The Brookings Institution, 1970), pp. 77-110. The data we used are taken from Tables 2 and 3 of this article.

27. For example, see M.L. Weidenbaun, "Impact of the Vietnam War on the American Economy," in *Economic Effect of Vietnam Spending Hearings* before the JEC, 90th Cong., 1st sess., 1967.

28. Harvey Galper, "The Timing of Federal Expenditure Impacts," in President's Commission on Budget Concepts, *Staff Paper* (Washington, D.C.: G.P.O., 1967), pp. 416-30. (Table 3.) We used Galper's estimate from his Table 3 for this adjustment to the expenditure side of the FES measure. Since these estimates are available only through 1966, we had to use a rough approximating procedure to obtain observations for '67, '68, and '69. This was done as follows: Okun (*Brookings Papers* 1, no. 1, p. 89) cites the estimates of the OBE for Galper's adjustment for the years 1965-69 on an annual basis. We took the average ratio of Galper's estimate to the OBE's for 1965, 1966 and applied it to the OBE data for '67, '68, '69 in order to obtain estimates comparable to Galper's. This figure was entered for F_2 for each quarter of the year.

29. If they are significant. Also a constant term should be included and would be expected to be significant and negative whenever the coefficient of the fiscal variable is significant and positive since F is a number close to unity—it never takes on a value of zero.

30. See Shirley Almon, "The Distributed Lag between Capital Appropriations and Expenditures," *Econometrica* (January 1965). We experimented with both second and third degree polynomials, restricted at the far end (i.e., the weights are forced to zero). The results of the third degree are far superior on the usual grounds of high R^2's, significance of estimated coefficients, and lower degrees of serial correlation.

31. Use of unsmoothed data for estimating $\dot{p}_i = f(\dot{M}, F)$ contrasts with our use of seasonally adjusted quarterly data for all other variables. A critical reader might well wonder what our estimates would be with all observations unadjusted. One run on unsmoothed data was made with $\dot{p}_i = f(\dot{M}_3, F_2)$. (Before the reader can fully understand these results and their comparison to regressions reported later, he must read the material leading up to the reporting of those later regressions.)

$$\dot{w} = 1.22 + 0.72\,\hat{\dot{w}} - 0.19\ U_{pd} + 0.70\,(\dot{p}^c - \hat{\dot{p}}_c)_{-2} - 0.09\,(\dot{w} - \hat{\dot{w}})_{-1}$$
$$\quad (0.71)\quad (1.75)\quad (-0.45)\quad (2.30)\quad\quad\quad (-0.59)$$

$$R^2 = 0.40$$
$$\text{D.W.} = 2.11$$

$$\dot{p}_o = 0.05 + 1.10\,\hat{\dot{p}}_o - 0.36\,(\dot{p}^o - \hat{\dot{p}}_o)_{-1} + 0.24\,(\dot{w} - \hat{\dot{w}})_{-1}\quad R^2 = 0.42$$
$$\quad (-0.09)\ (4.96)\quad (-2.07)\quad\quad\quad (1.89)\quad\quad \text{D.W.} = 2.12$$

$$\dot{p}_c = -0.08 + 1.16\,\hat{\dot{p}}_c + 0.19\,(\dot{p}^o - \hat{\dot{p}}_o)_{-2} - 0.47\,(\dot{p}^c - \hat{\dot{p}}_c)_{-1}$$

$$R^2 = 0.63$$
$$\text{D.W.} = 1.73$$

$$U_p = 3.23 + 0.05\,(\dot{w} - \hat{\dot{w}}) - 0.81\,(\dot{p} - \hat{\dot{p}}) - 0.16\,(\dot{p} - \hat{\dot{p}})\quad R^2 = 0.20$$
$$\quad (18.36)\ (0.34)\quad\quad (-2.85)\quad\quad (-1.21)$$

The main results are: The R^2's are much lower and the D.W.'s slightly higher than with the corresponding equations (10.40.1)-(10.40.4) run on unsmoothed data. The constant terms and the coefficients on expected wages and prices are consistent with the neoclassical hypothesis (the $\dot{w}$ equation is distinctly improved in this respect and the coefficient on U_{pd} is insignificant). However, the signs of the deviation terms are more erratic than when smoothed data are used implying that the coefficients of the deviated terms are very sensitive to seasonal factors, and that great care must be taken in the deseasonalizing process. However, our principal findings still emerge from the unsmoothed data.

32. The results using the more conventional (adaptive expectations) measure of price expectations with $\dot{M}_1$, F_1, and $\dot{M}_3$, F_2 are reported in the first eight regressions; those with the interest rate measure and $\dot{M}_3$, F_2 in the last four (indicated by use of a primed $p-p'$). The underlined expectations measures indicate that unsmoothed data were used. The lag structure for all the $\dot{p}$

regressions is over the previous ten quarters since coefficients before -10 contributed very little to the explanatory power of the regressions. For similar reasons the $\dot{p}'$ regressions have a lag structure for $\dot{M}_3$ from $t-5$ to $t-20$ and for F_3, $t-4$ to $t-14$. The figures in brackets are standard errors. The numbers just to the side of those in brackets are the mean lags of the weight distributions.

33. The form of the unemployment rate that is entered in some of the wage equations here is $U_{pd} = (1/U_p - 1/3.6)$ since we obtained a value of 3.6 for the natural rate of U in our earlier analysis. This makes no difference to the regression results that would have been obtained using $1/U_p$ except to add $Z/3.6$ to the constant where Z is the estimated coefficient of U_{dp}.

34. To facilitate comparison of our results with those of other authors who frequently measure $\dot{w}$ by straight-time hourly earnings in manufacturing, we have run several regressions in which $\dot{w}$ is measured as percentage change in straight-time hourly earnings in manufacturing, $\dot{w}_m$. (All these regressions are run as OLS.)

(i) $\quad \dot{w}_m \;=\; .20 \;+\; 1.1\,\dot{w}_m$ $\qquad\qquad\qquad\qquad R^2 = .80$
$\qquad\qquad\qquad (-.62)\ (12.5)$ $\qquad\qquad\qquad\qquad\quad$ D.W. $= 1.55$

(ii) $\quad \dot{w}_m \;=\; .06 \;+\; 1.05\,\dot{w}_m \;+\; .24\,(\dot{w}_m - \dot{w}_m)_{-1}$ $\qquad R^2 = .81$
$\qquad\qquad\qquad (-.15)\ (11.3) \qquad (1.52)$ $\qquad\qquad\qquad$ D.W. $= 2.0$

(iii) $\quad \dot{w}_m \;=\; .14 \;+\; .98\,\dot{w}_m \;+\; .17\,(\dot{w}_m - \dot{w}_m)_{-1}$ $\qquad R^2 = .83$
$\qquad\qquad\qquad (.41)\ (9.99) \qquad (1.08)$ $\qquad\qquad\qquad$ D.W. $= 1.98$

$\qquad\qquad\qquad +\; .53\,(\dot{p}_c - \dot{p}_c)_{-2}$
$\qquad\qquad\qquad\quad (1.89)$

(iv) $\quad \dot{w}_m \;=\; -.07 \;+\; .63\,\dot{w}_m \;+\; 4.53\,\dfrac{1}{U_p}$ $\qquad\quad R^2 = .85$
$\qquad\qquad\qquad (-.18)\ (4.2) \qquad (3.7)$ $\qquad\qquad\qquad$ D.W. $= 1.81$

(v) $\quad \dot{w} \;=\; 1.11 \;+\; .72\,\dot{w} \;+\; 3.58\,U_{pd}$
$\qquad\qquad\quad (1.37)\ (3.4) \quad (2.08)$

(v) $\quad \dot{w} \;=\; 1.11 \;+\; .72\,\dot{w} \;+\; 3.58\,U_{pd}$ $\qquad\qquad R^2 = .80$
$\qquad\qquad\quad (1.37)\ (3.4) \quad (2.08)$ $\qquad\qquad\qquad$ D.W. $= 1.13$

(vi) $\quad \dot{w} \;=\; .54 \;+\; .69\,\dot{w} \;+\; 9.33\,\dfrac{1}{U} \;+\; 21.1\,\left(\dfrac{1}{U} - \dfrac{1}{U}\right)_{-1}$ $\quad R^2 = .80$
$\qquad\qquad\quad (-1.2)\ (3.8) \quad (2.0) \qquad\quad (1.68)$ $\qquad\qquad\qquad$ D.W. $= 1.05$

As can be seen from the first three equations, the constant terms are not significantly different from zero and the coefficient on the expected wage rate not significantly different from unity. The coefficients on the "correction" terms are all positive, though not twice their standard errors, and the D.W.'s respectable. When U_p^{-1} is introduced in (iv) as a replacement for $(\dot{p}_c - \hat{\dot{p}}_c)_{-2}$ and $(\dot{w}_m - \hat{\dot{w}}_m)_{-1}$ the coefficient on $\dot{w}_m$ falls sharply and it becomes significantly lower than one.

In (v) and (vi) when we replace $\dot{w}_m$ with $\dot{w}$, the coefficients on the wage expectation terms stay significantly below unity, the constants become appreciably greater than those in (i-iv), though not significantly different from zero, but the D.W.'s fall to unacceptably low levels. Briefly, the use of $\dot{w}$ instead of $\dot{w}_m$ and U^{-1} instead of $(\dot{w} - \hat{\dot{w}})_{-1}$ and/or $(\dot{p} - \hat{\dot{p}}_c)_{-2}$ drastically "worsens" the performance of the wage equation.

35. The reestimation involves reestimating the dependent variables in Table 10-3 using the aforementioned dummy as a regressor in the estimating equations. The results are as follows:

$$\dot{w} = \underset{(1.48)}{0.64} + \underset{(8.61)}{0.85\,\hat{\dot{w}}} + \underset{(2.39)}{0.69\,(\dot{p}_c - \hat{\dot{p}})_{-2}} + \underset{(3.76)}{0.52\,(\dot{w} - \hat{\dot{w}})_{-1}} \quad \begin{array}{l} R^2 = 0.85 \\ \text{D.W.} = 1.67 \end{array}$$

$$\dot{p}_o = \underset{(-0.30)}{0.05} + \underset{(3.7)}{1.04\,\hat{\dot{p}}} + \underset{(3.64)}{0.52\,(\dot{p}_o - \hat{\dot{p}}_o)_{-1}} + \underset{(1.62)}{0.19\,(\dot{w} - \hat{\dot{w}})_{-1}} \quad \begin{array}{l} R^2 = 0.90 \\ \text{D.W.} = 1.65 \end{array}$$

$$\dot{p}_c = 0.02 + 1.02\,\hat{\dot{p}}_c + 0.18\,(\dot{p}_o - \hat{\dot{p}}_o)_{-2} + 0.48\,(\dot{p}_c - \hat{\dot{p}}_c)_{-1}$$

$$\begin{array}{l} R^2 = 0.89 \\ \text{D.W.} = 1.63 \end{array}$$

36. The U_p equations with the zero-one dummy for the pro and post 1964 periods are as follows:

$$\begin{aligned} U_p = {} & \underset{(51.6)}{4.18} - \underset{(-6.82)}{1.81\,(\dot{p}_c - \hat{\dot{p}}_c)} - \underset{(-1.06)}{-0.15\,(\dot{p}_o - \hat{\dot{p}}_o)} \\ & + \underset{(.42)}{.05\,(\dot{w} - \hat{\dot{w}})} - \underset{(-8.09)}{1.27\,\text{dummy}} \end{aligned}$$

$$\begin{array}{l} R^2 = .92 \\ \text{D.W.} = 1.14 \end{array}$$

$$\begin{aligned} U_p = {} & \underset{(25.2)}{5.25} - \underset{(-6.95)}{1.45\,(\dot{p}_c - \hat{\dot{p}}_c)} - \underset{(-.27)}{.03\,(\dot{p}_o - \hat{\dot{p}}_o)} \\ & + \underset{(2.72)}{.25\,(\dot{w} - \hat{\dot{w}})} - \underset{(-5.90)}{.28\,\dot{w}} - \underset{(-8.21)}{1.03\,\text{dummy}} \end{aligned}$$

$$\begin{array}{l} R^2 = .96 \\ \text{D.W.} = 1.73 \end{array}$$

$$U_p = 3.93 - .89\,(\dot{p}_c - \hat{\dot{p}}_c') - .11\,(\dot{p}_o - \hat{\dot{p}}_o')$$
$$\ (59.5)\ (-10.5)\qquad\qquad (-2.28)$$
$$\ + .04\,(\dot{w} - \hat{\dot{w}}) - .71\ \text{dummy}$$
$$\quad (.86)\qquad\qquad (-5.75)$$

$R^2 = .97$
D.W. = 1.50

$$U_p = 3.76 - .93\,(\dot{p}_c - \hat{\dot{p}}_c') - .11\,(\dot{p}_o - \hat{\dot{p}}_o')$$
$$\ (13.8)\ (-8.84)\qquad\qquad (-2.29)$$
$$\ + .01\,(\dot{w} - \hat{\dot{w}}') + .04'\dot{w} - .69\ \text{dummy}$$
$$\quad (.21)\qquad\quad (.64)\qquad (-5.51)$$

$R^2 = .97$
D.W. = 1.57

37. After this study was completed, we received, O. Eckstein and R. Brinner, *The Inflation Process in the United States*, a study prepared for the use of the JEC (Washington, D.C.: G.P.O., 1972). In this paper, wage and price equations in which lagged wages and prices play an important role are fitted to quarterly data. A dummy called the "inflation severity factor" is found to have great explanatory power. This dummy is (roughly) the excess of the annual rate of price increase over 2.5 percent. *Ad hoc* devices such as this can usually be found to explain any behavior. ("Accurate prediction is formula plus an adjustment.") But they do not advance our knowledge of economic structure.

38. The means of $|(\dot{w} - \hat{\dot{w}})|$ and of $|(\dot{p}_c - \hat{\dot{p}}_c)|$ are about equal and hence their relative impacts upon U are determined by the relative sizes of their coefficients.

39. N.B. It is necessary to postulate that an increase in $(\dot{M},F)$ has this effect; our model does not imply that it will. $(\dot{p}_c - \hat{\dot{p}}_c)$, $(\dot{p}_o - \hat{\dot{p}}_o)$, and $(\dot{w} - \hat{\dot{w}})$ all are predetermined (endogenous) variables; $(\dot{M},F)$ operates with a distributed lag upon $\dot{p}_c$ and $\dot{p}_o$ only.

40. A fully anticipated inflation has no effect on the distribution of wealth or income, except that which occurs via changes in the share of wealth held in real cash balances.

41. The unemployment rate is a "net" supply variable and as such does not have the properties that theory would seem to call for. It may be a "proxy" for the tightness of the labor market, but it may be a poor one. Better measures would take into account such things as vacancy rates, turnover rates and the like as well as strict supply measures.

Chapter 11
Implications for Policy and Research

1. There is no such thing as "no policy" in the utilization of fiscal and monetary tools.

2. See the third section of Chapter 6, "Distribution and the Level of Economic Activity."

3. The Phillips curve is usually depicted roughly as a parabola in $\dot{w}$ or $\dot{p}$, U space, with the latter on the horizontal axis.

4. A point at which rates of inflation and unemployment were simultaneously about 6 percent as they were in 1971 was not remotely near to any Phillips curve estimated for the United States prior to 1970. We have suggested that one reason for this is the improper approach taken by most authors in examining the relationship between inflation and unemployment.

5. To understand what we have in mind here, the Phillips curve should be conceived of as a frontier of all feasible combinations of rates of inflation and unemployment achieved through conventional means at a given point in time. Since the rates of inflation and unemployment are jointly determined, endogenous variables, there is no unique Phillips curve that exists for any economy at any given point in time, but an infinite number depending upon the types of macroeconomic policies that are pursued and the manner in which people and institutions react to them. However, we can assume that, at any given time, for a given economy, there is a frontier of feasible points.

6. When one considers the difficulty we had in Chapter 10 of obtaining a good Phillips curve relationship, the general problems involved in specification, the "interesting" results that other authors have obtained by various *ad hoc* changes in their specifications, and so forth, it is difficult to see how the Phillips curve characterization of the economy can be defended in the practical sense (as opposed to the esoteric).

7. Given present institutional arrangements concerning labor contracts and other relevant structural aspects of our economy.

8. It is also unlikely that such controls, their undesirability for many reasons aside, can be very effective in any but the short run.

9. Increasing the flow and accuracy of information will not necessarily lower the unemployment rate (by decreasing the average duration of search unemployment), *ceteris paribus*; however, it will increase the efficiency of the labor market and expand outward the Pareto optimal frontier. This is to say that under such conditions the same, or even slightly higher, rate of unemployment may have better welfare consequences.

10. This is not to suggest that policies to promote less discrimination should not be pursued with more vigor than has been the case in the past, but merely that new policies ought to direct themselves to neglected areas.

11. That is, the magnitude, sign, and significance of the estimated coefficients were quite similar in both instances. However, obtaining the same magnitude for the estimated coefficient of the price expectations term in both cases does imply different reactions to past rates of increase of prices since the Feldstein-Eckstein weights decrease more slowly going back in quarters than do the assumed adaptive expectations weights.

Bibliography

Bibliography

Books and Pamphlets

Abramovitz, Moses et al. *The Allocation of Economic Resources*. Stanford University Press, 1965.

Bach, G.L. *Inflation: A Study in Economics, Ethics and Politics*. Providence, R.I.: Brown University Press, 1958.

Ball, R.J. *Inflation and the Theory of Money*. London: George Allen and Unwin, 1964.

Beveridge, Lord William. *Full Employment in a Free Society*. London: George Allen and Unwin, 1944.

Blackman, Jules, and Gainsbrugh, Martin R. *Inflation and the Price Indices*. The National Industrial Conference Board Studies in Business Economics, no. 94, New York: National Industrial Conference Board, 1966.

Boulding, Kenneth, and Pfaff, Martin (eds). *Redistribution to the Rich and Poor: The Grants Economics of Income Redistribution*. Belmont, Calif., Wadsworth Publishing Co., 1971.

Brunner, Karl (ed.). *Targets and Indicators of Monetary Policy*. San Francisco: Chandler Publishing Co., 1969.

Charlesworth, Harold K. *Economics of Repressed Inflation*. London, 1956.

Doeringer, Peter B., and Piore, Michael J. *Internal Labor Markets and Manpower Analysis*. Lexington, Massachusetts: D.C. Heath and Co., 1971.

Eckstein, Otto (ed.). *The Econometrics of Price Determination*. Washington, D.C.: Board of Governors of the Federal Reserve System, 1972.

Evans, Michael K. *Macroeconomic Activity*. New York: Harper and Row, 1969.

Friedman, Milton (ed.). *Studies in the Quantity Theory of Money*. Chicago: University of Chicago Press, 1956.

Lerner, Abba. *The Economics of Employment*. New York: McGraw-Hill, 1951.

Lindauer, John. *Macroeconomics*. New York: Wiley, 1968.

Margret, Arthur. *The Theory of Prices*. New York: Prentice-Hall, 1938.

Metcalf, Charles E. *An Econometric Model of the Income Distribution*. Institute for Research on Poverty Monograph Series, Chicago: Markham Publishing Co., 1972.

Okun, Arthur M. "Inflation: The Problems and Propsects Before Us." The Brookings Institution, reprint 182, Washington, D.C., 1970.

Okun et al. (eds.). *Brookings Papers on Economic Activity*. Vol. 1, no. 1, Washington, D.C.: The Brookings Institution, 1970, pp. 77-110.

_____ . *Brookings Papers on Economic Activity*. Vol. 2, Washington, D.C.: The Brookings Institution, 1970, pp. 8-47.

_____ . *Brookings Papers on Economic Activity*. Vol. 2, no. 1, Washington, D.C.: The Brookings Institution, 1971, pp. 105-158.

Okun et al. (eds.). *Brookings Papers on Economic Activity*. Vol. 3, Washington, D.C.: The Brookings Institution, 1970, pp. 369-411.

_____. *Brookings Papers on Economic Activity*. Vol. 3, no. 2. Washington, D.C.: The Brookings Institution, 1972, pp. 385-421.

Ohlin, Bertil. *The Problem of Economic Stabilization*. New York: Columbia University Press, 1949.

Paish, Frank W. *Studies in an Inflationary Economy*. London: Macmillan Press, 1962.

Parsons, Talcott, and Clark, Kenneth (eds.). *The Negro American*. Boston: Beacon Press, 1966.

Perry, George. *Unemployment, Money Wage Rates, and Inflation*. Cambridge: MIT Press, 1966.

Phelps, Edmund et al. *Microeconomic Foundation of Employment and Inflation Theory*. New York: W.W. Norton and Co., 1970.

Shultz, George, and Aliber, R.Z. *Guidelines, Informal Controls, and the Market Place*. Chicago: University of Chicago Press, 1966.

Solow, Robert. *Price Expectations and the Behavior of the Price Level*. Manchester: Manchester University Press, 1969.

Soltow, Lee (ed.). *Six Papers on the Size Distribution of Wealth and Income*. New York: NBER, 1969.

Thurow, Lester. *Poverty and Discrimination*. Washington, D.C.: The Brookings Institution, 1969.

Weintraub, Sidney. *Growth Without Inflation*. New Delhi: National Council of Applied Economic Research, 1965.

Government Documents

President's Commission on Budget Concepts, *Staff Papers*, Washington, D.C.: U.S. G.P.O., 1967.

U.S. Congress, Joint Economic Committee, *Hearings*, 90th Cong., 1st sess., 1967; Murray L. Wiedenbaum, "Impact of the Vietnam War on the American Economy," *Economic Effect of Vietnam Spending*.

U.S. Congress, Joint Economic Committee, "Price Level Stability and Economic Policy," by Albert Rees. *Compendium on the Relationship of Prices to Economic Stability and Growth*, 86th Cong., Washington, D.C.: G.P.O., 1958.

U.S. Congress, Joint Economic Committee, *The Inflation Process in the United States*, by O. Eckstein and R. Brinner, A study prepared for the use of the Joint Economic Committee, Washington, D.C.: G.P.O., 1972.

U.S. Congress, Joint Economic Committee, *Recent Inflation in the United States*, by Charles L. Schultze, Study Paper 1, prepared in connection with the study of employment, growth and price levels, Washington, D.C.: G.P.O., 1959.

U.S. Congress, Senate, Subcommittee of the Committee on Appropriations, *Hearings*, on labor-health, welfare and education appropriations for 1965, 88th Cong., 2nd sess., 1964.

U.S. Department of Commerce, Census Bureau, *Survey of Current Business*.

U.S. Department of H.E.W., Social Security Administration, "Counting the Poor: Another Look at the Poverty Profile," by Mollie Orshansky, *Social Security Bulletin*, January 1965.

U.S. Department of H.E.W., Social Security Administration, "OASDI Benefits, Prices and Wages: 1966 Experience," by Saul Waldman, *Social Security Bulletin*, June 1967, p. 9.

U.S. Department of H.E.W., Social Security Administration, "Personal Health Care Expenditures of the Aged and Non-Aged, Fiscal Years 1966 and 1967," by Rice Anderson and Cooper, *Research and Statistical Note No. 11*, Washington, D.C.: G.P.O., June 1968.

U.S. Department of H.E.W., Social Security Administration, "Who's Who Among the Poor: A Demographic View of Poverty," by Mollie Orshansky, *Social Security Bulletin*, July 1965.

U.S. Department of Labor, Bureau of Labor Statistics, *Handbook of Labor Statistics*, 1968, Bulletin No. 1600, Washington, D.C.: G.P.O., 1969.

U.S. Department of Labor, Bureau of Labor Statistics, *Monthly Labor Review*.

Journal Articles

Aaron, Henry. "The Foundations of the War on Poverty Re-examined." *American Economic Review* 57 (December 1967), pp. 1229-43.

Alchian, A.A., and Kessel, R.A. "Effects of Inflation." *The Journal of Political Economy* 70, no. 6 (December 1962), pp. 521-37.

_____. "The Meaning and Validity of the Inflation Induced Lag of Wages Behind Prices." *American Economic Review* 50 (March 1960), pp. 43-66.

Almon, Shirley. "The Distributed Lag between Capital Appropriations and Expenditures." *Econometrica* (January 1965).

Anderson, Leonall. "Three Approaches to Monetary Stock Determination." *Review* of the Federal Reserve Bank of St. Louis (October 1967), pp. 6-13.

Anderson, Locke. "Trickling Down: The Relationship between Economic Growth and the Extent of Poverty Among American Families." *Quarterly Journal of Economics* 78, no. 4 (November 1964), pp. 511-24.

Ando, Albert, and Bach, G.L. "The Redistributional Effects of Inflation." *The Review of Economics and Statistics* 39, no. 1 (February 1957), pp. 1-13.

Bailey, Martin J. "The Welfare Costs of Inflationary Finance." *Journal of Political Economy* 64 (April 1956), pp. 93-110.

Black, S.W., and Kelegian, H.H. "A Macro Model of the U.S. Labor Market." *Econometrica* 38, no. 5 (September 1970), pp. 712-41.

Brimmer, Andrew. "Inflation and Income Distribution in the United States." *The Review of Economics and Statistics* 53, no. 1 (February 1971), pp. 37-49.

Bronfenbrenner, Martin, and Holtzman, Franklyn D. "Survey of Inflation Theory." *American Economic Review* 53, no. 4 (September 1963), pp. 595-661.

Brown, E. Cary. "Fiscal Policy in the Thirties: A Reappraisal." *American Economic Review* 46 (December 1956), pp. 857-79.

Budd, Edward C. "Postwar Changes in the Size Distribution of Income in the U.S." *American Economic Review* 60 (May 1970), pp. 247-60.

Budd, Edward C. and Seiders, David. "The Impact of Inflation on the Distribution of Income and Wealth." *American Economic Review, Papers and Proceedings* (May 1971).

Burger, Albert E. "Relative Movement in Wages and Profits." *Review* of the Federal Reserve Bank of St. Louis, 55, no. 2 (February 1973), pp. 8-16.

Burns, Arthur. "The Perils of Inflation." *Tax Review* 29, no. 5 (May 1968), pp. 17-24.

Cargill, Thomas. "An Empirical Investigation of the Wage Lag Hypothesis." *American Economic Review* 59, no. 5 (December 1969).

Durbin, J. "Testing for Serial Correlation in Least Squares Regression When Some of the Regressors are Lagged Dependent Variables." *Econometrica* 38, no. 3 (May 1970), pp. 410-21.

Galloway, Lowell. "The Foundations of the War On Poverty." *American Economic Review* 55 (March 1965), pp. 122-30.

Gramlich, Edward. "The Behavior and Adequacy of the United States Federal Budget, 1952-64." *Yale Economic Essays* 6 (Spring 1966).

Griliches, Zvi. "Distributed Lags: A Survey." *Econometrica* 35, no. 1 (January 1967), pp. 16-49.

Haberler, Gottfried. "Incomes Policy and Inflation: Some Further Reflections." *American Economic Review* 62 (May 1972), pp. 234-42.

Hansen, W. Lee, and Weisbrod, Burton. "An Income-Net Worth Approach to Measuring Economic Welfare." *American Economic Review* 58 (December 1968).

Holt, Charles. "Improving the Labor Market Trade-Off between Inflation and Unemployment." *American Economic Review, Papers and Proceedings* (May 1968).

Lipsey, Richard G. "The Relation between Unemployment and the Rate of Change of Money Wage Rates: A Further Analysis." *Economica* 27 (February 1960), pp. 1-31.

Litavian, Nissan, and Patinkin, Don. "On the Economic Theory of Price Indexes." *Economic Development and Cultural Change*, 1961.

Lucas, R.E. Jr., and Rapping, L.A. "Price Expectations and the Phillips Curve." *American Economic Review* 59 (June 1969), pp. 342-50.

Marty, Alvin L. "Growth and the Welfare Cost of Inflationary Finance." *Journal of Political Economy* 75 (February 1967), pp. 71-76.

_____. "Money Is a Theory of Finance," *Journal of Finance* (January 1964).

Metcalf, Charles. "Fiscal Policy and the Poor: The Case of Vietnam." *Public Policy* 18, no. 2 (Winter 1970), pp. 187-211.

Mundell, Robert A. "Growth, Stability, and Inflationary Finance." *Journal of Political Economy* 23 (April 1965), pp. 97-109.

_____. "Inflation and Real Interest." *Journal of Political Economy* 21 (June 1963), pp. 280-83.

Musgrave, Richard. "On Measuring Fiscal Performance." *Review of Economics and Statistics* 46 (May 1964).

Nourse, Edmund. "Concepts of Full Employment." *American Economic Review* 47 (May 1957).

Phelps, Edmund S. "Anticipated Inflation and Economic Welfare." *Journal of Political Economy* 73 (February 1965), pp. 1-17.

_____. "Phillips Curves, Expectations of Inflation and Optimal Unemployment Over Time." *Economica* 34 (August 1967), pp. 254-81.

Phillips, A.W. "The Relationship between Unemployment and the Rate of Change of Money Wages in the United Kingdom, 1862-1957." *Economica* 25 (November 1958), pp. 283-99.

Reder, Melvin W., "The Theory of Occupational Wage Differentials." *American Economic Review* 45 (December 1955), pp. 833-52.

_____. "The Theoretical Problems of a National Wage-Price Policy." *Canadian Journal of Economics* 14 (February 1948), pp. 46-61.

Rees, Albert. "The Phillips Curve as a Menu for Policy Choice." *Economica* (August 1970).

Stigler, George. "Information in the Labor Market." *Journal of Political Economy, Supplement*, no. 5, pt 2 (October 1962), pp. 94-105.

Thurow, Lester C. "Analyzing the American Income Distribution." *American Economic Review* 60 (May 1970), pp. 261-69.

Tobin, James. "Inflation and Unemployment." *American Economic Review* 62 (March 1972), pp. 1-18.

Turnovsky, S., and Wachter, M. "A Test of the 'Expectations Hypothesis' Using Directly Observed Wage and Price Expectations." *Review of Economics and Statistics* 54, no. 1 (February 1972).

Turvey, Ralph. "Some Aspects of Inflation in a Closed Economy." *Economic Journal* 61 (September 1951), pp. 532-43.

Ulman, Lloyd. "Cost Push and Some Policy Alternatives." *American Economic Review* 62 (May 1972), pp. 242-50.

Wallis, Kenneth. "Some Recent Developments in Applied Econometrics." *Journal of Economic Literature* 7, no. 3 (September 1969), pp. 771-96.

Zarnowitz, Victor. "Unfilled Business Orders, Price Changes, and Business Fluctuations." *Review of Economics and Statistics* 44, no. 4 (November 1962), pp. 362-94.

Unpublished Works

Beach, Charles M. "Cyclical Impacts on the Distribution of Income." Working Paper, Department of Economics, Queen's University, 1973.

_____. "Estimating Distributional Impacts of Macroeconomic Activity." Working Paper No. 38, Industrial Relations Section, Princeton University, April 1972.

Bodkin, R.G. "Wage and Price Formation in Selected Econometric Models." Research Report 2023, Department of Economics, University of Western Ontario, September 1970.

Feldstein, Martin, and Eckstein, Otto. "The Fundamental Determinants of the Interest Rate," mimeo.

Friedman, M. "A Theroretical Framework for Monetary Analysis." National Bureau of Economic Research, Occasional Paper 112-1971.

Hashmi, R.M.H. "Studies in Functional Income Distribution." Occasional Paper No. 3, Bureau of Business and Economic Research, Michigan State University, 1960.

Mirer, Thad W. "The Distributional Impact of the 1970 Recession." Institute for Research on Poverty Discussion Paper 136-72, Madison, Wisconsin, July 1972.

_____. "The Effects of Macroeconomic Fluctuations on the Distribution of Income." Institute for Research on Poverty Discussion Paper 110-72, Madison, Wisconsin, January 1972.

Perry, George. "Inflation and Unemployment." The Brookings Institution, December 1970, mimeo.

Phelps, Edmund S. "Rational Inflation Policy and the Consequences of Unemployment." Draft, April 1970.

Reder, Melvin W. "Social Mobility and Labor Market Structure." Stanford, 1971, mimeo.

_____. "Unemployment Among New Labor Market Entrants." Stanford, 1970, mimeo.

Swan, Neil. "Inflation and the Distribution of Income." Ph.D. dissertation, University of Pennsylvania, 1969.

Index

About the Author

John L. Palmer received the B.A. in mathematics from Williams College in 1965 and the Ph.D. in economics from Stanford University in 1971. He has been a member of the Faculty of the Department of Economics of Stanford University and affiliated with The Rand Corporation, The Institute for Public Policy Analysis of Stanford University, The Institute for Research on Poverty of the University of Wisconsin and the Office of Policy, Research and Evaluation of the Office of Economic Opportunity. Since 1971 he has been with the Office of the Assistant Secretary for Planning and Evaluation of DHEW in Washington where he is currently the Acting Deputy Assistant Secretary for Income Maintenance and Social Services.